Designing Out Crime

Edited by R. V. G. Clarke and P. Mayhew

HOME OFFICE RESEARCH UNIT

LONDON: HER MAJESTY'S STATIONERY OFFICE

HOME OFFICE RESEARCH UNIT PUBLICATIONS

The studies collected together in this book were first published in the *Home Office Research Studies* series. Titles in this series are listed at the end of the book, together with titles in the earlier series, *Studies in the Causes of Delinquency and the Treatment of Offenders*. Also listed are *Research Unit Papers* which contain material of a rather more specialised nature. All Research Unit publications result from research undertaken within the Home Office to assist in the exercise of its administrative functions, and for the information of the judicature, the services for which the Home Secretary has responsibility (direct or indirect) and the general public.

HER MAJESTY'S STATIONERY OFFICE
Government Bookshops
49 High Holborn, London WC1V 6HB
13a Castle Street, Edinburgh EH2 3AR
41 The Hayes, Cardiff CF1 1JW
Brazennose Street, Manchester M60 8AS
Southey House, Wine Street, Bristol BS1 2BQ
258 Broad Street Birmingham B1 2HE
80 Chichester Street, Belfast BT1 4JY

Government publications are also available
through booksellers

ISBN 0 11 340732 7

Contents

Foreword

Recent criminological research, some of it undertaken by the Home Office Research Unit, has made apparent the limited potential for bringing about reductions in crime through adjustments to the penal system. For this reason, the Research Unit has been engaged in a programme of work which has sought alternative means of preventing crime. The origins of this programme are fairly diverse. In the mid-1970s a clear demand emerged for research into the nature and prevention of vandalism. At the same time, the Unit began to undertake research concerned with the relationship between crime levels and criminal opportunities. More recently, in the course of research on the police, it has evaluated amongst other things, certain crime prevention initiatives conducted by forces.

The element common to the studies is the concern with situational factors surrounding the commission of crime and the way they might be manipulated to reduce opportunities for crime. This approach has been called 'situational' crime prevention, and the findings of a dozen or so studies relevant to this have now been published in separate reports in the *Home Office Research Studies* series. The interest that these studies have provoked warrants their re-issue in a single volume, but an additional reason for producing this book is that 'situational' crime prevention depends for its success on the support and interest of a wide range of people—architects, planners and those in education, housing and transport authorities—who might not ordinarily see the *Home Office Research Studies*.

Social scientists must be wary of raising expectations that cannot be fulfilled. The suggestion that crime rates might be controlled by reducing opportunities for crime was originally greeted with considerable scepticism; it was widely believed that the approach was vitiated by the phenomenon of 'displacement'—that reducing opportunities at one point would simply displace crime elsewhere.

The findings presented in this book may help to allay such scepticism, though there is still a need to clarify the limits of displacement. Research might also attempt to incorporate situational factors more adequately into criminological theory, and to identify and evaluate the role of opportunity-reducing measures with respect to different forms of crime. But there are some other problems which more urgently call for research effort. The first of these concerns implementation. Broadly put, it could now be said that the problem of preventing crime is not so much of knowing what to do but of persuading people to undertake the necessary action.

v

Some of the reasons why situational measures may be difficult to implement are discussed in the introduction to the book. They include costs, problems of co-ordinating different groups of people to a common end, and a general dislike of what can be seen as mechanistic solutions to complex social problems. It may be, of course, that this opposition will diminish as people come to recognise more clearly the limits of alternative ways of preventing crime. But it is important to see if research can help to find ways round these obstacles. One requirement would seem to be for clearer information (which victim surveys would provide) about the risks of specific forms of crime in particular places or at particular times. This might be helpful in focussing crime prevention where is it most needed and in helping to determine the most promising form of such effort. More precise information about the fear of crime and the effects of this fear on the lives of different segments of the population (for example the elderly) might also be useful in galvanising voluntary and official bodies into action and in ensuring the co-ordination of their efforts. These various directions for research could form the basis for an extended programme of work and are at present under consideration by the Research Unit.

JOHN CROFT
Head of the Research Unit

May 1980

Editors' note

The studies collected together in this book are illustrative of the 'situational' approach to crime prevention. They have all been previously published in the *Home Office Research Studies* series, for the most part in reports containing introductory and concluding chapters which place the empirical work in some broader criminological context. These chapters not only overlap considerably with one another but at times deal with topics beyond the scope of this book. For this reason they have not been reprinted here but have been replaced by a fresh introductory chapter (Chapter 1).

Chapter 2 originally appeared in *Home Office Research Study No. 34: Crime as Opportunity* (1976). The study examines the impact on car theft in Greater London of the introduction of steering column locks on all new cars manufactured after 1970. It is predicted that levels of car theft should begin to fall at the end of the 1970s as the proportion of cars with steering column locks reaches 75–80%. This prediction has not been borne out (there were 32% more thefts of cars in the Metropolitan Police District in 1978 than in 1974 when the study was carried out), perhaps because there may still be enough unprotected cars, or enough carelessness on the part of owners, to provide ample opportunities to maintain car theft at high levels. Or it may be, as the police believe, that ways have been found of overcoming at least some of the early steering column locks.

Chapter 3 originally appeared in *Home Office Research Study No. 34: Crime as Opportunity* (1976). The study is concerned with the effects of surveillance by bus crews on bus vandalism; it was designed by R. V. G. Clarke and carried out by A. Sturman under the supervision of T. F. Marshall. It formed part of a wide-ranging programme of research into vandalism, which included the studies reprinted in Chapters 4 and 5 as well as a self-report survey of vandalism by schoolboys and a study of the extent of vandalism in a city suburb. This programme of research was intended to illuminate the value of various ways of preventing vandalism, as discussed in *Home Office Research Study No. 47: Tackling Vandalism.*

Chapter 4 originally appeared in *Home Office Research Study No. 47: Tackling Vandalism* (1978). The study tests the 'defensible space' hypothesis of Oscar Newman in relation to two London housing estates; it was carried out by Sheena Wilson under the supervision of T. F. Marshall. Some methodological short-comings of the study have been noted by Trasler (1979), stemming from what he calls the 'tug of war' between the need to tackle socially-important questions and the requirements of scientific methodology. These do not seriously throw into doubt the main conclusions of the study, particularly as regards the current status of 'defensible space' (cf. Mayhew, 1979).

Chapter 5 originally appeared in *Home Office Research Study No. 49: Crime in Public View* (1979). The study assesses the effects of 'natural surveillance' on telephone kiosk vandalism in a London borough.

Chapter 6 originally appeared in *Home Office Research Study No. 49: Crime in Public View* (1979). The study evaluates the experimental introduction of closed circuit television surveillance at four stations in the London Underground in order to cut theft and robbery. The experiment was judged successful, though the number of thefts on the Underground system as a whole has shown subsequent increases, standing at 7494 in 1979. Encouraged by the experiment with C.C.T.V., London Transport has recently announced its intention—finances permitting—to cover the entire Underground network with television observation cameras.

Chapter 7 originally appeared in *Home Office Research Study No. 55: Crime Prevention and the Police* (1979). The study evaluates a 'truancy sweep' conducted by the police in Bristol.

Chapter 8 originally appeared in *Home Office Research Study No. 55: Crime Prevention and the Police* (1979). The study examined the effect of a publicity campaign mounted by the police in Plymouth to persuade car owners to be more careful about locking their cars.

Chapters 9 and 10 originally appeared in *Home Office Research Study No. 63: Crime Prevention Publicity: an Assessment* (1980). The studies examine respectively a Home Office autocrime publicity campaign conducted in the north of England in 1979, and a Home Office anti-vandalism publicity campaign, conducted in north-west England in 1978.

Chapter 11 originally comprised *Home Office Research Study No. 62: Co-ordinating Crime Prevention Efforts* (1980). This reports the progress of a project conducted by the Crime Policy Planning Unit of the Home Office, intended to test out the feasibility of achieving inter-agency co-operation in implementing preventive measures to curb a localised crime problem. This 'demonstration project' focussed on vandalism in Manchester schools, and the report outlines the agreed solutions and some of the early problems of implementation. It is stated in the report that about a year would be required for implementation of the measures which had been selected. In the event, it has taken longer than this for some of the measures to come into effect, and it now seems that the 'social' remedies that were suggested may have more difficulty in getting off the ground.

Because of some overlap with the discussion in the early part of Chapter 1, the first part of *Co-ordinating Crime Prevention Efforts* as it originally appeared has been omitted in this book. (A summary of what has been omitted is given at the beginning of Chapter 11). Also, three appendices to the report have not been reprinted here including a 'Guide to Good Practice' in preventing school vandalism.

1 Introduction

J. M. Hough, R. V. G. Clarke and P. Mayhew

Crime prevention is a rather elastic term, which at its broadest can encompass any activity intended to reduce the frequency of events defined as crimes by the criminal law. Under this umbrella, it includes the crime-related work of the police, the work of the courts, prison and probation services, some kinds of social work and social intervention programmes, as well as 'physical' crime prevention - the use of locks and bolts and other security devices. But usually crime prevention has more specific connotations, referring to pre-emptive measures which avoid the need to invoke the law. These are often equated with the physical security concerns of police crime prevention officers, sometimes with conventional police strategies such as preventive patrolling, and sometimes with small-scale 'social' prevention activities such as youth work or community development schemes.

This book collects together a number of research studies concerned with crime prevention which have been carried out within the Home Office over the last five years or so. The measures under examination all fall within a specific approach, cutting across some of the distinction made above, referred to here as 'situational' prevention. They can be characterised as:

  i measures directed at highly specific forms of crime;

 ii which involve the management, design or manipulation of the immediate environment in which these crimes occur;

iii in as systematic and permanent way as possible;

iv so as to reduce the opportunities for these crimes;

 v as perceived by a broad range of potential offenders.

These measures encompass but are broader in scope than the work of police crime prevention officers. They are contrasted in the following discussion with measures intended to reshape people's dispositions.

Many situational measures are not in themselves new and are often little more than commonsense precautions; individuals, as well as organisations in both private and public sectors, have consistently made wide use of them. Locksmiths, for example, can hardly count as a new profession; and few people would doubt that some situational measures can provide those who use them with protection against crime. However, they have been neglected by administrators and criminologists as a means of bringing about *overall* reductions in the crimes to which they are applied.

There are some signs that academic interest in the situational aspects of crime is now growing. Within the criminological tradition of ecological research, for instance, attention is being focussed on the places where crimes occur, as well as on the social and physical features of the places where offenders live (cf. Herbert, 1977; Winchester, 1978). There has also been a number of 'crime specific' studies (e.g. Reppetto, 1974; Walsh, 1978) in which the spatial and temporal distribution of burglary, shoplifting or robbery has been examined in relation to measurable aspects of the physical environment in which these offences occur. Another significant factor behind the increasing interest in situational measures has been the popularity of Oscar Newman's (1972) theory of 'defensible space' - the essence of which is that good housing design can engender a sense of territoriality amongst residents and opportunities for surveillance by them, both of which work against crime. Many 'defensible space' measures have now been extensively tested in the United States, for instance in the *Crime Prevention Through Environmental Design* programme conducted by the Westinghouse Corporation under federal sponsorship (*Nation's Cities, 1977*); and despite some equivocal research findings, the measures have retained their popularity and continue to attract federal funds (Rouse and Rubenstein, 1978).

The studies in this book primarily address criminologists, and through them criminal justice administrators responsible for the prevention of crime. But if the situational approach is to achieve any impact, it needs the understanding and support of practitioners and academics in related fields such as social administration, planning and architecture. Such readers are unlikely to be aware of the limitations of other means of reducing crime and of the scepticism of most criminologists concerning the crime preventive potential of the criminal justice system. Assessing the situational approach out of context they may see little promise in it; and for this reason it is necessary to make brief reference to current trends in criminological thought before examining situational measures in detail.

No-one would suggest that the criminal justice system and other formal systems of social control are without impact. This would be facile: the organisations which comprise the criminal justice system are social institutions which sustain a sense of public and consensual morality (cf. Manning, 1977). Nor would criminologists deny any absence of scope for improving the equity of the criminal justice system - which may in the long term consolidate popular acceptance of the system and thus its effectiveness. Most of them, however, as well as an increasing number of politicians, administrators and practitioners, now accept that there is little promise in attempts to reduce present levels of crime through different kinds of therapeutic intervention (cf. Brody, 1976; Martinson 1974), through exploiting the deterrent effects of punishment (Beyleveld, 1979; Walker, 1979), or through 'containment' - imprisoning offenders in order to keep them 'out of circulation' (see e.g. Brody and Tarling, 1980). Many would also accept that the case for reducing overall levels of crime through improvements in policing or increases in police resources has been overstated (see Clarke and Hough, 1980, for a review). And though research has had less to say on these

2

issues, it is now becoming recognised that there are great practical and political difficulties with policies of diversion (cf. Lerman, 1975) and decriminalisation as means of reducing levels of 'crime', as popularly defined. Finally, there are growing doubts about the impact of liberal programmes of social reform outside the criminal justice system, whether these are broad social policies to reduce inequalities thought to be criminogenic or more localised schemes to increase social solidarity or improve police-community relations (Wilson, 1975). Few people would question the value of these on other grounds but their effectiveness in preventing crime is still more a matter of faith than fact.

The reasons for the neglect of situational measures by criminologists may lie in what has been described as the dispositional bias of much criminological theory (cf. Rutter, 1979). In explaining the occurrence of crime, attention can be drawn to a wide range of factors - some of which are illustrated schematically in Figure 1:1 in relation to vandalism. It is broadly true that criminologists over the last hundred years have been concerned to explain crime in terms of factors occupying groups 1–5 of the figure - to explain what in biological, psychological or social terms differentiates people who commit crime from those who do not. Few criminological theories have been concerned with the 'situational' factors of groups 6 and 7 - which help to explain why a particular criminal act has taken place - and where attention has been paid to these, they have rarely been fully integrated into explanations of offending. At an applied level interest has been correctional - the practical concern has been to alter criminal disposition. The dispositional bias is also present in theories developed in response to the perceived inadequacies of mainstream criminology (e.g. Matza, 1964; Becker, 1962; Quinney, 1970). This work is characterised not by an absence of dispositional explanations but by an explicit rejection of correctional objectives.

Whilst the dispositional bias reflects the tendency of its parent disciplines, particularly psychology, to explain social phenomena in terms of individual differences (cf. Tizard, 1976; Ross, 1977), it is also the result of the specific problems which a neo-classical system of criminal justice creates. Once the classical principle of equality in the eyes of the law has been abandoned, questions of demarcation - between those who are responsible to the law and those who are not, those who should be punished and those who should be cured - become central. An understanding of individual pathology is therefore needed, which dispositional theory can provide.

However, this theoretical emphasis has had an unfortunate consequence. It has encouraged a view of crime whereby criminality in some way inheres in the personality of offenders, so that, come what may, they will seek out their opportunities for crime. In terms of prevention too much effort has been expended on unproductive attempts to change the 'criminal disposition' of offenders. Morris and Hawkins (1970) and Wilson (1975) have argued that many of the causes of crime identified by criminologists are impossible to manipulate. For example, there seems to be no acceptable way of modifying temperament

3

Fig.1:1 Explanations of vandalism*

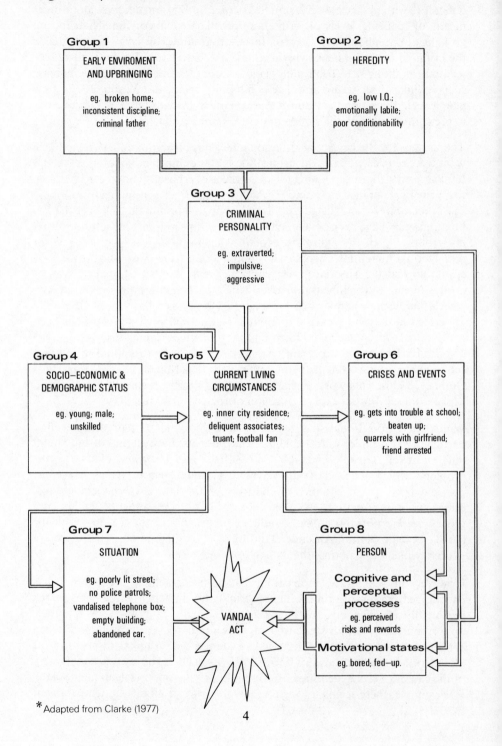

*Adapted from Clarke (1977)

and other biological variables, and it is difficult to know what can be done to make parents love their children or exercise more consistent discipline. At the same time, attention has been diverted from the situational determinants of offending (which will vary greatly from offence to offence) and thus from preventive measures focussed on these (cf. Ohlin, 1970; Gibbons, 1971; Jeffery, 1971).

The boundary between the 'dispositional' factors of groups 1–5 of Figure 1:1 and the 'situational' factors of groups 6 and 7 is of course somewhat artificial. In varying degrees people select their situations and control rather than merely respond to them. So for some offences, where offenders clearly seek out their opportunities, explanations involving situational factors will carry less weight. The activities of 'career criminals' as reported by Peterson and Braiker (1980) fall into this category. But in explaining the occurrence of other offences such as vandalism, considerably more attention might need to be paid to situational variables; indeed, for many purposes much crime is best understood as rational action performed by fairly ordinary people acting under particular pressures and exposed to specific opportunities and situational inducements (cf. Taylor *et al.*, 1973; Clarke, 1980); and this crime is best prevented by manipulating opportunities and inducements.

DESIGNING OUT CRIME: THE 'SITUATIONAL' APPROACH
In defining the 'situational' approach, opportunity is thus a key concept. (The use of 'opportunity' here is to be distinguished from that associated with Cloward and Ohlin (1961) which refers to the legitimate and illegitimate opportunities to acquire socially-accepted goals.) The term criminal opportunity has several shades of meaning. First it can refer simply to the material conditions in which a potential offender is competent or able to commit a crime. And, of course, for those crimes which are the result of impulse or temptation, the opportunity for crime consists simultaneously in the material conditions and the inducement: a car with a key in the ignition provides both conditions and inducement. But it has a still broader meaning which includes the element of chance - criminal opportunities exist not only where the material conditions are present but where benefits can be gained at low risk. The broader definition, including both material conditions and risk, is employed throughout this book.

Situational measures are exemplified below under eight headings. The first three groups comprise measures which reduce opportunity by making crime physically harder to commit. The remainder involve the manipulation of the costs and benefits, as well as the material conditions, of offending in ways which are considerably more complex.

i. Target hardening
The most obvious way of reducing criminal opportunities is to obstruct or 'target harden' - to increase the physical security of targets of theft through the use of locks, reinforced materials and immobilising devices, to protect against vandal-

5

ism by installing unbreakable and paint-resistant materials, and by placing vulnerable objects behind grills or meshes. Some forms of target hardening have proved highly successful. In West Germany steering column locks or equivalent immobilising devices were in 1963 made compulsory on all cars (old and new) with a consequent and apparently permanent reduction of more than 60% in the rate of car thefts (see Chapter 2). There is further unexploited potential for designing out theft of and from cars, for example by centrally activated locking systems, and replacement of keys with electronically-read magnetic or punched cards (Ekblom, 1979). In this country, the Post Office have succeeded virtually eliminating theft from telephone kiosks by the wholesale replacement of vulnerable aluminium coin boxes with stronger steel ones.

ii. Target removal

A second group of measures consists in the removal of targets of crime from the environment. Thus the opportunities for wage-snatches are reduced if employers are encouraged to pay their staff by cheque rather than cash. Robberies of takings in New York buses were greatly reduced with the introduction of automated flat-fare collection (Chaiken *et al.*, 1974). Large scale thefts of copper from one of Britain's major ports have been greatly reduced simply by the port authority refusing to accept consignments until immediately before the date of sailing. In Italy, theft of car radios has become so prevalent that a radio is now marketed with a small but essential and expensive component which can be removed when the car is left parked. Thefts from electricity and gas meters can be eliminated where coin meters are replaced by quarterly billing systems. Target removal can also be applied to some crimes against the person; some people run material risks of victimisation in certain conditions - for example girls hitch-hiking by themselves or walking alone late at night - and it may be possible to discourage people from putting themselves in such situations. A further variant of target removal is to be found in measures which disguise the opportunities for crime or make temptations less blatant, even if in these cases the target is only removed from the subjective world of potential offenders. For example, the rapid repair of vandalism damage may prevent further attacks. A study by Zimbardo (1973) showed that a car left in poor condition in a 'rough' inner city area rapidly attracted further depredation. And for whatever reason, walls carrying mural paintings appear not to attract graffiti to the extent that blank walls do.

iii. Removing the means to crime

Some sorts of crime have been dramatically reduced by removing the means to commit them. For example the incidence of aircraft 'skyjacking' has been reduced from an annual average of around 70 in the early seventies to the present rate of about 15 a year by screening passengers and baggage to detect weapons and bombs (Wilkinson, 1977). Gun control, including the control of imitation firearms, has been advocated as a method of reducing robbery and other crimes involving the threat or use of violence. The Scottish Council on Crime (1975) has proposed that pubs in which violence is frequent should serve drinks in plastic containers rather than glasses, to avoid their use as offensive weapons. It has been proposed, for example in Western Australia, that drunken driving could be reduced if offenders convicted of these offences were required to equip their vehicles with a breathalyser system connected to the ignition: only sober people would thus be able to start such a car. At a rather more mundane level, children can be denied the opportunities for some sorts of vandalism if, for example, they are not allowed to buy aerosol paint sprays. Legal but dangerous behaviour such as glue-sniffing can also be reduced by similar means.

iv. Reducing the pay-off

Some preventive measures are designed to reduce the incentives to crime, or the pay-off accruing to successful offenders. Most of these are applicable only to property crime and rest on making stolen goods less valuable to people who acquire them illegitimately. One example is to be found in the 'Operation Identification' schemes now popular in North America whereby households are encouraged to mark valuable possession with indelible codes which render the goods uniquely identifiable and thus of less value to the thief. Evaluation of such schemes (see Zaharchuk and Lynch, 1977; Heller *et al.*, 1975) point to a number of difficulties, including that of encouraging people to join. Participating households, however, have usually enjoyed some protection from burglary, which has been reflected in reduced overall levels of burglary in specific areas if - and this is unusual - the majority of householders have been involved. Another example of measures intending to disrupt the market for stolen goods is to be found in 'sting' operations which have been mounted by some American police departments. In these, under-cover police set themselves up as 'fences' with a view to make a mass arrest when they have acquired a sufficiently large 'clientele' of burglars (L.E.A.A., 1979). The rationale of these schemes lies less in the arrests themselves than in destroying the trust between thieves and fence, thus making the disposal of stolen goods more difficult. A final example is to be found in the theft of cheque books, which by themselves became of less value to thieves once credit cards were required to guarantee cheques. A further disincentive against the theft of both cheque books and credit cards would exist if the cards carried photographs. This measure has been resisted in this country, though there are many precedents elsewhere.

v. Formal surveillance

Formal surveillance refers to the activities of those whose sole or primary function is to provide a threat of apprehension sufficient to deter potential offenders. The police, of course, are the main agency to provide formal surveillance, but as discussed above there seem to be few realistic policies open to them which would achieve any further substantial impact on crime. Under certain circumstances, however, it may be worthwhile for public authorities or private organisations to provide themselves with formal surveillance for high risk targets. Some local authorities have set up special patrols to protect their parks, for example, and the private sector is making increasing use of private security services. The extent to which these are cost-effective is not known (and difficult to assess) but the provision of effective and continuous formal surveillance can prove very expensive. Another type of formal surveillance is to be found in community surveillance schemes promoted in the United States. It seems that these 'block watches' and vigilante patrols reduce fear of crime, but have minimal impact on actual levels of offending crime (e.g. Yin *et al.*, 1977); the sustained enthusiasm they require also tends to dissipate rapidly.

vi. Natural surveillance

The 'natural' surveillance afforded by people going about their everyday affairs can afford a source of (free) protection against crime, the potential of which can be exploited by intelligent design. 'Planning' solutions of this kind are associated most with Jane Jacobs (1961), who argued that increased population densities and 'mixed' land use (shared between housing, schools, recreational facilities and so on) would lead to a stronger sense of community and higher levels of street activity - conditions which she thought would provide considerable informal surveillance. These ideas are not unattractive, though their implementation would involve large-scale change and would conflict with current principles of town planning. They probably serve better as arguments for the conservation of existing communities than as guidelines for new development. There is no guarantee either that busier streets would lead to social cohesiveness, or that they would not simply attract more offenders wanting crowds as a cover.

The 'architectural' solutions of Oscar Newman have centred on the design of housing estates to give residents a better view of vulnerable areas and an increased sense of responsibility for the areas surrounding their homes. These have had particular appeal in combining solutions to the problem of crime with the promise of more attractive and less alienating environments. Both here and abroad 'action' projects to build or modify housing complexes along defensible space lines have been initiated as well as a number of empirical studies relating levels of crime and vandalism to defensible space features. Two such studies are presented in this book. Chapter 4 shows that the 'defensibility' of the design of different housing estates in London was of some importance in determining the degree of vandalism on the estates though a good deal less so than the number of children in residence. Chapter 5 shows that telephone kiosk vandalism was to a small extent dependent on the degree to which kiosks could be overlooked by domestic dwellings, but again other factors were overriding. These results are in line with other research findings, which taken together suggest that the gains to be had from defensible space measures are less than originally claimed (Mayhew, 1979). There is good reason to think that housing design plays a small part in determining levels of residential crime in comparison with other factors such as the characteristics of the residents and the quality of management (as Newman (1980) argues in his latest book). And besides, there are practical difficulties in modifying existing complexes, as well as competing priorities in designing new ones, such as fire regulations and the desire for privacy on the part of residents.

Other 'natural' surveillance measures aim to increase the visibility of crime by upgrading the quality of street lighting and designing out features such as pedestrian tunnels, which are susceptible to very little surveillance. Evidence as to the effectiveness of these measures is mixed. For example improvements in street lighting have often left crime rates unaffected (Tien *et al.*, 1979), though fear of crime seems to decrease - in itself a valuable result.

These findings may seem puzzling in view of the undeniable responsiveness of people to forms of self-policing - where, for example, those waiting for a bus criticise queue-jumpers. But studies of bystander intervention suggest that people are very reluctant to intervene in any occurrence which is out of the ordinary. People in their daily round rarely see a crime in progress; and if they do they are likely to place some innocent interpretation on what they see; they may be afraid to intervene or they may feel that the witness would resent interference; and they may be unable to summon the police or other help in time to achieve anything (cf. Mayhew *et al.*, 1979, Chapter 1).

vii. Surveillance by employees

If formal surveillance encounters problems of cost and natural surveillance is of limited effectiveness, there is rather more promise in exploiting the surveillance role of certain sorts of employee such as caretakers in schools and on housing estates, doormen, shop assistants, bus-conductors and so on. Research in North America has shown that apartment blocks with doormen are less vulnerable to burglary (e.g. Waller and Okihiro, 1978). In this country, vandalism has been shown to be less on housing estates with resident caretakers (D.O.E., 1977), and, as Chapter 3 describes, the problem of vandalism on buses is very considerably less where there is a driver and conductor rather than a driver alone. It also seems that public telephones in places such as pubs or launderettes, which are given some supervison by staff, suffer almost no vandalism in comparison with those in kiosks; that car parks with attendants in control have lower rates of car theft; that football hooliganism on trains can be reduced by giving permission for club stewards to travel free of charge; and that shoplifting is discouraged by the presence of assistants who are there to serve the customers (Walsh, 1978). The use of surveillance aids for employees can also help. The study reported in Chapter 6 shows that the installation of closed circuit television in four London Underground stations substantially reduced the incidence of theft and robbery.

viii. Environmental management

A final group of situational measures can be loosely identified under the heading of environmental management. These measures have some but not all the characteristics of the situational approach, and some are opportunity-reducing only in an extended sense. Insofar as a distinction can be drawn between the social and physical environment, this group tends to involve manipulation of the former. Perhaps the best example is to be found in the organisation of events such as football matches. Good liaison between the police, the two football clubs and

9

supporters' clubs can reduce the opportunities and temptations for vandalism and violence; arrival and departure of supporters can be better managed so as to avoid long periods of delay; within the grounds routes of access to stands and occupation of stands can be co-ordinated so as to minimise contact between rival supporters; sale of alcohol can be controlled within, and possibly around, the grounds. Again, public transport services in many towns shut down before the pubs have closed, leaving some customers stranded and in high spirits - a recipe for vandalism, thefts of cars and bicycles and so on. Co-ordination of transport and pub closing would eliminate the precipitating conditions. Housing allocation policies can be pursued which avoid high concentrations of children on certain sorts of estate, or which place families in accommodation that makes it easier for parents to supervise their children. Attempts to reduce truancy may also have a crime preventive rationale - the idea being that so long as they are at school, children have no opportunities to shoplift, vandalise property or steal cars. Chapter 7 describes an evaluation of a 'truancy sweep' run by the police, whereby truants were returned to their schools. In fact, in this particular case it emerged that truants could only have been responsible for a very small amount of crime, and the lesson to be drawn concerns less the effectiveness of the sweep and more the need for comprehensive problem analysis before instituting any preventive measure. Finally, some forms of environmental management whose main objectives are independent of crime control can have preventive effects. The recent law in this country requiring all motorcyclists to wear crash helmets was introduced to save lives, but it had the unintended effect of reducing the theft of motorcycles - no doubt because few potential thieves have a helmet with them at the right time and place, and without one they run a disproportionate risk of being stopped by the police.

DISPLACEMENT

The objection most often raised to opportunity-reducing measures is that they are subject to 'displacement' - either in causing offenders to choose their *time* carefully; shift their attention to other *places* where there are unprotected targets; employ a different *method* of committing crime; or turn instead to some completely different *form* of illegal activity (cf. Reppetto, 1976). To the extent that displacement occurs, then, situational measures might be effective only in protecting individual targets, leaving overall crime levels intact. There are reasons for thinking, however, that the problem of displacement has been overestimated. The dispositional bias in theory has tended to reinforce popular beliefs in the inevitability of displacement ('bad will out'). People find it hard to accept that actions with often momentous consequences for both victim and offender can turn on apparently trivial situational contingencies. But shifts in opportunities do affect levels of behaviour such as suicide, which not unlike many forms of crime is usually thought to be the result of deep-seated motivation. Hassall and Trethowan (1972) and Brown (1979) have provided convincing evidence that the marked reductions in suicide in this country in recent years can be attributed to reduction in the toxicity of gas used in houses for cooking and heating. Similar considerations apply to crime, though due regard must be paid to differences in motivation underlying different sorts of crime. Reducing opportunities for 'professional' criminal may be relatively ineffective, and indeed there is ample evidence of displacement in crimes such as bank robbery. Safe-cracking was the favoured form of bank robbery until the technology of safe outreached that of the 'cracksman'; over-the-counter armed robberies then became prevalent until preventive technology within banks displaced attacks to cash in transit. And at each stage in displacement there was an escalation of violence used (see, for example, Ball *et al.*, 1978). But even then there is no reason to suppose that the displacement was total. It is popularly believed that bank robbery in London was only brought under control with the aid of 'supergrasses' who provided Queen's evidence against their accomplice. But there would probably have been very many more robberies if the banks had taken no such situational measures.

It is also clear that at the other end of the spectrum there is an enormous number of people whose engagement in crime is marginal and who would be seen by very few people as 'real' criminals; these people, as almost all of us know from personal experience, commit offences which are defined by themselves as relatively trivial, are easy to commit and have a low probability of detection. There are very few people, according to self-report studies, who have not at some time or other committed offences such as shoplifting, theft from their employers or vandalism. A sizeable proportion of the population regularly evades income tax, drives whilst drunk, or commits drugs offences. It is unlikely that reducing opportunities for these sort of offences will displace energies to other illegal activities: if employees, for example, are thwarted from using the office phone for personal use, it offends commonsense to think that they will turn their attention to the office stationery supply; or that with the office stationery safely locked up they will pillage the local stationery shop.

It is the bulk of offences, however, that are neither 'professional' nor 'opportunistic' that pose the most difficult questions about displacement. These offences include many burglaries and instances of autocrime, where the offender, who may merely supplement his normal income through the proceeds of crime, has gone with the deliberate intention of committing the offence and has sought out the opportunity to do so. The difficulty posed for situational measures is one of the vast number of potential targets combined with the generally low overall level of security. Within easy reach of every house with a burglar alarm, or car with an anti-theft device, are many others without such protection. Chapter 2 provides an example: when steering column locks were introduced in this country in 1971 it was only to new cars; and whilst the risk of these cars being stolen was reduced, the risk to older cars increased, presumably as a result of displacement. Another case of possible displacement is to be found in the study of the use of C.C.T.V. in London Underground stations, described in Chapter 6. Whilst thefts and robberies declined in the stations equipped with C.C.T.V. there is some evidence to suggest a degree of displacement to adjacent stations.

11

It is sometimes possible to protect a whole class of property, as West Germany's experience with car theft shows (see Chapter 2). Even if these instances are comparatively few, this does not constitute a fatal difficulty. There must be geographical and temporal limits to displacement, and provided that a sufficient number of targets within these limits receive protection, an overall reduction in the crime in question will result. The less determined the offender, the easier this will be - evidence for which comes from a study (Decker, 1972) showing that the use of 'slugs' in parking meters in a New York district was greatly reduced by replacing the meters with ones which incorporated a slug-rejector device and in which the last coin inserted was visible in a plastic window. For most drivers there would be little advantage in parking their car in some other district just because they could continue to use slugs there.

Except perhaps for the most opportunist offenders, it is difficult to know for certain whether if stopped from committing one crime, people would turn instead to some other form of illegal activity. The methodological problems in identifying displacement effects of this kind are formidable. Commonsense, however, suggests that total displacement, especially to more harmful forms of offending, is most unlikely. It is telling, as Pease (1979) has argued, that nobody advocates preventive strategies which exploit the displacement effect; for example if displacement were inevitable, it would be possible to provide valuable targets with a degree of protection by leaving less vulnerable targets unprotected. For any particular form of crime, the rewards have to be commensurate with the risks taken; and the offender must be able to justify the offence to himself. A housewife thwarted from shoplifting in her local supermarket is most unlikely to turn to burglary.

The discussion of displacement has largely concentrated on the response of specific individuals to blocked opportunities. It is worth noting, however, that there is another form of displacement which operates at a societal level. Opportunities for one sort of offence might be greatly reduced but only at the expense of creating an entirely new set of criminal opportunities for a different group of people. For instance, the movement to a 'cashless' society in which financial transactions are largely computerised would greatly reduce the scope for petty pilfering but would create opportunities for theft of a very different order - large-scale computer crime.

In sum, then displacement is clearly not an 'all or none' phenomenon. Measures applied with varying degrees of comprehensiveness will result in different levels of displacement within and between categories of crime. A certain amount of displacement does not vitiate a preventive measure; so long as the benefits accruing from a reduction in crime exceed the social cost of a measure, it can be regarded as a success not only by the individuals receiving the protection but also by those who have a responsibility for crime control.

IMPLEMENTATION

Although criminologists and administrators may come increasingly to accept the logic of the situational approach, they may nevertheless regard it as either distasteful or impossible to implement sufficiently comprehensively to achieve any real impact.

First, there are those who would see the approach as little more than an attempt to paper over the cracks of an inequitable (and criminogenic) social system. This is an objection which is applicable to any form of ameliorative social intervention, and one can only reply that there is a case for seeing incremental change as the safest strategy for achieving a fairer society. Nor does the application of one ameliorative strategy necessarily exclude other reforms. Indeed, if effectively implemented the situational approach could reduce the use of arguably more repressive forms of social control.

A more widely held though less articulated objection is often formulated in terms of the erosion of human dignity. The situational approach may be seen at best as representing an over-simplified, mechanistic view of human behaviour and at worst a slur on human nature; the assumptions of the approach may be seen as environmentally determinist and at odds with the idea of people as moral agents. But the approach is predicated on a view of criminal behaviour as predominantly rational, and is thus entirely compatible with concepts of moral responsibility.

Rather more specifically, people tend to identify situational measures with their more unattractive aspects - barbed-wire, heavy padlocks, guard dogs, and private security forces. And in some of their more sophisticated forms (C.C.T.V. and electronic intruder alarms) they provoke fears on the one hand of totalitarian forms of state control where people's privacy is grossly abused, and on the other, of a 'fortress society' in which citizens scuttle from one fortified environment to another in perpetual fear and suspicion of their fellows. Against these criticisms it should be said that design measures rely on co-operation as much as compulsion and need not be obtrusive or inconvenient. Steel cash compartments in telephone kiosks are indistinguishable from aluminium ones, and vandal-resistant polycarbonate looks similar to glass. Steering-column locks are automatically brought into operation on removing the ignition keys of cars, and many people are quite unaware that their cars are fitted with them.

Where resistance to the situational approach on such grounds is overcome, people may still regard it as impracticable. They may believe that there is little scope for additional situational measures, in that sensible preventive measures are in the natural course of events discovered and employed. Against this however, it should be recognised that *systematic* attempts to implement situational measures are very rare indeed. People may also think the effective protection can only be bought through situational measures at unrealistic cost. Clearly it is a prerequisite that a preventive measure should be cost-effective though assessment of this ratio can be much more complicated than appears at first sight. Another criticism is that the limitations to the approach lie in the practical problems of implementation. For example, there are limits to what can be achieved through legislative action. Though some countries such as Greece have

13

made it illegal to leave ignition keys in unattended motor vehicles and gun control legislation operates in this country, the range of measures which can be compulsorily enforced is limited. There is strong opposition to legislation which can be construed as a sacrifice of individual freedom to the general good. Many Americans, for example, believe in an inalienable right to possess fire arms. And indeed, penalising people for creating criminal opportunities amounts to a reduction in their freedom which can only be justified if this loss is outweighted by gains in other freedoms resulting from such legislation. Moreover, when such legislation reaches the statute book there are consequent problems and costs of enforcement.

However, there are a number of other approaches to implementation. Many manufacturing and service industries in economically developed countries are dominated by cartels - small numbers of large organisations which collectively enjoy a virtual monopoly of the market. These will often respond favourably to pressures to incorporate crime preventive technology in their products or to adopt codes of practice to increases security. It may be against a company's interest to introduce a preventive measure in isolation from its competitors, but in its interest to do so in concert with them. The voluntary undertaking by motor manufacturers made in 1971 to introduce steering column locks is a case in point. There may also be more scope for persuading shops and supermarkets to introduce preventive measures. Retailers at the moment carry none of the public expense of prosecution (cf. Pease, 1979) and may be disinclined to change marketing techniques so long as these gain more in sales than they lose in theft. There may, however, be unexploited potential for negotiation between either central or local authorities and retailers' associations, in which the continued provision of free prosecution is only one bargaining counter. It is interesting to note in this context that the Danish police now refuse to bring prosecutions against shoplifters unless they have stolen goods in excess of £40 (Pease, 1979).

Negotiation between public authorities and the private sector is only possible when the relevant part of the private sector is already organised and has representative bodies. But the victims of a large amount of crime are private individuals, who cannot be reached so easily by negotiation. Except for the few measures where legislation is a real possibility, the only option is persuasion. This is offered on an individual basis to victims of crime by police crime prevention officers, and through mass-media publicity campaigns - mounted either by the police themselves or by central or local authorities. The degree to which advice given by crime prevention officers is taken up has not been rigorously evaluated. Though some recipients of the advice may, for example, install better locks to prevent burglary, many others may continue to rely on insurance cover. The problem here is that though the public costs of crime such as burglary and car theft can be high, the private costs sustained by an insured victim can be negligible - and indeed an unscrupulous claimant can make a profit. The advice of the police would probably achieve considerably more impact if it were possible to underpin this by some form of financial incentive from insurance companies themselves, such as 'no claims' bonuses.

Evaluations of the effectiveness of mass-media publicity are not very encouraging. Three such studies are presented in Chapters 8, 9 and 10 of this book. Two campaigns - one at local and one at national level - aimed to persuade motorists to lock their vehicles more securely, and both clearly failed to achieve this. The third campaign aimed to reduce vandalism. One of its strategies was to deter potential offenders; the other was to encourage parents to exercise greater supervision over their children. Like the car security campaigns, the publicity concerned with vandalism met with no measurable success. Vandalism rates were unaffected; and parents made no more effort to supervise their children after the campaign than before it. All three studies are consistent with a large body of research which suggests that crime prevention publicity has a minimal impact on behaviour, whatever other gains there are to be had in terms of attitude shifts (cf. Riley and Mayhew, 1980, Chapter 1).

The limitations of crime prevention campaigns in changing behaviour may appear surprising in view of the apparent good sense of the advice they offer. But possible explanations are to be found in the low levels of risk attached to victimisation. People leave their houses and their cars unlocked day after day without falling victim to theft. For example, in Chapter 8 it is estimated that, in 1977, cars without steering column locks (some ten times more at risk than those with them) face a one in eighteen chance of being stolen. This figure is less than at first appears when it is considered that it means that *on average* an owner of an unprotected car will be a victim of theft only once every eighteen years. And as for burglary, an 'average' household will fall victim only once every 30 years or so (taking into account crimes both reported and unreported to the police). The perceptions of 'negligent' members of the public may be more consistent with these realities than with the exaggerated picture of risks drawn by most campaigns.

Campaigns may also have limited impact because of simple forgetfulness on the part of potential victims, or because campaigns take insufficient account of the costs of the behaviour they promote, in relation to these low risks. The costs are in part financial - increasing household or vehicle security, for example, can cost money - but they also include inconvenience and loss of time. These competing influences on behaviour may counterbalance any belief that people might hold about the value of security, and undermine their good intentions.

A great many crimes are committed against public property or against institutions which are publicly-owned. Burglary and theft from schools and other public institutions are commonplace, while vandalism is particularly prevalent against public housing, schools, telephone kiosks, and transport systems. On the face of it, implementation of situational measures may appear relatively unproblematic in the public sector once their value has been demonstrated. However, where several agencies are involved, co-operation can prove harder to

15

achieve than it should do, as illustrated in Chapter 11. Again, the initial expense of the measures may need time to be recouped. They may also conflict with other priorities and constraints such as safety regulations. For example, restricting unauthorised access to public buildings through target hardening measures may make it difficult for legitimate occupants to leave quickly in the event of fire; polycarbonate glass effectively resists attacks by vandals, but also constitutes a greater fire hazard than conventional glass. Finally, though surveillance by public employees may reduce crime, it could prove unacceptable to such personnel to be given additional surveillance functions - a difficulty which has already arisen with school caretakers.

The varying problems which can be encountered in the situational approach underscore the need for comprehensive analysis of the problems to be solved before measures are implemented. Such analysis involves an assessment of the nature and range of opportunities to commit the offence in question; an assessment of environmental changes which would reduce the opportunities (without leading to undue displacement); and an assessment of the practicality and costs of the means available to bring about the environmental change. The analysis has to identify people or organisations which have the competence to reduce criminal opportunities effectively, and it has to assess both whether these have a responsibility to do so and whether this responsibility can be enforced (cf. Engstad and Evans, 1980).

To talk of problem analysis of this sort presupposes that official agencies already exist with the competence and preparedness to undertake it. Unfortunately, this is not yet the case. The police have a limited capability to analyse crime problems at local level; and central government, in shape of the Home Office, is similarly restricted in undertaking analysis of more global problems. As described in Chapter 11, some headway has been made by central government to stimulate and co-ordinate initiatives at local level. In this project, set in Manchester, the Home Office acted as a catalyst in encouraging schools to implement situational measures and other preventive steps to reduce vandalism. The experience gained was valuable but there is no prospect at present for developing this work. At local level, the police may seem the obvious agency to promote the situational approach, and there is certainly nothing to lose in encouraging the police to analyse crime problems more appropriately. Against this, it is questionable whether the police are always the appropriate body to co-ordinate the activities of other local authority agencies such as housing, planning, and education departments. Many local authorities are now creating policy-planning units, and it is possible that these may be better suited to the function.

SUMMARY
Against a general background of pessimism regarding the effectiveness of the criminal justice system, it has been argued that a situational approach to prevention affords considerable promise. Through the careful description and analysis of highly specific forms of offending it is possible to identify effective ways of

reducing opportunities for their commission. Many examples of this relating to offences of theft and vandalism are now to hand and there is every reason to think that as the technology of the situational approach improves, it will be success-fully applied to a much greater range of offences. Indeed some successes have already been chalked up in regard to some exotic forms of crime such as airline hijacking and the wholesale theft of high-value lorry loads. There are many crimes, however, where the offender is either so determined or emotionally disturbed as to invalidate the approach, and there are others where the costs of prevention may exceed the benefits. It should be clear, therefore, that a panacea for crime is not being offered. What does seem to be true, however, is that careful application of the situational approach can lead to substantial reductions in the incidence of specific though nonetheless troublesome forms of offending.

It was suggested that the neglect of the situational approach was a partial consequence of the dispositional bias of much criminological theory. This bias results from, and further encourages, a view of offenders as being somehow different from other members of soecicty, driven to commit crime by forces beyond their control. But a great deal of crime is committed by quite ordinary members of society who choose to break the law in response to particular situations and temptations. It seems therefore that theories of crime causation need to pay much more attention to situational factors, though it is important to maintain a balance between them and dispositional ones. A predominantly situational bias would be as unhelpful as a dispositional one in that it would be difficult to account for the behaviour of the small minority of people who persistently engage in offending.

Some of the drawbacks to the approach have been examined. The most frequent objection raised to situational measures is that they merely displace crime. It has been argued here that the extent of displacement has been considerably overesti-mated - this stemming at least in part from dispositional stereotypes of offenders as people whose *raison d'être* is to break the law. Problems of implementation include cost, difficulties in persuading people to take and co-ordinate action, and resistance arising out of a general distaste of what can be seen as mechanistic and illiberal solutions to complex social problems. These objections are neither specific to the situational approach nor sufficient to invalidate it. Like any form of social control, the situational approach is open to both use and abuse. Assessed in context - in the light of the costliness, unwieldiness and doubtful effectiveness of our existing criminal justice system – it is clear that it merits a great deal more support.

2 Steering column locks and car theft

P. Mayhew, R. V. G. Clarke and J. M. Hough

Since January 1971, all new cars imported to and manufactured in this country have been fitted with a steering column lock as standard equipment. These locks, which are automatically brought into operation when the ignition key is removed, were introduced in the face of increasing autocrime in preceding years to make it more difficult for vehicles to be illegally driven away[1]. The potential savings to be offset against the cost of fitting new vehicles with anti-theft equipment (approximately £10 a vehicle at 1971 prices) were considerable. Autocrime involves a great deal of police time and effort (it accounts for no less than 24% of recorded known indictable crime[2]), and there are losses to insurance companies which are passed on to car owners through the premiums they are required to pay. It also presents considerable hazards to road safety: according to a recent, unpublished paper by the Federal Bureau of Investigation, a stolen vehicle is 200 times more likely to be involved in a car accident than one which is not stolen. This may be because many of those who take cars are young and inexperienced drivers: 76% of those caught for taking cars in England and Wales in 1973 were under the age of 21, and of these almost half were under the minimum legal driving age of 17.

Although it was hoped that fitting new cars with steering column locks, would lead to a reduction in the overall level of vehicle theft and unauthorised taking, this has already been confounded by a remarkable increase in these offences since the beginning of 1971. In the Metropolitan Police District in 1974, for instance, vehicle theft and unauthorised taking was some 80% higher than in 1970. (Other indictable crime rose by 22% over the same period.) This increase, however, does not necessarily mean that steering column locks are ineffective, since published statistics make no distinction between cars protected by locks and those not[3]; the

---

[1] The agreement to fit steering column locks to cars (and vans derived from cars) was a voluntary one negotiated by the Home Office with the Society of Motor Manufacturers and Traders. Though the agreement allowed for alternative anti-theft devices, in practice most cars have been fitted with steering column locks. Thus, for convenience, all devices covered by the 1971 agreement are referred to in this report as steering column locks.

[2] *Criminal Statistics: England and Wales, 1973*. Autocrime here is unauthorised taking of vehicles, vehicle theft and the theft of property from vehicles. Vehicles in this case comprise commercial vehicles and two-wheelers as well as private cars and vans.

[3] At the same time, given increasing scepticism about the validity and reliability of official criminal statistics, it is worth making the point that statistics relating to cars which are illegally driven away are unusually accurate, at least as far as the reporting of offences is concerned. Because of insurers' requirements that the police be notified when a claim for theft is made, and because of the owner's dependence on the police to help retrieve cars, failure to report missing vehicles is rare (cf. Mansfield *et al.*, 1974).

overall increase in theft and unauthorised taking may well be accounted for by offences involving unprotected vehicles.

The study reported below aimed to assess the extent to which the increased security of vehicles manufactured since 1971 has prevented their unauthorised use, and given the continuing increase in theft and unauthorised taking, to examine the question of whether higher levels of protected cars will eventually reduce the overall incidence of these offences. Thus, the study analyses car theft in terms of one of the sources of opportunities for crime, namely lack of physical security. At the same time, it also provided a chance to study another aspect of opportunity through an examination of Wilkins' (1964) hypothesis of a direct relationship between the abundance of vehicles on the road and the frequency of their unauthorised use and, more generally, to comment on the long-standing question of whether preventive measures actually reduce crime or simply displace its pattern.

THE EFFECTIVENESS OF STEERING COLUMN LOCKS

The method employed in evaluating the effectiveness of steering column locks was to see whether a smaller proportion of 'new' cars were stolen or driven away in 1973 (i.e. since the introduction of the locks) than in 1969 (before their introduction). In both years 'new' cars were defined as those which, according to their licence numbers were three years old or less[1]. In 1973 all 'new' cars would have steering column locks, whereas in 1969 the great majority would not.

1969 rather than 1970 was taken to represent the 'before' situation since a small number of new cars introduced in 1970 were fitted with anti-theft devices in anticipation of the 1971 measure. Cars on the road in 1969 would have included a number of foreign models some of which had anti-theft devices and, although for strict accuracy some account should have been taken of these, the difficulties of doing so were incommensurate. In any case, the numbers involved would have been small; from information given to us by the Society of Motor Manufacturers relating to new foreign cars registered in this country in can be estimated that in 1969, in the country as a whole, foreign cars accounted for about 5% of the total cars on the road. And not all of them were fitted with anti-theft devices.

Sample

The sample was drawn from the Metropolitan Police District's statistical records. These maintain a distinction between theft of vehicles and unauthorised taking: a vehicle is considered stolen if it is not recovered with 30 days, otherwise

---

[1] The age of a vehicle cannot always be determined from its registration number. For example, second-hand cars imported from abroad are registered by year of import rather than manufacture, and some owners of new cars, especially expensive ones, obtain personalised number plates. These and other exceptions were rare enough to be discounted in the analysis.

Because of the practice since 1967 of changing the suffix to licence numbers on August 1, J registration cars were subdivided into those registered before February 1, 1971 (assumed to be without security protection) and those registered after that date (assumed to be fitted with anti-theft devices).

it is recorded as having been taken without authority. The sample comprised, in 1969 and 1973, the last 20 cars recorded as taken without authority and the last 20 (or as many as were available) recorded as stolen in each of the 23 main divisional stations of the MPD. Most of the cars in the sample were taken between August and December; although in 1969 and 1973 the number of cars taken at the very end of the year was rather high, there is no reason to think that for our purposes bias has been introduced by sampling car theft and unauthorised taking mainly from the second half of the year.

Results

Table 2:1 shows that in 1969 'new' cars represented 20·9% of all cars illegally taken, whereas in 1973 the figure had dropped to 5·1%, a difference we would attribute to the protection afforded by anti-theft devices[1]. Moreover, since in 1973 'new' cars represented a greater proportion of the total number of cars on the road (an estimated 37%) than in 1969 (34%), the difference is a little more accentuated than it appears.

Table 2:1
'New' cars (i.e. those 3 years old or less) as a proportion of cars stolen and taken without authority in the Metropolitan Police District in 1969 and 1973.

	1969			1973		
	Unauthorised taking	Theft	Total	Unauthorised taking	Theft	Total
All cars taken	460	457	917	460	458	918
New cars taken	93	99	192	30	17	47
% new cars	20·2%	21·7%	20·9%	6·5%	3·7%	5·1%

The 47 'new' cars sampled which were stolen or taken without authority in 1973 despite being protected by steering column locks were not all, of course, necessarily moved by tampering with the locks themselves. Although from the data examined it was not possible to tell how many of the 'new' cars were left insecure, it is quite likely that some of the cars would have been left with the keys either in them or readily available. A United States President's Commission report (1967) on crime suggested that 42% of cars stolen had unlocked ignitions, while in this country Baldwin (1974) has shown, similarly, that a disproportionate number of cars left insecure are taken and driven away, or have property stolen from them.

---

[1] Two other categories of autocrime maintained in MPD statistics are theft of property from a vehicle which is not moved and theft from a vehicle which is moved. Since 1969, theft from vehicles which have been moved has continued to rise along with unauthorised taking and theft, confirming that steering column locks have not improved the overall picture of car theft. At the same time, it appears from some rather limited data we collected that moving a car and taking property from it occurred very infrequently among vehicles fitted with steering column locks, again suggesting that such locks are effective anti-theft devices.

21

Thus, if steering column locks are less effective than might be expected from their technical design, some degree of carelessness on the part of car owners is likely to provide part of the explanation.

Although Table 2:1 shows a greater decline in theft than in unauthorised taking, this was not statistically significant ($\chi^2 = 3\cdot6$; 1 df). Steering column locks might have been expected, in fact, to have had a greater impact on unauthorised taking than on theft, given that 'stolen' cars are often regarded as being taken by determined thieves interested in resale, but cars recovered within 30 days as being taken by more opportunistic 'joy-riders', or those in need of transport. It is becoming increasingly difficult, however, to maintain the distinction between theft and unauthorised taking on the basis of a 30-day retrieval period, since more than half the cars recorded as stolen in the MPD are eventually recovered. In easier circumstances, they might have been recovered sooner and thereby have been classified as taken without authority. Moreover, in the present sample, there was no evidence, as one might have expected, that stolen cars were newer than those taken for more casual purposes, since the distribution of cars of various ages between the two categories of theft and unauthorised taking was statistically indistinguishable. This again suggests that the present distinction between the two categories is insufficiently sound to test whether steering column locks have less of a deterrent effect on professional thieves than on more casual cartakers.

The possibility that some factor other than increased vehicle security had inter-vened since 1969 to reduce the vulnerability of 'new' cars in 1973 was dismissed as remote given that the theft of 'new' commercial vehicles and 'new' motorcycles (neither of which had been covered by any comparable requirement for addi-tional security) had not dropped since 1969. On the contrary, a limited sample of these vehicles was examined, and the proportion of 'new' models stolen was found to have increased from 19% in 1969 to 22·5% in 1973.

It seems, then, that steering column locks are efficient in reducing the risk of cars fitted with them being illegally driven away. In fact, extrapolating from our sample, the risk of a 'new' car being stolen or taken without authority in the MPD was about three times less in 1973 than in 1969. The risk to 'old' cars, on the other hand, nearly doubled over the same period and it seems most likely that part of this increase in risk reflects the greater security of 'new' cars - protecting these may well have re-directed some thieves to easier targets.

FUTURE LEVELS OF THEFT AND UNAUTHORISED TAKING

While, at present, steering column locks are not providing the police with any overall benefit, their effectiveness in preventing the theft and unauthorised taking of cars to which they are fitted suggests that as the proportion of protected cars increases, the numbers of these offences might fall. For various reasons, however, it is difficult to make any precise estimate of when steering column locks might begin to have such an effect. In the first place, like other locks, steering column locks become easier to 'break' as they become worn, so that the protection they

22

give may diminish with age. Again, as more cars have locks, it is arguable that the need for the unauthorised user to 'break' them will increase and he may become increasingly ingenious in his attempts. This might be especially applicable to those who make a living from stealing cars (by resale of the vehicle, or its parts) since the value of old, unprotected cars will diminish as the proportion of cars with locks increases. Lastly (and this is particularly likely if locks maintain their effectiveness, or are supplemented by more elaborate security devices), professional thieves may respond by changing their *modus operandi*. For instance, they may increasingly acquire cars from locations such as garage forecourts where the keys are likely to be available, or by fraudulent means from car hire firms.

The central difficulty in making reliable predictions about future levels of auto-crime, however, is that our findings show that the number of 'stealable' cars[1] on the road (i.e. those without steering column locks) does not clearly or directly influence the level of theft and unauthorised taking. Figure 2:1 shows a progressive increase in theft and unauthorised taking since 1961 (notably sharp in 1974) which has not been affected by the reduction in the number of 'stealable' vehicles following the 1971 measures. Although the number of 'stealable' vehicles was even lower in 1974 than in 1961, the volume of car theft and unauthorised taking was 160% higher at the later date than at the earlier one. Theft and unauthorised taking is apparently not dictated solely by the number of easy opportunities available, and reducing opportunities by fitting an increasing proportion of cars with anti-theft devices might not effect the level of theft in any predictable way.

The increase in theft and unauthorised taking shown in Figure 2:1 also calls into question the hypothesis that autocrime is fairly closely related to the number of vehicles registered, as Wilkins (1964) has argued was the case in England and Wales between 1938 and 1961. If the number of cars *without* steering column locks is taken as an index of opportunity to steal cars, his hypothesis is, as indicated above, clearly untenable; if the total number of cars *registered* is taken as this index, the data still disproves the hypothesis as it stands: for instance, in 1974 there was a 34% increase over 1973 in the number of thefts and unauthorised takings, but a slight decrease in the total number of cars registered[2].

A more sophisticated model to explain levels of car theft has been proposed by Gould and his associates (Gould, 1969; Mansfield *et al.*, 1974) which takes into account the changing relationship between the 'supply' of vehicles and the 'demand' for them from various sections of the population. Explaining varying

---

[1] 'Stealable' cars are those assumed to be without steering column locks on the grounds that they were first registered before 1971. The number of such vehicles on the road in subsequent years was estimated by subtracting new registrations from the total number registered in each year, allowing for a small amount of 'wastage' of vehicles first registered after January 1971.

[2] There are other problems with Wilkins's analysis. In relating the level of vehicle registration to the volume of *theft from* motor vehicles, rather than to the *theft of* or to the *unauthorised taking* of these vehicles, Wilkins appears to have chosen the index of autocrime which supported his proposition best. Moreover, even this rather convenient measure of autocrime has not related well since 1961 (when his analysis finished) to the increase in vehicle registration.

Figure 2:1

THEFT AND UNAUTHORISED TAKING OF MOTOR VEHICLES IN THE
METROPOLITAN POLICE DISTRICT AND NUMBERS OF 'STEALABLE'
CARS (i.e. WITHOUT STEERING COLUMN LOCKS) REGISTERED, 1961-1974

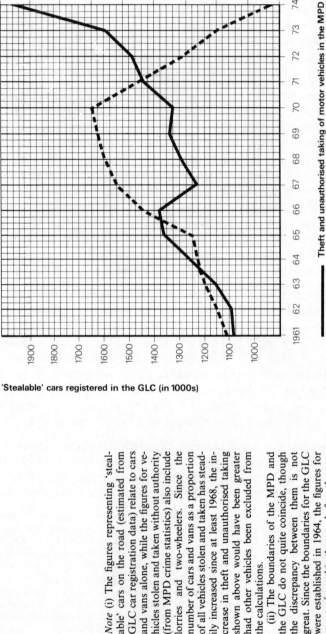

Motor vehicles stolen or taken without authority in the MPD (in 1000s)

'Stealable' cars registered in the GLC (in 1000s)

———— Theft and unauthorised taking of motor vehicles in the MPD

- - - - - 'Stealable' cars registered in the Greater London Council

Note (i) The figures representing 'stealable' cars on the road (estimated from GLC car registration data) relate to cars and vans alone, while the figures for vehicles stolen and taken without authority (from MPD crime statistics) also include lorries and two-wheelers. Since the number of cars and vans as a proportion of all vehicles stolen and taken has steadily increased since at least 1968, the increase in theft and unauthorised taking shown above would have been greater had other vehicles been excluded from the calculations.

(ii) The boundaries of the MPD and the GLC do not quite coincide, though the discrepancy between them is not great. Since the boundaries for the GLC were established in 1964, the figures for cars registered in the area before then are estimated.

24

levels of autocrime at different periods and in different countries, they have claimed that when vehicles are in short supply they are the preserve of the professional thief, but when they are abundant they are stolen mainly by amateurs (for instance by those who wish to keep a vehicle for their own use). The model, however, does not adequately accommodate the pattern of autocrime in this country. For instance, while it is claimed that vehicle thefts peak and begin to decline when there are about 160–200 cars per thousand of population, there is no sign that vehicle thefts in this country are beginning to decline even though vehicle registrations are now well beyond the level specified. Moreover, the steep increase in theft and unauthorised taking that has occurred in this country recently cannot be easily explained in terms of supply and demand since the number of vehicles on the road has not greatly altered.

One shortcoming of the predictive models of both Wilkins and Gould would appear to be that no weight is given to varying levels of vehicle security. More precisely, their models may only be tenable when the abundance of similarly insecure vehicles is the only changing factor over time. They fail to accommodate situations in which the overall level of vehicle security is raised, as we explain below has been the case in the German Federal Republic, and those in which a proportion of the cars on the road are made more secure.

The importance of vehicle security has been confirmed by our findings that cars protected with locks are much less likely to be taken or stolen than they would otherwise have been. Other evidence (Bundeskriminalamt, 1973) of its importance is provided by the pattern of autocrime in the German Federal Republic since 1963 when all cars, both new and old, were required to be fitted with anti-theft devices (see Figure 2:2). Increasing the security of the total population of cars in this way produced a very marked decrease (62%) in car theft during the first complete year (1963) when all cars were protected over the last complete year when no cars were protected (1960). In fact, security protection decreased the risk of a car being stolen or taken without authority by a factor of nearly *four*, and this decrease has endured: the risk of a car being stolen was virtually identical in 1972 as in 1963, taking into account an 86% increase in registrations. In other words, the German case indicates that the incidence of car theft is related not only to the number of cars on the road (as Wilkins suggests), or the changing demand for them by different types of car thief (as on Gould's argument), but also to the degree to which they are secured.

There are considerable problems, therefore, in accurately predicting future levels of car theft and unauthorised taking in this country. The apparent fact, however, that a substantial proportion of cars taken involve youths who 'joy-ride' or miss the last bus home perhaps suggests that anti-theft devices will eventually reduce the overall level of autocrime. According to MPD statistics for 1973, 85% of cars stolen or taken without authority were recovered, the great majority of them within 30 days. For the most part, these cars can reasonably be assumed to have been taken by casual unauthorised users who were probably responding to the

25

Figure 2:2

THEFT AND UNAUTHORISED TAKING OF CARS IN THE GERMAN FEDERAL REPUBLIC, AND NUMBERS OF CARS REGISTERED, 1957-1972

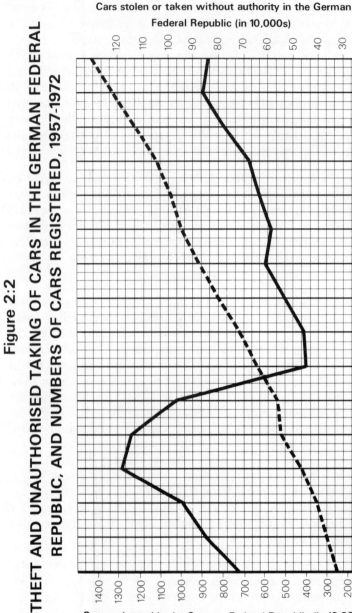

Cars stolen or taken without authority in the German Federal Republic (in 10,000s)

Cars registered in the German Federal Republic (in 10,000s)

Theft and unauthorised taking of cars in the German Federal Republic

All cars registered in the German Federal Republic

26

opportunity presented by the large number of relatively insecure vehicles on the road. One might well expect that the fitting of steering column locks to an increasing proportion of vehicles will eventually be reflected in a lower incidence of 'joy-riding' and 'journey-making' on the part of the less painstaking, more opportunist thief. For eventually the absolute numbers of unprotected cars on the road will fall to figures low enough to alter materially the ease of finding a car for illegitimate use. Thus in the MPD in 1973, 1:32 unprotected cars were stolen or used without authority at a time when cars with steering column locks accounted for about 37% of cars on the road. In the MPD in 1977, protected cars will account for about 68% of cars, and in 1980 for about 81%[1]. It is worth noting that at these two levels some 1:20 and 1:13 unprotected cars would have to be stolen or taken without authority if the same number of such vehicles were to be taken as in 1973. On the face of it, either proportion seems untenably high given (apart from anything else) that risks of these magnitudes would hardly be accepted complacently by owners of old cars - or by their insurers.

DISPLACEMENT*

A main finding of the present study is that although steering column locks have substantially reduced the risk of cars fitted with them being illegally driven away, they seem also to have had the effect of redirecting thieves to cars without them. The results are therefore compatible with a 'specific' displacement effect. Or, at least, the findings support 'specific' displacement in the current situation when, given the 1973 level of cars with steering column locks (in the MPD about 37%) the absolute number of unprotected cars (some 1·2 million) seemed quite adequate to allow displacement to these: the potential thief or joy-rider would have little difficulty in finding an unprotected car when he wanted one. We have already pointed out, however, some of the difficulties of knowing whether displacement to unprotected targets will as readily occur when the number of these is heavily outweighed by the number of cars protected by anti-theft devices.

As it becomes increasingly difficult to find unprotected cars, the 'specific' displacement that will occur may be of the kind whereby car thieves - or, more precisely, some car thieves - change their methods of operation. It seems likely that those who at the moment steal cars for re-sale will, as well as developing more sophisticated methods of moving secure cars and devoting more effort to the fraudulent acquisition of cars, also displace some of their present activities to related offences such as stealing parts and contents without moving the car and stealing relatively vulnerable commercial vehicles. In contrast, displacement to other autocrime is less likely to occur among those who casually and opportunis-

---

[1] These estimates assume that the yearly level of new registrations will remain constant at its 1973 level, and that the 'fall-off' in registrations of old cars will conform to present patterns in the GLC (as they appear from GLC car registration data). No attempt has been made to predict the situation beyond 1980.

* *Editors' Note: A more up-to-date discussion of displacement, including rather finer distinctions than are made here, can be found in Chapter 1.*

tically take cars for purposes (for instance, a ride home) which would not be obviously served in other ways.

While this study provides evidence that curtailing opportunities for autocrime might lead to a degree of 'specific' displacement, it says nothing of course about the extent to which reduced opportunities for car theft will 'generally' displace behaviour to other forms of deviance. We ourselves would be hesitant to suggest that, with higher levels of vehicle security, there will be any greater incidence of other crimes whose ends are not congruent with those presently served by autocrime, and for which different internal and external sanctions might apply. Thus, in relation to those casual car users whose activities are unlikely to be 'specifically' displaced to other forms of autocrime, we would argue also that their energies are unlikely to be 'generally' displaced to mugging passers-by for money to get home, hijacking taxis, or assaulting bus conductors.

GENERAL IMPLICATIONS FOR CRIME PREVENTION

The implications of this study for crime prevention, then, are of some weight. For having shown that steering column locks have, for the time being at least, probably displaced some autocrime to unprotected cars, we have shown how optimistic was the hope that overall levels of car theft might be reduced through a securing of a proportion of those vehicles at risk. A clear lesson of this research is that the police will derive only limited benefit from preventive measures which protect only a proportion of vulnerable property - as indeed has already been argued by Riccio (1974) in relation to autocrime in the United States. If within easy reach there is equally vulnerable and equally attractive property, anti-social behaviour will probably be displaced to this. To derive real benefit the whole class of property must simultaneously be secured - a principle, of course, which has been borne out by the successful German experience of anti-theft devices on cars[1].

Inevitably, however, a total securing of a class of property will cost more than a partial securing of it; and it is worthwhile trying to assess whether, in Germany

---

[1] Another interesting example of a legislative measure which has been applied to a total class of vulnerable property is the requirement brought into operation on 1 June 1973, that all riders of motor-cycles (and similar two-wheelers) wear protective headgear. While the measure was introduced for reasons of road safety, there is evidence that an unintended but valuable consequence of the regulation has been a reduction in the number of two-wheelers stolen and taken without authorisation. The number of two-wheelers so removed in the MPD fell from 5280 in the 12 month period immediately prior to the introduction of the protective headgear regulations to 3997 in the subsequent twelve months (a decrease of 24%). This was particularly noticeable in relation to unauthorised taking, and contrasts with a rise of 35% in the theft and unauthorised taking of other motor vehicles in the same period. To the extent that vehicle theft is opportunist, it is reasonable to think that some potential users (aware of what was a well-published requirement) have been deterred from illegally taking two-wheelers because of their increased visibility if not wearing a crash helmet. It is not unlikely, of course, that some small proportion of the rise in 1973 in the theft and unauthorised taking of other motor vehicles could be accounted for by displaced two-wheeler theft. Indeed, such an effect would be a good illustration of how 'specific' displacement might operate between two categories of similar offences involving property which serves generally similar ends.

for instance, the cumulative cost of fitting all cars on the road with anti-theft devices has been justified in terms of some of the more definable savings made. Indeed, since locks on cars serve no obvious purpose other than increasing car security, their cost-effectiveness as a crime prevention measure is particularly well worth considering.

Between 1961 and 1973, the cost of fitting all cars at risk in the German Federal Republic with anti-theft devices can be estimated at £177m, on the assumption that the cost of equipping each existing car was £15 and each newly-produced car £10. On the further assumption (and it is a very optimistic one) that, of all cars registered, the proportion stolen or taken without authority in each year since 1960 would have stayed at the 1960 level, the loss of some 2·6m cars has been prevented over the 12-year period - apparently by the universal fitting of anti-theft devices. Leaving aside that the protection of many newer vehicles will be of continuing benefit after 1973, the total cost to car-owners of £177m, when averaged over these 2·6m cars, gives a figure of about £70 per theft prevented, i.e. to prevent the loss of one car, some seven individual car-owners have each had to bear the relatively small expense of £10 to protect their car with an anti-theft device. This cost can be offset against the cumulative savings made from the total number of prevented losses in terms of police time, the costs to insurance companies, the material costs to owners of stolen vehicles, and the cost associated with the road accidents in which stolen vehicles are often involved. While it is difficult to put a figure on these savings (and we acknowledge that for cars retrieved quickly and undamaged, the inconvenience costs might be greater than the material ones) it would seem, on the face of it, that the fitting of steering column locks in Germany has been cost-effective.

Up to the present time, steering column locks have been cost-effective in this country only for the owners of cars to which they have been fitted - a small additional sum on the price of a new car has conferred the benefit on these owners of a substantially reduced chance of their car being stolen. But the fitting of steering column locks to new cars has not been of any great collective benefit since, on our argument, the protection of only a proportion of cars on the road has in all probability meant that car theft has been displaced to continuingly vulnerable (though admittedly less valuable) older vehicles.

At first sight, then, the argument for requiring old cars as well as new ones to be fitted with anti-theft devices might seem a strong one. In fact, even discounting the difficulties of gaining public agreement, the time that would elapse before action could be taken (realistically perhaps three years) might render the measure superfluous. By 1978, an estimated 73% of cars in the GLC will be protected by anti-theft devices anyway, and as we have said, the owners and insurers of the remaining vehicles may not be prepared to run the enhanced risks of these cars being removed illegally.

In the meanwhile, the disproportionate increase in theft and unauthorised taking over the past few years requires some explanation, and this will be helped by more accurate information about the purposes for which cars are taken, the immediate inducements which operate, and the ways in which different types of illegal users acquire cars. Nevertheless, it would seen - given the still large proportion of cars recovered intact - that casual offenders are heavily implicated in the recent increase in autocrime. In direct practical terms, then, though we have argued that steering column locks will ultimately prevent much casual taking of vehicles, perhaps the benefits of such locks should be maximised by making it more difficult for drivers to leave keys in the car (through the use of spring-ejection locks and key warning systems), and more difficult for keys to be acquired fraudulently. To the extent, however, that some of the increase in car-taking is in the furtherance of theft of contents, it would be worth trying to improve door locks. In any event, a technical approach to the problem of vehicle security is likely to prove more acceptable than at least the alternative of introducing legal sanctions against drivers who leave their cars insecure.

3 Damage on buses: The effects of supervision

A. Sturman

On the argument (cf. Clinard and Wade, 1957; Wade, 1967) that vandalism tends to be committed spontaneously rather than after deliberate planning, it would seem a particularly appropriate offence to include in any examination of the role of opportunity in crime. Vandalism is particularly likely to be directed at abandoned houses, buildings under construction and closed school buildings in secluded areas (Wade, 1967), all of which present opportunities for damage perhaps largely to the extent that they are left unsupervised. Certainly, experimental research in social psychology has indicated that under conditions of little supervision, the occurrence of various forms of dishonest or irresponsible behaviour increases (Hartshorne and May, 1928; Mischel and Gilligan, 1964; Medinnus, 1966; Aronson and Mettee, 1968) while, in another context, attention has been drawn to how urban street crime can be reduced through intensified police activity (e.g. Press, 1971). With the exception of Newman's (1972) research on public housing estates in the United States, however, little empirical work has been done relating vandalism specifically to levels of supervision in the community.

The small-scale research project reported below provided a chance to study how opportunities for vandalism on buses might be mediated by the ability of drivers and conductors to supervise passengers. Recognising that supervision is affected by design features of the bus - closer supervision of passengers is possible, for example, on buses with conductors and on the lower deck of a double deck bus (where the conductor would normally be) - the location and extent of damage on four different types of double deck buses were related to the different levels of supervision which the crew were able to provide. It was hoped that the results, by elucidating factors in vandalism over which bus operators might have some control, could provide a sound empirical base for attempts to minimise damage.

THE STUDY

Sample

The sample of 99 buses was chosen from the two garages which service the Southern Area of the Central Divisions of Greater Manchester Transport. A 25% random sample was taken, stratifying for the four main types of double deck bus - one-man operated, dual purpose, front-entrance conventional, and rear-entrance conventional. The numbers of each type of bus making up the sample and their principal characteristics are shown below:

Type	No. in Sample	Conductor	Average age of sample buses	Staircase position	Number of seats	
					Lower	Upper
One-man operated	48	No	3·5 yrs	Centre	26–30	45–47
Dual purpose	22	Yes - 80% of journeys	6·4 yrs	Front	32–33	43
Front-entrance conventional	12	Yes	8·8 yrs	Front	33	43
Rear-entrance conventional	17	Yes	16·4 yrs	Rear	28	32–37

Method

Since the bus company kept no individual job records of repair work related to vandalism, damage was directly recorded by the research worker. Four different types of damage were distinguished - holes, tears, scratches and writing - which depending on their size were given a score of between 1 and 3. Damage was recorded for individual seating units, defined as the seat itself and its immediately surrounding area. Although these units varied slightly in size, analysis showed that this was not an important factor in the results. For the main analysis of the data, damage was scored for the seating units in four locations of the bus: the front, middle and rear third (excluding the back seat) and the back seat itself. In comparing damage between these different locations, mean seating unit damage scores were calculated to take account of the fact that the number of units in each location varied between buses.

Damage was recorded over a period of five evenings when the buses were in the garage. No reliability checks were made of the ratings as this was only intended to be a small-scale exploratory study. As the damage was recorded by one observer, however, it was not expected that the assessments would vary greatly between parts of the bus or from one bus to another. In recording damage, no allowance was made for the age of the bus or for when it had last been renovated[1], though account was taken of these factors in the analysis. Nor was any attempt made at the recording stage to distinguish between accidental and deliberate damage, though writing and many of the larger holes and tears (which would attract larger damage scores) were quite obviously the result of vandalism.

Although four types of damage were distinguished at the recording stage, they

---

[1] An exception to this was that on the few occasions when parts of seats or complete seats had been replaced they were separately recorded. As a result of such replacements, not all seats on a particular bus would have been at risk for the same amount of time. In order to test whether this affected the comparisons the two types of conventional bus, which had had most of the seat changes, were compared both overall and by different locations without including any seat which had been changed: differences in damage scores found between the bus types were, however, unaffected.

were re-grouped for the purpose of analysis since when considered separately there were too many zero scores to make detailed comparisons between buses possible. In order to arrive at a basis for re-grouping, principal component analyses were performed on the damage scores in the four different locations and overall. As the results were very much the same whatever location was studied, only the factor loadings from the overall analysis were used. Holes, tears, and writing had roughly equal loadings on the first factor while scratches alone loaded highly on the second (see Table 3:1) - the first two factors being the only two with an eigenvalue of 1 or more. This suggested that holes, tears, and writing had much in common, i.e. they may all have been the result of vandalism, whereas the scratches were of a different order of damage - perhaps caused accidentally by large objects such as baskets or umbrellas. It was therefore decided to sum scores for holes, tears and writing and to omit scratches altogether.

Table 3:1
Correlation coefficients and factor loadings (all seat positions)

	Holes	Tears	Writing	Factor 1	Factor 2
Holes	1·00			0·80	−0·11
Tears	0·57	1·00		0·86	0·01
Writing	0·35	0·45	1·00	0·70	−0·34
Scratches	0·13	0·24	0·05	0·34	0·92

RESULTS

Damage on the lower and upper decks

For all four types of bus the seats on the upper deck suffered much more damage than those on the lower deck (see Table 3:2). The difference was least pronounced on rear-entrance conventional buses - mean seat damage on the upper deck being *five times* as great as on the lower deck - and most pronounced on one-man operated buses and on dual purpose buses - where damage on the upper deck was over *twenty times* greater than on the lower deck.

Table 3:2 highlights, secondly, the particularly great amount of damage on the upper deck of one-man operated buses: they suffered almost twice as much damage there as any of the other three types of bus ($p < ·001$) where the extent of upper deck damage did not vary significantly. Another indication of the severity of damage on one-man operated buses was that some of the seats on twelve of these buses (a quarter of the total) had been replaced by hard wearing plastic seats which are fitted only where vandalism is prevalent. None of the other buses had been fitted with these seats.

Table 3:2
Mean seat damage score by deck and type of bus

	One-man operated (n=48)	Dual purpose (n=22)	Conventional with front entrances (n=12)	Conventional with rear entrances (n=17)
Lower deck	0·22	0·12	0·23	0·37
Upper deck	5·12	2·47	2·70	1·97

The greater vulnerability of seats on the upper deck of all bus types was not unexpected given that the upper deck would be less supervised than the lower deck. On conductor-operated buses the conductor would spend most of his time on the lower deck, leaving the upper deck unattended for long periods. Lack of supervision, of course, could also explain the particular vulnerability of upper deck seats on buses operated without a conductor: drivers would observe the activities of passengers on the upper deck only through the observation mirrors sited at the front of the bus. The fact that the dual purpose buses are more similar to conventional buses than to one-man operated buses in the extent of damage suffered on the upper deck is probably explained by the bus company's estimate that dual purpose buses operate with conductors on about 80% of their journeys.

From Table 3:2 it can be seen, thirdly, that on the lower deck, despite relatively small amounts of damage, there were again differences between bus types. Analysis of variance showed these to be significant ($p < ·05$). While one-man operated buses suffered most damage on the upper deck, it was rear-entrance conventional buses which suffered most from damage committed on the lower deck. Although conventional buses are slowly being phased out - the older rear-entrance ones first - the bus company has not adopted a policy of letting the damage to the oldest buses go unrepaired. Indeed, if there had been such a policy, one would have expected such buses to have suffered more damage on the upper deck than was the case.

The probable explanation for this difference in damage on the two decks is that, in addition to the effect of supervision, the effect of the buses' age has also to be taken in account. Separate analyses of damage to buses within each of the four types had not shown any direct relationship between age and extent of damage, but this was probably because the age range was too narrow for each bus type. To have treated all buses together, however, would have confounded the analysis by inclusion of the supervision factor. On the upper deck, the amount of supervision was clearly a more important factor than the age of the bus because the one-man operated buses, despite being at risk for the least time, had suffered most damage and the oldest buses with a conventional rear-entrance had suffered the least. On the lower deck, however, the oldest buses, in particular the rear-entrance conventional ones, had suffered the most damage, some of it possibly caused not by vandalism but by extensive ordinary wear. Nevertheless, supervision may still have had a limited effect upon the extent of damage on the lower deck, as the least supervised one-man operated buses had suffered more damage than the older dual purpose ones.

The location of damage on the upper deck within different bus types

Analysis of variance of damage scores for the upper deck again revealed that there were significant differences between the bus types in the location of damage ($p < .001$), the greatest differences being between the one-man operated and all the others, for each of the locations.

Table 3:3
Bus type by location of damage on upper deck - mean seat damage scores

	One-man operated (n=48)	Dual purpose (n=22)	Conventional with front entrances (n=12)	Conventional with rear entrances (n=17)
Front	2·55	0·81	1·30	1·68
Centre	3·25	1·27	0·91	1·16
Rear	6·22	2·42	2·83	1·58
Back seat	18·10	11·55	12·96	9·53

It can be seen from Table 3:3 that for all bus types, the back seat had suffered far more damage than any other location and, with the exception of the rear-entrance conventional buses, the damage generally got worse towards the back of the bus. These results were not unexpected given the particular perspectives of this study: the back seat would be the only seat where the activities of the occupants would be unobserved by other passengers, and the rear of the bus would also be less visible to most passengers than the front.

On the rear-entrance conventional buses, although the back seat was still most severely damaged, there was a greater amount of damage at the front of the bus than in the centre or rear. It was thought that these findings might partially be accounted for by a 'displacement' of damage resulting from the position of the staircase - rear-entrance conventional buses being the only buses with their staircases at the back. People sitting near to the staircase might be more reluctant to commit acts of vandalism when there would be a danger of being surprised by another passenger or the conductor[1]. At the same time, the relatively small amount of damage on the back seat of rear-entrance conventional buses and, indeed, the relatively small amount of damage on the upper deck in general (see

---

[1] In fact, when the two types of conventional bus were separately examined, no significant difference was recorded in the location of damage, although the tendency for rear-entrance buses to suffer more damage at the front and less at the back was consistently found for each of the individual damage types which make up the aggregate score.

Table 3:2) suggests that the position of the staircase on these buses, as well as displacing some vandalism, might also have prevented some.

On the one-man operated and dual purpose buses with, respectively, staircases situated at the centre and the front, it is not possible to estimate whether the location of damage has similarly been affected by staircase position because any 'displacement' would be in the direction of the back of the bus, which was likely to be most severely damaged wherever the staircase was positioned.

DISCUSSION

Two main findings, then, emerge from this study: first, damage was greatest on buses without a conductor, even though these were the newest of the buses studied[1]; second, on all buses, including those with conductors, damage was greatest in areas of low supervision (especially the upper deck and the back seat). Neither of these findings may be surprising, but the magnitude of the differences in the damage recorded should not be overlooked. For example, on one-man operated and dual purpose buses there was about 20 times as much damage on the upper as on the lower deck. The finding of a relationship between the supervision of passengers and the amounts of damage on buses is broadly in agreement with Newman's (1972) finding reported in *Defensible Space* that the least observed parts of housing estates, such as lifts and staircases, suffered the highest rates of crime.

Although a relationship was found in this study between lack of supervision and damage, it is conceivable that the location of damage *within* buses, but not the extent of damage *between* different types, may be affected by where different people choose to sit. With this in mind a small observational study involving 47 bus journeys was conducted to find out where people of different age and sex tend to sit. On any one journey only passengers on one deck of the bus were studied. For practical reasons the study took place during Monday to Friday of one week, and only on one-man operated buses, although it was accepted that on other types of bus and at weekends the age and sex of passengers might be different. The results showed that slightly more people travel on the lower deck, and that about 60% of them were women and girls. On the upper deck about 70% of the passengers were male and 21% were estimated, again without checking reliability, to be under 16; on the lower deck 14% were estimated to be of that age. A separate analysis of where people choose to sit on the upper deck showed that children (especially boys) are more likely to be found at the back of the bus, especially on the back seat (48% of the back seat passengers were under 16), while the older passengers who travel on the upper deck more often sit at the front (60% of passengers over 16 sat at the front).

These results, then, show that those people who are considered least likely to engage in acts of vandalism (older passengers, women and girls) have a tendency

---

[1] Although conductor operated buses tended to serve certain routes, there was no reason to think that these would attract more or less vandals than the routes served by one-man operated buses.

to sit in the areas least damaged (the lower deck and the front of the upper). Nevertheless, these differences between groups of people in where they choose to sit are not nearly as large as the differences in the amount of damage to the various seat locations. Moreover, it should not be overlooked that very substantial differences were found between bus types in amount of damage and that these were most likely to have resulted from differential supervision. It would seem likely, therefore, that differences in amount of damage between the various parts of the bus are also largely due to supervision factors, with perhaps a smaller part of the differences attributable to different kinds of passengers choosing particular seats. Even more likely is that these two factors are to some extent interdependent - potential vandals probably choose unsupervised areas even if they do not intend to cause damage. Vandalism itself might still be a spontaneous reaction to the opportunties that the situation presents.

Further knowledge about this process could be achieved in several ways. A study of where people sat on the upper deck of the two types of conventional bus might show whether those types of people who sat at the back of the bus of the front entrance buses were more likely to be found at the front of the rear entrance buses, given the effects that the staircase would have on the levels of supervision. Failing this, interviews with bus passengers might reveal reasons for seat choices.

To find out more about the circumstances of acts of vandalism it would be necessary to undertake an observational study (with the difficulty that the observation might inhibit the behaviour being studied). It would be valuable to know when vandalism is most likely to occur and which sort of bus vandalism is an individual pursuit and which a group one, since it has been argued that groups are likely to take greater risks than individuals (Rettig, 1966; Wallach, Kogan and Bem, 1965). It might be expected, for example, that vandalism occurring in the more supervised areas was more likely to be committed when there was a group of two or three children together.

Thus, while the findings of the present study may not greatly enhance our understanding of, say, the motivational factors involved in vandalism, they certainly point to powerful situational determinants of the behaviour and, moreover, they have important implications for its prevention. The findings suggest that, in considering the design and manning of buses, bus companies should take into account the possible effects of their policies on the prevention of vandalism. Quite clearly, though, bus companies have other factors than vandalism to consider, in particular staff recruitment and wages. Given the policy of operating buses with a minimum of staff, it would seem that the only way to reduce vandalism is the short term is to reduce the opportunity for offences to be committed in ways other than providing conductor supervision. Greater Manchester Transport is already trying to do this by colouring flat surfaces so that they do not show felt-tip writing, by using non-flammable materials wherever possible, and by ensuring that fixtures and fittings cannot easily be removed. The company is also experimenting with more elaborate devices to minimise damage, such as closed circuit television on the upper deck and warning devices fitted to seats. All of this adds to the cost of vandalism (already estimated by GMT to be about £150,000 a year) and it may be that one-man operated buses will only prove less expensive to operate if most of the damage is left unrepaired or if more hard wearing seats are fitted, especially on the upper deck.

SUMMARY

This chapter has been concerned with the effect of supervision by drivers and conductors on the location and extent of damage on four different types of bus operating in Manchester. From the particularly large amount of damage to seats on the upper deck of one-man operated buses, it appeared that, for this deck at least, the absence of conductor supervision was the most important factor affecting the amount of damage sustained. At the same time, on all types of bus, including those with conductor supervision, the degree to which passengers were supervised by the bus crew seemed to relate clearly to the extent and location of damage, in that areas of low supervision (such as the upper deck and the back seats) were damaged most.

There was some evidence that the position of the staircase can lead to a displacement of damage, probably because vandals seated near to the stairs can be surprised by anyone climbing them. This displacement can be advantageous overall if it is in a direction away from the back seat where most vandalism occurs; this was illustrated by the lower rate of damage on the upper deck of conventional rear-entrance buses compared with the front entrance ones.

Although the least supervised areas of the bus were the most damaged, it was also found that younger male passengers - perhaps the ones who would more often commit damage - were somewhat more likely than others to sit in these places. While this finding suggests that any explanation of the different levels of damage *within* different parts of the bus needs to account for the interrelationship between seat choice and supervision factors, it does not, of course, undermine the importance of the differences found in damage committed *between* bus types. Thus the results indicate that situational factors, such as supervision, can play an important part in determining the extent of damage on buses, and indeed, that to reduce bus vandalism, these factors must be taken into account.

4 Vandalism and 'defensible space' on London housing estates

Sheena Wilson

AIMS OF THE STUDY

New each day is the love and care tendered to the few precious feet of private garden on an estate in South London; yet where the front doors open onto the public footway the litter is allowed to gather in windblown swirls and aerosol sprayed paint fades into the brickwork. The contrast in attitudes illustrated here is a puzzle to many municipal housing officers; if only those attitudes of private care and pride could extend to the public sphere then the problem of estate vandalism would be solved (Burbidge, 1973; 1975). The implication is that vandalism denotes too little care and pride. But equally it could denote too much public space, space which is seen as the responsibility of 'other' people.

The research reported here did not set out to provide a comprehensive explanation of estate vandalism, but to see how far the variations in the extent and pattern of vandalism on a large sample of inner London estates could be explained by variations in their lay-out and design. A principal influence on the study was the work done in the United States by Oscar Newman (1972). In his book, *Defensible Space*, he analyses the crime rates on 100 corporation estates in New York and demonstrates that crime rates increase with the height of the building, from an average felony rate per annum of 8·3 per 1,000 people in three-storey buildings, to one of 20·2 in buildings of 16 storeys or over. Moreover, whereas 17% of all crimes in low-rise buildings occur in communal areas, the comparable figure for high-rise buildings is 55%.

In explaining these findings Newman claims that large apartment blocks, particularly high-rise, are crime-prone because substantial areas within and around them are neither private (and therefore supervised by the residents), nor truly public (and therefore constantly used and overlooked by passers-by). The internal access routes, external circulation routes, and entrances are described by Newman as 'semi-public'. They are not seen to belong to a particular group of dwellings so residents fail to adopt proprietary attitudes towards them. Any kind of surveillance is difficult as windows often do not open on to the access routes, nor do the dwellings have direct access to the common grounds. Where areas are overlooked, outsiders are unlikely to be questioned because the terrain is impersonal and the numbers using it make it difficult for residents to distinguish intruders from inhabitants. In short, these buildings are crime-prone because they lack 'defensible space'.

Newman identifies four major, interrelated components of 'defensible space'. As he puts it, these are:

(1) The capacity of the physical environment to create perceived zones of territorial influence ('territorial definition').
(2) The capacity of physical design to provide surveillance opportunities for residents and their agents.
(3) The capacity of design to influence the perception of a project's uniqueness, isolation and stigma.
(4) The influence of geographical juxtaposition with 'safe zones' on the security of adjacent areas. This last component refers to the general quality of an estate's location, including environmental and socio-economic character-istics, both of which may be related to crime rates.

Within this framework, Newman describes in detail how each aspect of design influences the behaviour of potential offenders and potential witnesses. Design which increases defensible space reduces opportunities for criminal activity to take place undisturbed by exploiting the safeguards inherent in certain forms of building which afford better surveillance and more positive use of shared space by residents. Both in his early book and in later writings (notably Newman, 1976), he deals in detail with methods of achieving defensible space through site planning, and the positioning of windows, paths, doors and lifts. It is these practical implications that make his ideas so attractive for further research.

Newman's thesis, stimulating though it may be, has not escaped criticism. Bottoms (1974), for instance, concludes that the methodological shortcomings of the work are such that the relationship between crime and design cannot be seen as established. Criticisms have centred largely on the presentation of results; detailed findings are scarce, and where they are presented they show a weaker statistical relationship between crime and design than Newman claims. Multi-variate analysis of the data (the original method of analysis) is said not to give much support to Newman's theory, while the alternative presentation of results, based on 'comparison of coupled projects' is less rigorous than might be expected. Only two housing projects are compared in detail; and there is no way of confirming that these were chosen for any other reason than that they provided the best results.

In addition, in *Defensible Space* Newman tended to play down the effect of social factors on crime (thus laying his ideas open to the charge of 'architectural determinism'), although in later work (Newman, 1975; 1976), he found the influence of social factors to exceed that of physical design; the number of teenage children, one-parent and welfare-dependent families were particularly important. Nevertheless, although crime rates were lower where the average income of residents was higher, his results continued to show an increase in crime rates with building height. The highest crime rates were found to occur where the most vulnerable populations were housed in the least defensible buildings. In accordance with these findings, Newman is currently concerned with evaluating the effects of 'matching' different household types and income groups with the buildings most suited to their needs.

At the time of planning the present research, *Defensible Space* was the only publication by Newman available. Therefore it is his earlier theories, which focus on architectural design and crime, specifically those concerning the principle of 'territorial definition', that are chiefly explored here. In view of the much lower crime rates on housing estates in Britain, which would have made it virtually impossible to establish relationships between selected types of crime and defensible space, it is appropriate that the research deals with vandalism - which has a much higher incidence than other forms of crime.

METHODS

The sample
The original sample covered all estates of over 100 dwellings in two inner London boroughs numbering 52 estates in all. The findings reported here are based only on the 38 estates of just one of the boroughs which comprised a total of 285 separate blocks of dwellings[1]. The main analysis was based on scores for each block (rather than whole estates) and these were placed in one of five general design categories as follows (see also Figure 4:1):

(1) *Gallery or balcony access* (N = 152). Walk-up blocks (such as 4–5 storey pre-war blocks or lift access 'slabs' of up to 9 storeys). Corridor blocks were included in this category because there were so few in the sample.

(2) *Staircase access* (N = 70). Blocks divided into sections, each having a stair-well around which the dwellings are grouped; they are from 2–10 storeys high, the higher ones having lifts.

(3) *Tower blocks* (N = 30). All buildings 11 storeys or over (the tallest was 22 storeys).

(4) *Deck access* (N = 27). Blocks of 3–6 storeys on high density estates (a design type increasingly employed since the 1960s). Decks are wider than galleries, usually giving access to a greater number of dwellings. Most deck access blocks in the sample had decks linking them with other blocks so that circulation round the estate was possible above ground level.

(5) *Houses* (N = 6). Rows of dwellings with no shared entrance.

'Defensible space' characteristics
Data on the design and layout of blocks were collected through observation. To classify blocks along defensible space lines - a rather difficult task in practice - information was collected on:

(1) *The height* of blocks (number of storeys); and

---

[1] Data from the other borough were omitted from the main analysis because split-half reliability tests showed that information on vandalism was less reliably recorded; also differences in rates of vandalism between estates were markedly less (probably because there was less variety in the estates and less variety in estate populations) so results were less clearcut. Nonetheless the main deter-minant of levels of estate vandalism appeared from preliminary analysis to be similar in both boroughs.

Fig 4:1 Design classifications

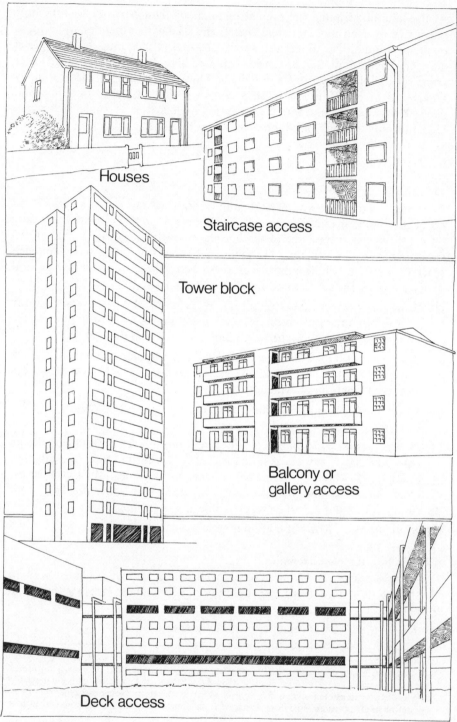

Houses

Staircase access

Tower block

Balcony or
gallery access

Deck access

(2) The *size* of blocks (number of dwellings per building);

as these clearly affected the amount of shared internal access required and the number of people likely to use it.

In addition, each block was rated in terms of four aspects relating to territorial definition[1]:

(3) *The average number of dwellings sharing each entrance of the block.* This is a measure of territorial definition commonly used by Newman. It varied in both the low and high-rise buildings studied here.

(4) *Entranceways which act as a through-route.* It was noted if blocks had entranceways which *de facto* or by design acted as a through-route to non-residents, as in the case of blocks straddling a path which clearly leads to other blocks (see Figure 4:2).

(5) *Entranceways which imply resident access only.* It was noted if the path leading to the entrance of the block was marked with a real or symbolic barrier which implied resident access only (see Figure 4:3).

(6) *Privacy.* Ratings of the degree of privacy afforded by layout were applied only to the front of blocks. They were as follows:

    (i) *private* if individual gardens or patios fronted the block;

    (ii) *semi-private* if an area was assigned for the use of one block only (see Figure 4:4);

    (iii) *semi-public* if an area served more than one block (see Figure 4:5); and

    (iv) *public* if there was no intermediate zone between the block and the public domain.

Other physical characteristics

Preliminary visits to estates in a number of London boroughs suggested that there was no simple relationship between vandalism and those features of defensibility which were being studied, and that information about the age of the blocks and certain environmental provisions should also be included:

(1) *The age of blocks.* According to the date of construction the age groups used were: pre-war; 1949–1958; 1959–1962; and 1963–1973.

(2) *Landscaping.* Each block was rated as being either:

    (i) *not landscaped* where there was no greenery or paved areas with shrubs for uses other than access or car parking;

    (ii) *minimally landscaped* where there were strips of green or flower beds but no area for residents' use;

    (iii) *partially landscaped* where there were areas of grass or pavement which could be used by residents for sitting or playing; or

    (iv) *fully landscaped* where flowers, trees and seats were provided.

---

[1] Due to the need to limit the study, no attempt was made to obtain a direct measure of surveillance (an important component of defensible space) which was independent of territoriality.

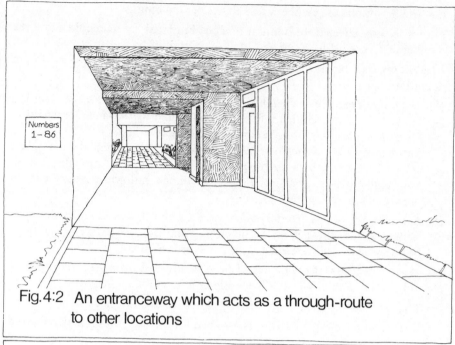

Numbers
1 – 86

Fig. 4:2 An entranceway which acts as a through-route to other locations

Numbers
1 to 8

Fig. 4:3 An entranceway which implies residents' access only

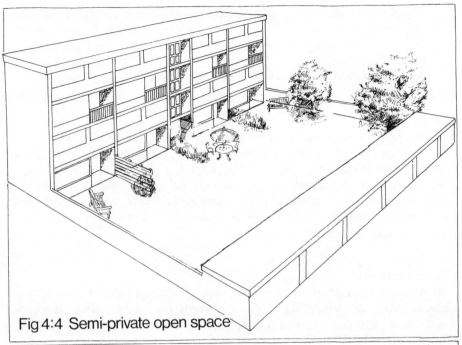

Fig 4:4 Semi-private open space

Fig 4:5 Semi-public open space

(3) *Play facilities*. Blocks were designated as having play facilities if these were adjacent to them. The term could refer to a fenced-in strip of tarmac, a group of swings, or specially-designed infant play spaces. (Initially these different types of facilities were separated out but since so few blocks had any provision they were collapsed to form one variable.)

(4) The amount of *glazing* used in design. Each block was assessed for amounts of glazing in entrance-ways and in access routes off the ground.

Landscaping was rated because it is often suggested that the austere appearance of many council estates and their lack of greenery discourage residents from taking pride in their environment. Similarly, any play facilities were noted because lack of such provision is commonly thought to lead to vandalism. Amounts of glazing were assessed, since there is evidence (e.g. Miller, 1973) that vulnerable finishes, such as glass and soft wall coverings which can be picked or burnt, seem to invite damage[1].

Maintenance and caretakers

Maintenance was looked at as another measure of the standard of provision on estates, taking into account litter, dirt and smells. Poor maintenance standards were found to be associated with vandalism, but as it could not be established whether this relationship was one of cause or effect the variable was not used in the analysis. In the light of the results of the Lambeth Inner Area Study (D.O.E., 1977) which suggested that estates with resident caretakers suffered less from vandalism, it is worth noting that all the estates in the present sample had caretakers resident at the time of the study.

Child population

As the local authority's records proved incomplete and sometimes out of date, variables describing the people living in the estates would have been difficult to collect so, regrettably, the study has limited itself to just one social variable. It seemed particularly important to make special efforts to obtain data about numbers of children on the estates as there was a widely-held belief among housing managers and others consulted about the design of the research that it was children living on the estates who were responsible for most of the damage. In the event, information about the *numbers* of children aged 6–16 living in each block was obtained from education welfare records. Using this information a measure of *child density* was calculated. This was a rate of children per dwelling and was obtained by dividing the number of children in each block by the number of dwellings. As vandalism rates per block were being compared, a measure of

---

[1] It proved impossible to classify adequately the wide variety of wall finishes used throughout the estates. Certainly, though, vulnerability appeared important: on one estate, 'false' panels which had the superficial appearance of invulnerability were all torn off once it was discovered that they were made of flimsy plastic.

the child density per block (i.e. the average numbers of children per dwelling) was thought to be more suitable than a measure of their number per acre[1].

Definition of vandalism

For the purposes of the research, vandalism was taken to mean damage to property whether due to accident (such as a football through a window); direct attack (such as air-gun pellet holes in glass); or misuse-cum-play (such as swinging on doors until they were off their hinges). This definition excluded wear and tear therefore, but no attempt was made (nor indeed would it have been possible) to differentiate the effects of intentional damage from those of less deliberate rowdyism. This perspective was applied both in interpreting local authority records and in rating vandalism on the basis of observation. It was a workaday definition, used because of the impossibility of imputing motives to damage already done. In each case it meant 'extra' repairs for the local authority over and above programmed maintenance and standard replacements for wear and tear.

Measurement of vandalism

Vandalism was assessed in two ways: first, as police records are a poor source of information (see Sturman, 1978), information was taken from local authority repair records; second, assessments of damage were made by direct observation of each block.

Local authority records of vandalism

Because vandalism repairs in the maintenance records were not always differentiated from repairs for other damage (though they were meant to be and, indeed, this was one of the reasons for undertaking the study in the boroughs chosen) it was necessary to examine all individual repair chits issued for each of the blocks in the sample and to decide which items repaired were due to vandalism. To obtain a sufficient number of incidents, chits were examined relating to a 15-month period, 1 January 1973 to 31 March 1974. Identifying vandalism in this way proved to be a fairly straightforward task; housing managers and technical officers were constantly consulted about the possible causes of breakage in order to sift out repairs needed due to wear and tear, faulty design, or unusual circumstances (for example, high winds blowing out glass).

The staff were also asked about methods of reporting damage in order to assess the reliability and completeness of the records. As a result, the final analyses concentrated on lifts, broken glass, and structural damage. Other types of

---

[1] In the analyses presented in the Appendix at the end of this Chapter, the measure of child density is based on the number of boys in each block. The number of boys and girls in residence was highly correlated, but the association between vandalism and the number of boys was slightly clearer than between vandalism and the number of boys and girls. For the sake of simplicity, in the rest of this report, the relationship between 'children' and vandalism is referred to where this is the relationship between 'boys' and vandalism. Where numbers of children or child densities are quoted, the appropriate number of boys has been doubled to provide an estimate of the overall number of children.

damage like graffiti, broken light bulbs, and ruined shrubs, appeared either to be inconsistently reported or dealt with by the caretaker on location, and these were excluded.

As some quantification is necessary in order to compare rates of vandalism in different buildings, the basic unit of analysis from local authority records has been an item of damage. Inevitably, this conceals the fact that there was variation in the degree of seriousness of each incident of damage; in the cost of repairs (accurate figures on the cost of damage were not available); and in the social costs (for example, the effect it has on the appearance of the block or the number of people inconvenienced by it).

Observed vandalism
Some indication of these social costs came from direct observation of the extent of vandalism to individual blocks. This complemented recorded data in giving an idea of the extent of damage occurring in certain locations, such as outside walls and stairways. Concentrations of damage in communal facilities could greatly affect the appearance of the buildings and cause much inconvenience, more so than when damage (which on the basis of recorded data could involve a substantial number of items) was piecemeal and dispersed. Moreover, whereas the recorded vandalism rate reflected the frequency of damage and its extent relative to the size of the building, the observed vandalism rate reflected the intensity of damage and the ability of maintenance staff to keep up with repairs. This distinction proved important in interpreting the results. Also some of the damage picked up by the observations (especially graffiti) was not included in recorded rates for reasons already given.

Each estate was visited on one occasion and individual blocks were scored for vandalism using a 4-point scale.

1 - minimal damage or none;
2 - a few panes broken or some graffiti;
3 - more than a few panes broken and considerable or extensive graffiti;
4 - extensive boarding up, breakage and graffiti.

The construction of vandalism rates for each block
Using *recorded* data, four rates of vandalism for each block were constructed and analysed:

(1) *Unit rate.* This was the number of items of damage to glass or structural fittings, divided by the number of dwellings in the block.

(2) *Rate of damage to dwellings.* Damage to dwellings as opposed to communal areas was calculated per 10 dwellings in each block.

(3) *Rate of damage to ground-floor communal areas.* Damage in these areas was divided by the number of entrances, as this was where most damage occurred[1].

---

[1] The rate of damage to communal areas off the ground was also measured per 10 dwellings in each block, but these rates were generally low and were not analysed.

(4) *Rate of damage to lifts.* In lift access blocks, call-outs for lift repairs were
   divided by the number of lifts.

In addition an observed rate of vandalism for each block (i.e. the 4-point scale
described above) was used.

In constructing the unit rate - the principal recorded measure of vandalism -
damage which was infrequently reported or which occurred in outside areas
shared by more than one block, was not included. This measure, therefore, has a
slight bias in that damage to dwellings, rather than public areas, is over-
represented. This has been borne in mind when interpretating the results.

The subdivision of the unit rate into damage to dwellings and damage to
ground-floor communal areas proved useful in that the level of unit damage
could mask differences in patterns of damage. In particular, buildings with
damage occurring predominantly in communal areas tended to have correspondingly lower rates of damage to the dwellings themselves. Damage to lifts was not
found to be strongly correlated with other types of vandalism. Some buildings
with high rates of lift damage had little other damage; possible reasons for this
are given below. The correlations between the different measures of vandalism
which are shown in Table 4:1 demonstrate that not all types of damage are highly
correlated.

Table 4:1
Correlations between the different measures of vandalism

	Observed vandalism score	Unit rate	Rate of damage to dwellings	Rate of damage to ground-floor communal areas
Unit rate	·42	—	—	—
Rate of damage to dwellings	·23	·60	—	—
Rate of damage to ground-floor communal areas	·34	·39	− ·01	—
Rate of damage to lifts	·34	·12	− ·14	·18

FINDINGS

Some basic statistics about the distribution of vandalism, some of which have
relevance to 'defensible space', are presented first. These are followed by more
detailed findings concerning the relationship between vandalism, child densities
and design features of the estates. (Some of the detailed findings are shown in
tables in the Appendix which are identified here by the prefix 'A' before table
numbers.)

a. The type and location of (recorded) vandalism

Altogether a total of 6,225 items of vandalism were recorded in the local authority's records for the 38 estates. The damage was categorised into six types (only the first three of which were used in constructing rates of 'recorded' vandalism - see above). Table 4:2 shows the distribution of damage between the various types.

Table 4:2
Types of vandalism

	Glazing	Lifts	Structure	Electrical equipment	Decoration	Miscellaneous	Total
Number of items of damage	3,294	1,643	960	177	79	72	6,225
Percentage	53	26	15	3	1	1	100%

Glazing was the item most frequently recorded as damaged. It included window panes, balcony panels, and louvred ventilation. In some instances glass had been placed at foot level, near a playground, or in some other clearly vulnerable position. On one newly-opened estate whole lengths of persistently broken balcony panels had had to be replaced by brick, with a consequent reduction in the bill for damage. In other buildings, glazing damage had been reduced through the introduction of thick plastic panelling, although few such finishes proved totally vandal-proof: they could be scratched, burnt or sprung out. The vulnerability of glass to damage was particularly apparent in blocks with high densities of children (see Table A6 and below for a discussion of child density).

The figure under the heading 'lifts', the second most frequently recorded item, represents the number of times an engineer had to be called to do repairs; it covers fairly minor damage, such as the removal of starter buttons, as well as more serious interference with the mechanics of the lift. Lifts, too, were particularly prone to damage in blocks with high child densities (Table A10). It is interesting to note (see Table A5) that the rate of damage to lifts tended to rise in buildings where there was little glazing in the entrance (despite a positive correlation of 0·32 between the existence of lifts in a building and the extensive use of glazing). Although, on the one hand, this finding might be interpreted as showing that vandalism is 'displaced' to lifts if there is little glazing around to damage, it might, on the other, indicate that lifts are particularly vulnerable to damage when situated in lobbies where the opportunities for residents and passers-by to see what is happening in the lift area are restricted by lack of glazing.

Structural damage, the third most frequent category, refers to doors, panelling, walls, railings, and cupboards containing electrical fittings.

Damage was also categorised according to its location within and around the blocks, as shown in Table 4:3.

Table 4:3
Location of damage

	Lifts	Private dwellings	Stairs, corridors, walkways	Communal facilities*	Entrances	Out-side areas	Under-ground garages†	Roofs	Total
Number of items of damage	1,643	1,475	1,416	776	361	289	176	89	6,225
Percentage	26	24	23	12	6	5	3	1	100%

* 'Communal facilities' covers tenants' store-sheds, cupboards for fittings, caretakers rooms, laundries, etc.
† Several underground garages had, because of vandalism, ceased to be used and had been left unrepaired, so the figure given is likely to be an underestimate.

It can be seen from Table 4:3 that only about one quarter of recorded vandalism on the estates was to dwellings. The majority of dwellings involved were at ground level and most of the damage (68%) was window breakage. (A significant minority of dwellings were vandalised while empty.) Most of the damage on the estates occurred in public areas many of which - lifts, stairways, underground garages, roofs, and, in some areas walkways and communal facilities - are out of sight from dwellings. This information on the location of damage therefore supports Newman's general contentions about the vulnerability to vandalism of those 'semi-public' areas on housing estates which are not readily given surveillance by residents.

b. Damage and storey height
It was found that some 60% of damage (excluding that to lifts) is done at ground level including outside areas and underground garages. One reason for this is that the ground level contains more breakable items such as entrance doors, fences, and store-sheds. Another reason (see below) is that children tend to play at ground level.

Unit rates of damage decreased steadily with height and most of the damage (75%) *above* ground level was in communal areas rather than to private dwellings. This damage was often to staircases which in buildings of five or more storeys were less frequently used as most people used the lift; being secluded these staircases offered greater opportunities for damage to take place unseen.

Though unit rates of damage decreased with building height, there was more damage to ground floor communal areas the higher the building (see Table 4:4). The latter result is consistent with Newman's findings.

Opportunities to commit damage around the entrances of tower blocks were enhanced by the fact that the ground floors of some were used as service areas for

Table 4:4

Storey height and damage in ground-floor communal areas

Storey height	Number of blocks	Damage in ground-floor communal areas	
		Percentage of blocks with less than one item per entrance	Percentage of blocks with one or more item per entrance
1–4	123	83%	17%
5	95	77%	23%
6–10	37	46%	54%
11–22	30	23%	77%
Total	285	70%	30%

$\chi^2 = 46\cdot4$; 3df; p < ·001

tenant store-sheds etc., which were separate from the dwellings and often hidden from public view. Another feature of tower blocks particularly vulnerable to damage were mezzanine levels giving pedestrian access from one block to another. The entrance-ways of tower blocks were also particularly public in nature as any one entrance could service up to 120 dwellings.

c. Child density and vandalism

Regression analyses performed on the vandalism rates for the 285 blocks showed that child density was the single most important factor in explaining variation in the observed vandalism rate and in all but one of the measures of recorded vandalism (see Tables A1–5)[1]. The exception was the rate of damage in communal areas on the ground floor where storey height was of more importance, although child density still contributed to higher rates. Table 4:5 shows the relationship between child density and two of the measures of vandalism, the unit rate and observed vandalism.

While the two variables of 'child density' and 'numbers of children' tend to be correlated, it is possible to find blocks with a low ratio of children to dwellings but which, because they are large, might house substantial total numbers of children. In these blocks the rate of observed vandalism and the rate of damage to communal access areas were also likely to be high (see Tables A11 and A12). In general, it seemed that where the total number of children in the block was 20 or more, vandalism was likely to be high. Details of lift call-outs for the 117 blocks with lifts, for instance, showed that only 32% of the blocks with less than 20 children had more than 4 call-outs per lift, compared to 70% of the blocks with greater numbers of children than this (see Table 4:6).

The relationship between the two measures of child population and vandalism is

---

[1] It is important to note that child density still only explained a small proportion of the variations in each of the rates of vandalism (explained variance ranged between 5% and 20% which is fairly standard for studies of this kind).

Table 4:5
Vandalism and child density

		Observed vandalism		Unit rate of vandalism	
Children per 10 dwellings	Number of blocks	Percentage of blocks with little or no vandalism*	Percentage of blocks with fair amount or extensive vandalism	Percentage of blocks with 0–2 items of damage per 10 dwellings	Percentage of blocks with 3 or more items of damage per 10 dwellings
Less than 1	41	93%	7%	68%	32%
1–2·9	74	69%	31%	57%	43%
3–5·9	106	60%	40%	44%	56%
6–8·9	40	45%	55%	35%	65%
9 or more	24	38%	62%	13%	87%
Total	285	63%	37%	47%	53%

* Blocks with little or no vandalism were those which scored 1 and 2 on the scale of observed vandalism (see page 48); blocks with a fair amount or extensive vandalism scored 3 or 4.

revealed to be more complicated still by consideration of the rate of vandalism per child in the different blocks. In fact it was found that the rate of vandalism per child *decreases* with both child density ($r = -0.26$) and number of children per block ($r = -0.27$). The relevance of these findings both for achieving and understanding of vandalism and for prevention will be discussed later.

The findings concerning child density suggested that the principal objective of the study, i.e. elucidation of the relationship between 'defensible space' characteristics and vandalism, might only be met by first controlling for the variable of child density in the analysis. The 285 blocks were therefore divided into a group of 'low' child density blocks (N = 115) and a 'high' child density (N = 170) group, taking a cut-off point of 3 or more children per 10 dwellings to define 'high'

Table 4:6
Damage to lifts in lift-access blocks and number of children in the blocks

		Lift call-outs	
Number of children in the blocks	Number of blocks	Percentage of blocks with 0–4 call-outs	Percentage of blocks with 5 or more call-outs
0–19	47	68%	32%
20–159	70	30%	70%
Total	117	45%	55%

$\chi^2 = 16.4$; 1df; $p < .001$

[1] The cut-off point of 3 or more children per 10 dwellings was chosen for blocks with 'high' child density because a higher cut-off point would have given too many blocks where the absolute number of children exceeded 19. Also, the results obtained by techniques of regression analysis on the sub-samples were clearer if a split was made at this point.

density[1]. The two groups of blocks were found to differ significantly on five variables apart from that of child density: the age of blocks, design type, number of storeys, degree of 'privacy' at the front of blocks, and amount of landscaping. These variables are all inter-related. It seems, therefore, that in this sample the higher child densities are found in post-war deck-access design types and in pre-war gallery access blocks; the latter in particular usually had little or no landscraping while deck-access blocks often had individual gardens provided at ground level. Low densities of children were more common in tower blocks or estates opened in the 1950s. These broad differences between the 'high' and 'low' child density blocks have been taken account of where necessary in interpreting the findings reported in the sections below.

d. Vandalism in 'high' child density blocks
The relationship between vandalism rates and child density and number of children was still paramount within this group of 170 'high' child density blocks (Tables A6, A7, A10). The overall impression gained was that most design types can be vulnerable if child densities are high and that children will play and cause damage in most parts of an estate wherever the finish and lay-out of facilities affords opportunities for this. None of the defensible space measures were found to be significantly related to measures of vandalism for the group. Nor was vandalism related to age and design type. The analysis did show the importance, however, of some other aspects of design and lay-out, particularly of landscaping and playing facilities.

Landscaping
Both the level of observed vandalism and the unit rate of recorded vandalism were higher in blocks with little or no landscaping irrespective of child density (see Table A1 and A2), though the strongest correlation between absence of landscaping and damage was for damage to dwellings in blocks with high child densities (Table A8). The landscaping scores were based on such things as the presence of flower beds, trees and grass; these may have reflected amounts of open space, although no exact measure of the ratio of dwellings to amounts of open space was obtained. Nevertheless the provision of landscaping was associated with less vandalism only in those blocks, such as some built before the war, where most children's play was likely to take place outside (because the internal communal areas were too cramped or private). Many of the pre-war blocks sat directly on tarmac courtyards so that ground floor dwellings were particularly vulnerable if children played there. In the large modern blocks, however, which had extensive areas of shared internal access, provision of landscaping was often generous, but did not appear to deter children from playing inside the building and causing damage there.

Play facilities
Similarly, the provision of play facilities adjacent to the blocks did not prevent children from playing elsewhere on the estates. In fact the existence of play facilities appeared to attract greater numbers of children to one location, poss-

ibly because play provision generally was so scarce. Unit rates of damage, observed vandalism, and rates of damage to dwellings were higher in blocks with play facilities adjacent to them, especially where child densities were high (see Tables A3, A6 and A8 respectively).

e. Vandalism in 'low' child density blocks
The main finding to emerge from the analysis of blocks with a low child density was that rates of damage were influenced by design factors apparently relevant to 'defensible space'. In this regard, type of entrance was particularly important: vandalism was higher where there was a 'through' entrance (see Table A11), possibly because of the easy access it afforded to outsiders. The entrances of many of the larger, modern blocks were particularly impersonal because they could be used as a throughway which made any form of 'neighbour recognition' exceedingly difficult. In contrast, where it was implied, through the positioning of paths or fences, that the entrance was for the residents' use only, vandalism in blocks with a low child density was lower (see Table A11).

Lifts
It has already been mentioned (in the section on *The type and location of recorded vandalism*) that once the child density was high all types of lift access blocks were vulnerable to lift vandalism, but in blocks with a *low* child density there was considerable variation in damage to the lifts and, again, the degree of territorial definition in entrance-ways seems to be important. First, damage to lifts was lower if the entrance implied residents' access only. Second, through-routes seemed to result in damage to lifts: of those blocks with an entrance acting as a throughway, for instance, 76% had 5 or more lift call-outs; for blocks with a discrete entrance, only 30% had this number of call-outs (see Table 4:7).

In certain tower blocks with very few children, lift damage was the only type of damage experienced. Lifts in tall buildings may attract children from outside or provoke the otherwise property-regarding residents to vent their frustrations on

Table 4:7
Damage to lifts in blocks with a low density, and type of entrance

Type of entrance	Number of blocks	Lift call-outs	
		Percentage of blocks with 0–4 call-outs	Percentage of blocks with 5 or more call-outs
Discrete entrance	30	70%	30%
Entrance acting as a throughway	21	24%	76%
Total	51	51%	49%

$\chi^2 = 10\cdot5$; 1df; p < ·01

them when they are too slow or break down. Greater damage to these lifts may also to some extent reflect the possibility that they are subject to greater use.

Building size

As indicated above the measure of observed vandalism reflected a particular dimension of vandalism: its intensity, and the rate of repairs. One factor in particular - building size - was correlated with observed vandalism in low child density blocks although it did not appear to affect recorded rates of vandalism. Observed vandalism was greater in blocks with 30 dwellings or more (see Table A11). Blocks of this size were particularly prone to damage in communal areas (a form of damage difficult to keep up with by regular repairs) as the amount of shared space within them was necessarily greater, and more public[1]. In addition, much of the shared space served the very limited function of giving access; it did not lend itself to further use by the residents as a place to sit or to socialise with neighbours, and in so doing enable them to act as natural policing agents. The access ways were also often austere and uniform, discouraging efforts by residents to personalize them by putting territorial markers, in the form of mats and tubs of flowers, outside their front doors. There was little evidence of such personal touches, for example, on the wide walkways of the deck access design which linked one block to another, whereas the more private access balconies of smaller blocks frequently sported pots of thriving geraniums.

IMPLICATIONS FOR PREVENTION

'Defensible space'

The main objective of this study was to see how far variability in the vandalism rates of inner London council housing estates could be explained by their differing levels of 'defensible space' (Newman, 1972), although in the event certain other variables were looked at, some of which were found to correlate with rates of vandalism. The study does not purport, however, to provide a comprehensive explanation of vandalism on municipal estates.

The study found that the principal factor related to levels of vandalism in the sample of estates studied was child density. Thus, the implication of Newman's early work that design features exert the primary influence on vandalism rates did not receive support. However, in later work (Newman, 1975; 1976), Newman himself has been more precise about the relative importance of 'social' versus design factors, and has presented findings which show that the influence of social factors (for instance, the percentage of residents receiving welfare, and *per capita* income of estate residents) exceed that of physical design. The present research was limited by the fact that due to practical difficulties in obtaining data the only variables measured relating to the social composition of estates were the numbers and densities of children. (Other variables likely to be important are the social

---

[1] Landings and corridors off the ground in tower blocks, however, were not necessarily much used. They often gave the impression of seclusion and privacy and they rarely suffered from damage.

aspirations and demographic and socio-economic characteristics of the tenants as well as the standard of management and caretaking (D.O.E., 1977).) Nothing can be said, therefore, about the possible importance of those other social variables which Newman found relevant to vandalism and crime rates in public housing projects in America. The influence of children on levels of vandalism found in this study, however, can be seen to echo the results of Newman's analysis of 100,000 units of public housing in New York (Newman, 1975) which showed that the number of teenage children was second in importance in determining levels of crime only to the percentage of one-parent families on welfare.

With regard to the secondary importance of defensible space itself, this study gave some limited support to Newman's contentions. Although the influence of defensible space design features seemed to be swamped by high concentrations of children, in blocks with low child densities design features which reduced the ability of residents to defend semi-public space appeared to be associated with vandalism. The evidence derived from the study supporting the importance of defensible space can be summarized as follows:

(1) The relatively small amount of damage to dwellings themselves supported the notion that impersonal (and more accessible) space is more vulnerable to damage than targets towards which residents can adopt proprietary attitudes.

(2) Levels of *observed* vandalism in particular were high in large blocks (not necessarily high-rise) characterized by extensive semi-public space which could not be easily supervised by residents.

(3) High-rise blocks experienced more vandalism in ground-floor communal areas - space to which residents feelings of 'territoriality' were unlikely to extend.

(4) In low child density blocks, vandalism was greater if entrances were impersonal and could be used as a through-way to other locations.

Although these findings are consistent with Newman's theories, the study was by no means a complete test of them. In the first place it was concerned only with vandalism and not with other forms of crime since in the English context of generally much less serious crime rates, it is vandalism that is of most salience; whether vandalism, which may be a relatively opportunist and casual form of behaviour, is more or less influenced by design than more intentional and serious types of criminal behaviour remains an open question. Second, the study was conducted in the relatively limited though important architectural context of housing estates comprising mainly flats, and for methodological reasons no assessment was made of vandalism levels in areas between blocks (see page 49). In retrospect had the study included more houses - which are closest to the ideal of defensible space - and had it been able to take into account damage in public areas shared by more than one block, evidence relevant to theories of defensible space might have been clearer. Third, testing of the rest of the different components of the concept of 'defensible space' (see pp. 39–40) was not complete. In the main this study has centred on the first of Newman's four defensible space components: the way in which design can create 'perceived zones of territorial influence'. Thus, it did not include, for instance, an attempt to construct a measure of residents' surveillance opportunities - an important factor in Newman's scheme - and it might have been possible to devise different measures of territoriality.

Since the beginning of the present study, the popularity of Newman's thesis has been reflected in a growing body of work, emanating principally from America, which has incorporated either theoretical discussion, or more occasionally, empirical testing of defensible space. In this body of work, Newman's ideas have usually been dealt with in conjunction with other techniques (such as the use of security hardware) under the heading of what is often called 'crime prevention through environmental design'[1]. In relation to Newman's theories in particular, most attention appears to have been given to the importance of natural surveillance opportunities that flow from housing and street design for residents and pedestrians to 'police' the environment (see, for example, Duffala, 1976; Molumby, 1976; Mawby, 1977). Although, at present, the evidence on the degree to which areas can be successfully 'defended' by natural surveillance is somewhat inconclusive, and although there are few results available from larger scale empirical tests of the defensible space hypothesis, it would seem, as this study confirms, that architectural design factors can be considered relevant to the explanation of the incidence and patterns of offending.*

In terms, then, of the suggestions about design that this research would support, housing estates should incorporate precepts of defensible space - the careful allocation of all space to defined groups of users both to increase feelings of territoriality and to maximise surveillance opportunities. One critical aspect is the territorial definition of shared entrance-ways. Entrances should be discrete (i.e. self-contained and enclosed, giving access only to dwellings within the block) and imply that access is for residents only; large blocks with few resident children will continue to be prone to damage if easy access is afforded to outsiders. Since modifications to existing blocks of flats will in many cases be too expensive to undertake or be unfeasible for design reasons, recommendations with regard to defensible space apply more to the design of future estates.

Child density
In that child density and numbers of children resident were the single variables most strongly related to both observed and recorded vandalism in the present study, it might appear that one solution to the problem would be to disperse

---

[1] For instance, in America Westinghouse Corporation, with Federal assistance, is currently undertaking a large research programme to test the influence of the physical environment on crime (Rau, 1975). Model programmes aim to reduce crime through environmental techniques in homes, schools, commercial business and transportation.

* *Editor's Note: A more recent assessment of the evidence from various tests of Newman's defensible space theory can be found in Mayhew (1979).*

families with children more equitably among estates. However, the point should be reiterated that child density and numbers of children accounted for only a proportion of the variance in vandalism rates and that other variables (not measured or immeasurable) are also likely to be important. In addition it was found that the rate of recorded vandalism per child was lower with both increasing child density and numbers of children per block[1]. This may have been due to the fact that there is a limit to the level of damage possible in a particular block; also the rate of reporting and carrying out repairs might slow down once levels of vandalism reach a certain point (as was seen in the case of highly vandalised underground garages).

For these reasons - and, in particular, because there is no straightforward relationship between the rate of vandalism *per child* and concentrations of children - the effects on vandalism of lowering child densities cannot confidently be predicted. Dispersing the children may simply disperse the problem and result in greater overall numbers of tenants being offended. On the other hand, a reduction in the absolute levels of damage in one location would make it that much more tolerable to those residents affected and might ease problems of maintenance.

Should local authorities attempt to reduce child densities - as many are doing - they are likely to face a number of practical difficulties. For example on estates consisting for the most part of family-size dwellings, reducing the child density would involve a deliberate policy of under-occupation, which in the inner urban areas may not always be feasible. Where such a course can be followed, the aim of avoiding either the concentration of large families within blocks, or a great number of families in large blocks, may require a review of the whole system of lettings and transfers. It may involve in some instances the allocation of a certain quota of dwellings in any one block to all-adult households with a low priority rating on the waiting list; and where these include young married couples likely to have children, a flexible system of transfers would be necessary so that high child densities do not eventually develop.

Some local authorities have already taken such action, while others, when rehabilitating pre-war blocks for example, have modified the size of dwellings in order to achieve a mix of one, two and three bedroom dwellings. The scope for reducing child densities in high density areas is nevertheless limited although the

---

[1] Broadly speaking, our analysis suggests that when there are more than twenty children per block problems of vandalism become more acute. It is difficult to give a 'critical' figure for densities of children *per acre*, i.e. for the variable which planners and architects generally use. As will be seen from Table 4:5, vandalism increases rather steadily with child densities, though it is perhaps when these exceed six per 10 dwellings that the figures for vandalism worsen. On this somewhat subjective standard a very rough translation of six children per 10 dwellings on a per acre basis would be close to 20, assuming a high average density of 34 dwellings per acre. Since the records used for the present study probably underestimated the number of children living on the estates, and since they applied only to children over 5 years old, it would appear that the critical figure from our study broadly corresponds to the Lambeth Inner Area Study (D.O.E., 1977) 'cut off' figure of 30 children (of all ages) per acre.

Department of the Environment now recommends reduced overall densities (85–100 habitable rooms per acre) for new housing in inner areas and greater flexibility in setting densities to ensure that buildings are more suited to the requirements of those intended to live in them. It is already part of government policy to recommend that families with young children be housed on or near the ground, preferably in houses, due to the now recognised problems of rearing children in multi-storey buildings (Adams and Conway, 1974).

Play facilities and supervision of children

The provision of play space as such did not appear in the present study to prevent children from playing on other parts of the estate, and where provision was generally scarce it seemed likely to attract large numbers of children to one location, making the surrounding areas vulnerable to damage. Research by the Department of the Environment on children's play (D.O.E., 1973) found that never more than a fifth of a child's time was spent in play areas and concludes that the designer's primary concern should be to plan estates with the other four-fifths of a child's outdoor leisure time in mind. Specifically, in order to reduce vandalism it would seem that play facilities should be provided which adequately serve the number of likely users and which are not directly adjacent to living areas. Their benign effect will be limited to the extent that there are semi-public areas elsewhere likely to prove equally attractive as places to play.

The association between children and vandalism also raises the question of whether there is scope for closer supervision of children on estates. This might be organised around tenants themselves, so that, for instance, parents undertake play duties on some kind of rota basis. Present experience, at least in relation to other estate management schemes based on tenant participation suggests, however, that play supervision of this kind (even if financially rewarded) is likely to be severely hampered by general inertia and organisational problems. Many mothers have jobs making it difficult for them to spare the time for involvement of this kind. Also parents are very unwilling, unless confronted with evidence, to believe that it is their own children who may be responsible for the damage.

Alternatively, children might be supervised more formally either by trained play leaders, or by additional caretaking personnel. Clearly this would be a more costly arrangement which would need to be evaluated in terms of the financial savings made through reduced vandalism; it might be of only limited usefulness given the difficulties of supervising all play activity, and that the requirements of many children, of differing ages, would need to be catered for (D.O.E., 1973). Further investigation of the most effective forms of play supervision needs to be carried out; but any provision must be combined with designing estates along defensible space lines so that space where children are likely to play can be seen by parents from within their own dwellings.

SUMMARY OF THE CHAPTER

The study examined rates of vandalism in 285 'blocks' of dwellings on 38 inner

London public housing estates with the intention, primarily, of seeing how vandalism was related to certain 'defensible space' characteristics.

In addition to classifying blocks along defensible space lines in terms, for example, of height, size, design type and type of entrance-ways, information was collected on various other physical features such as landscaping and the provision of play facilities. Data were also collected on the numbers of children living in each block. Using this information a measure of child densities was calculated which was the average number of children per dwelling in each block.

Five measures of the amount of vandalism committed in and around individual blocks were used. Four of these were calculated from items of vandalism recorded on local authority repair notes: unit rate of damage; damage to dwellings; damage to ground-floor communal areas; and damage to lifts. (These measures did not take account of damage to territory shared by blocks.) The visibility and intensity of damage was gauged by the fifth measure of vandalism which was based on observation.

Vandalism on estates was found to occur mainly at ground-floor level where most breakable items are situated and where children usually play. Public areas (for instance, entrances and underground garages) were much more vandalised than dwellings, presumably because they were less visible to residents and less clearly part of their 'territory'. Glazing was the most frequently recorded item of damage (followed by lifts) and the amount of observed vandalism at any one time was substantially affected by the amount of glazing in entrances and access ways. Child density emerged as the single most important variable of those studied, though the overall number of children living in blocks was also important in relation to vandalism rates.

There was no direct relationship between design features and vandalism: all types of blocks could suffer from damage, and rates of vandalism varied between similar block types. In blocks with average to high child densities, defensible space attributes were either unimportant or obscured, although certain other provisions of design (landscaping, play facilities and robust finishes) may be especially necessary to reduce vandalism. In buildings with low child densities certain aspects of design which impede defensible space may have a critical effect on the amount of vandalism these buildings sustain: such blocks suffering damage tended to be large and high with damage to the lifts and in the extensive public areas. Vandalism was also higher in these blocks when entrances acted as through-ways to other locations, affording easy access to outsiders.

The study suggests that in the future design of housing estates principles of defensible space should be incorporated: dwellings should overlook outside areas so that children at play can be seen; impersonal space which is not part of residents' territory should be reduced; and entrances should be made discrete for residents' use only. Reducing child densities through dispersal of families with children is problematic but may have a significant part to play in prevention.

Where possible, families with children should be housed in buildings small enough not to need lifts or much semi-public access space. Landscaped areas may be used to demarcate physically dwellings from areas where children are likely to play. Play facilities may reduce vandalism only if they are adequate for the likely number of users, if they are located not too close to dwellings, and if semi-public space where children will inevitably play is not extensive. More robust materials should be used in construction and repair (this is particularly the case for lifts though it also applies to many other vulnerable fixtures and fittings), and where possible the use of glazing reduced. Finally, it is important to note that the suggestions for prevention, arising as they do out of a somewhat circumscribed study, may have only a limited part to play in dealing with the problem of vandalism on municipal housing estates.

Appendix Regression analyses for the study of London housing estates

N.B. Many different variables interact to produce the rates of vandalism calculated from observed and recorded data and multiple regression indicates which particular variables are most influential. Each vandalism measure was regressed against different sets of the independent variables (for instance child density, amount of landscaping, age of block). As a consequence of correlations between some of the independent variables the results from regressions vary considerably depending on which factors are included in the analysis; the 'sets' presented here are those where all the independent variables were included. Only those variables which made significant contributions ($p < .05$) are listed, unless otherwise stated. The possibility, of course, always remains that other unmeasured variables are influencing the results in unknown ways, and that different results would be obtained with a different sample of estates.

REGRESSIONS ON THE TOTAL SAMPLE OF 285 BLOCKS

Table A1
Regression of observed vandalism

Independent variables		Partial correlation
Child density		·36
Number of dwellings in the block		·35
Amount of glazing in the entrance		·26
Amount of landscaping		− ·14
Multiple correlation	·617	

Table A2
Regression of the unit rate of recorded vandalism

Independent variables		Partial correlation
Child density		·24
Play facilities		·15
Amount of landscaping		− ·14
Multiple correlation	·457	

Table A3
Regression of rate of damage to dwellings

Independent variables		Partial correlation
Child density		·26
'Newness' of the block		−·26
Play facilities by the block		·18
Number of dwellings in the block		−·14
Multiple correlation	·451	

Table A4
Regression of rate of damage in ground-floor communal areas

Independent variables		Partial correlation
Storey height		·33
Child density		·16
Privacy ratings on layout		·14
Multiple correlation	·504	

Table A5
Regression of number of call-outs per lift for lift access blocks

Independent variables		Partial correlation
Child density		·27
Amount of glazing in the entrance		−·22
Multiple correlation	·430	

REGRESSION ON THE 170 'HIGH CHILD DENSITY BLOCKS

Table A6
Regression of observed vandalism

Independent variables		Partial correlation
Total number of children in the block		·26
Amount of glazing in the entrance		·25
Play facilities by the block		−·18
Amount of landscaping		−·19
Storey height		·17
Multiple correlation	·541	

64

Table A7
Regression of the unit rate of recorded vandalism

Independent variables		Partial correlation
Child density		·31
Multiple correlation	·432	

Table A8
Regression of the rate of damage to dwellings

Independent variables		Partial correlation
Amount of landscaping		−·26
Play facilities by the block		·21
'Newness' of the block		−·16
Multiple correlation	·455	

Table A9
Regression of the rate of damage in ground-floor communal areas

Independent variables		Partial correlation
Storey height		·28
Privacy rating on layout		·16
Multiple correlation	·434	

Table A10
Regression of number of call-outs per lift, for lift access blocks

Independent variables		Partial correlation
Child density		·35
Multiple correlation	·505	

In the high child density sample, child density rather than the overall number of children continued to have the strongest influence on the overall rate of vandalism and damage to lifts.

REGRESSION ON THE 115 'LOW' CHILD DENSITY BLOCKS

Table A11
Regression of observed vandalism

Independent variables		Partial correlation
Entrance-way a 'through route'		·29
Entrance-way giving resident access only		− ·28
Number of dwellings in the block		·24
Total number of children in the block		·24
Multiple correlation	·722	

Table A12
Regression of the rate of damage in ground-floor communal areas

Independent variables		Partial correlation
Storey height		·40
'Newness' of the block		·22
Amount of glazing in the entrance		− ·22
Total number of children in the block		·21
Multiple correlation	·609	

Because rates of damage to dwellings in the low child density sample were very low, no regression was done on this measure. In the low child density sample, unit rates of vandalism were generally low and no independent variable was found to be significantly correlated with them. Similarly, in the regression on lift damage, none of the correlations were significant.

5 Natural surveillance and vandalism to telephone kiosks

P. Mayhew, R. V. G. Clarke, J. M. Hough
and S. W. C. Winchester

Telephone kiosks, like many other public facilities, are notoriously vulnerable to vandalism. Some kiosks suffer more than others, however, and it is reasonable to ask, following Oscar Newman (1972), whether the differing degrees of damage they sustain are influenced not just by the broader social characteristics of the neighbourhoods in which they are located, but also by the amount of 'natural' surveillance they receive from members of the public. This was the question investigated in the present study.

During the course of the present work, Mawby (1977) reported the results of a similar but smaller-scale study of vandalism to 27 telephone kiosks in residential areas of Sheffield. The strongest relationship he found was between vandalism and kiosk use: kiosks for which takings were highest were the most heavily vandalised, a finding which also held for the total number of kiosks in the Sheffield area. When kiosk use was controlled for, a weak relationship was found between vandalism and 'defensible space' in that of the 27 kiosks studied in detail, those on the least public roads and not near public amenities were the most vulnerable. There was no tendency, however, for areas of high-rise developments (generally seen as low on 'defensible space') to experience more kiosk vandalism than other areas. A further finding was that council housing areas had more kiosk vandalism than areas of privately-rented or owner-occupied accommodation, this being particularly true of council areas which experienced high rates of indictable crime known to the police.

There are three respects in which the present study can be seen as developing the work of Mawby. First, it is based on a much larger number of kiosks (217) which has made it easier to study the effect of the numerous variables related to vandalism. Second, it includes all the kiosks in one London borough and therefore covers a much wider range of settings than the residential ones Mawby examined. Third, and most important, Mawby's principal measure of 'defensibility' (the 'publicness' of the road in which a kiosk was situated), though admittedly showing some relationship with vandalism, is open to criticism. His emphasis on public visibility neglects the territorial component of defensible space, though he makes the reasonable point that it is not clear how far territorial responsibility can be induced in respect of public amenities. In addition, his measures of public visibility - the 'busyness' of the street and the proximity of the kiosk to public amenities (shops, parks, schools etc) - assumes that the busier a place is, the more surveillance will thereby be afforded to a kiosk. As argued in Chapter 1, however, more people do not necessarily mean more effective surveillance unless they are in some way 'committed' observers; and indeed more people may mean more potential offenders. Moreover, the number of people passing a kiosk, on foot or in cars, may not in fact be high or constant enough to deter potential vandals, who in any case can easily watch out for possible witnesses[1].

The measure of surveillance chosen for the present study was the number of domestic windows in a given radius overlooking the kiosk. This measure probably includes some component of territoriality as residents are more likely to feel responsible for public property which they constantly overlook. (Presumably territorial feelings will be even stronger where they make regular use of the kiosk, but this was something that could not be measured for the present study.) There are also some other theoretical advantages over the measures of public visibility used by Mawby. Those who may be watching from behind their windows cannot necessarily be seen and one might suppose therefore that they pose a continuous threat to the potential vandal. And this threat is likely to be particularly strong during the evenings and weekends when vandalism may most often occur. Moreover, even if nearby residents cannot actually see what is happening inside a kiosk, the vandal may not know this, or be prepared to risk it. The passers-by Mawby took account of may in any case be in no better a position especially if they are in cars rather than on foot.

METHOD

The sample consisted of 217 telephone kiosks in the London Borough of Greenwich, virtually all the kiosks in the borough (a few were omitted from analysis because of incomplete information). An analysis of data from the 1971 Census showed Greenwich to be typical of London boroughs on a range of census variables.

Four main sets of data were collected: the amount of vandalism sustained by each of the 217 kiosks in a twelve-month period; the social characteristics of the population living in the vicinity of each kiosk; the degree to which each of these kiosks was used; and the degree to which they were overlooked by residential dwellings.

Information about vandalism

Information about vandalism derives from records of visits made in the financial year 1973/74 by Post Office engineers to each kiosk in Greenwich to repair damage resulting from vandalism[2]. These visits were made either in response to calls from the public that the kiosk was out of order or in need of repair, or in

---

[1] In the pilot work for the present study it was found that two measures of defensibility which are akin to those of Mawby - land usage in the area surrounding the kiosk and levels of vehicle and pedestrian traffic passing the kiosk - were not related to vandalism. The latter measure is particularly inconvenient to take in any case as several observations are desirable over different times of the day and week.

[2] Other service work is separately recorded. Although it may be that some damage recorded as vandalism was in fact wear and tear, the nature of the repairs carried out (for instance, unblocking objects from coin slots) suggested deliberate rather than accidental damage. Furthermore, Post Office personnel offered assurances that vandalism in kiosks is easily recognised.

response to directions from Post Office personnel concerned with routine inspection. In the main, repairs were to the telephone instrument or to the coin box mechanism, the result usually of petty incidents of damage which nevertheless often upset the proper functioning of the telephone service. (At present, steel covers on cash compartments have made the theft of takings - at one time the cause of much kiosk damage - extremely difficult. Damage to the compartments is still committed, however, presumably by those who continue to try and break into them or by those who perhaps feel frustrated by the difficulty of doing so.)

While the data about vandalism are probably adequate for present purposes and appear to have been reliably kept[1], the records relate to the number of times an engineer is called out and may not have been a good indication of the number of individual incidents of damage a particular kiosk sustained. For example, in heavily-hit kiosks there may have been a policy of repairing a number of separate incidents of vandalism during the course of one visit. This would have tended to produce a negative correlation between call-outs and repair costs. In fact, the correlation between the number of call-outs and the costs of repair was positive and therefore in subsequent analysis call-outs in preference to costs were used.

Social characteristics
1971 Census data for Greenwich were used to characterise the small areas of population surrounding each kiosk from which it was assumed that vandals would be drawn. Data were collected at enumeration district (ED) level[2], and comprised information on a range of variables (for instance, social class, type of tenure and the age structure of the population) which evidence suggests are associated with criminal behaviour (see, for example, Wallis and Maliphant, 1967; Baldwin et al., 1976; Herbert, 1977).

For the purpose of examining the composition of local populations, data were collated on the main EDs (usually two or three in number) falling within a radius of 220 yards of each kiosk. (Nearly all kiosks were surrounded by some dwellings in the given radius, though a very small number were not.) The radius was decided upon because kiosks in urban areas are situated about a quarter of a mile apart, and because it seemed reasonable to suppose that kiosks are vandalised by those who live in the immediate vicinity. Probably juveniles are the most heavily involved, kiosk vandalism seeming to be one of the 'tough' activities that is an extension of their outdoor play[3]. Baldwin et al. (1976) found that three-quarters of young offenders operated within a mile of their homes, while Suttles (1968)

---

[1] A split-half reliability test showed that there was a close association between the number of vandalism incidents to each kiosk in the six 'even' months of the twelve-month period compared to the six 'odd' months. In other words, the recording of vandalism over the year in question seemed fairly consistent.

[2] An enumeration district is the smallest areal unit for which census data are collated. The average number of households per ED in Greenwich was 165.

[3] A self-report study of vandalism (Gladstone, 1978) by schoolboys in the 11–16 age group showed that telephone kiosk vandalism is one of the most common offences they said they committed.

found that two-thirds of juveniles who committed malicious damage offences did so within two blocks of their home.

Kiosk usage

As the easiest measures of kiosk use, information was obtained from the Post Office about cash takings during the financial year 1973/74 for 209 of the 217 kiosks.

Information about surveillance

The measure of surveillance used was the number of domestic windows (i.e. windows in residential properties) in a radius of 30 yards which overlooked a kiosk. (In the case of tall buildings, only windows of the first three floors were counted.) This was easy to record and reliable, serving as a measure of the amount of potential surveillance offered to kiosks by householders from within their homes.

RESULTS

Vandalism

The mean number of vandalism incidents to Greenwich kiosks over the twelve-month period was 4·7 (sd = 3·2), which compares with a national average for the same period of 2·2 incidents, a London average of 3·6, and a higher figure of 6·7 for the 27 kiosks in Sheffield studied by Mawby. (For Sheffield overall, Mawby found an average of 2·9 incidents repaired per kiosk.) In the worst cases, some 6% of Greenwich kiosks sustained more than 10 incidents in the period, while for 4% of the kiosks no reports of vandalism were made at all.

Social factors

Analysis of vandalism rates in terms of census variables showed that the amount of vandalism to individual kiosks was significantly related, in ways not unexpected, to the characteristics of the population from which vandals were likely to be drawn. (Most of the census variables associated with vandalism were themselves interrelated.) For example, vandalism rose as the average number of persons per household rose, and as the number of unemployed and one-parent families increased; it was more prevalent in lower social class areas and where there was a high turnover of population; and it rose together with the proportion of boys in the population aged 5–14 at the time of the Census[1].

The strongest factor, however, which discriminated between high and low vandalism rates was tenure type: the more that kiosks were surrounded by council housing, the more vandalism they suffered (p < ·001). One explanation which

---

[1] Mawby looked at boys aged 10–14 at the time of the 1971 Census in the nine residential areas in which his 27 kiosks were sited. Perhaps because of his small overall sample, the fact that his age range was small, or the fact that he looked at much wider surrounding areas, his results were inconsistent with ours in showing that the proportion of juveniles in the area had little effect on levels of damage.

suggests itself relates to the proportion of boys living in the close vicinity of kiosks. For 'council' areas (defined as those where 50% or more of the dwellings in the enumeration districts surrounding the kiosk were council-owned) the mean proportion of boys aged 5–14 at the time of the Census was 8·3% of the population. For 'non-council' areas (those where less than 50% of the dwellings were council-owned) the mean proportion of boys was significantly lower at 6·8% (p < ·001). However, despite this difference, rates of vandalism in non-council areas with unusually high boy densities suggested it was the presence of 'council' boys specifically which led to kiosk damage: a sample of 60 kiosks surrounded by very little council housing (on average 14% of the housing in the area) but with a high mean proportion of boys (8·2%) living in the vicinity, sustained on average 4·1 incidents of vandalism in the period compared to 6·4 for the 'council' kiosks themselves (p < ·001). This result may simply reflect a greater inclination to commit vandalism on the part of boys living in council areas, though it may also mean that council boys (particularly those living in flats) are more often out on the street than boys elsewhere.

Usage

Unlike Mawby's study, the present result revealed no strong effect whereby, for the sample of kiosks as a whole, vandalism increased as kiosk use increased. At the same time, looking at the council and non-council sectors separately (average takings per kiosk were similar in both sectors), there was a significant positive relationship (p < ·02) between use and vandalism for non-council kiosks, although this did not apply to kiosks in council areas. In other words, for areas with little or no council housing, heavy use was associated with vandalism. The explanation for this may be that while a relatively constant proportion of its users may damage a kiosk, in council areas this effect is masked by the fact that council boys may be attracted to, and may damage, a kiosk on occassions other than where they are using it. Alternatively it may be that in non-council areas the busy kiosks are likely to be in the more interesting and busy places which may attract the vandal.

Surveillance

With regard to surveillance, analysis of the sample as a whole, not controlling for population differences in the immediately surrounding areas, showed no straightforward effect whereby kiosk vandalism fell with increasing numbers of overlooking windows. However, a deterrent effect of windows became clearer when account was taken of the fact that kiosks in predominantly council housing areas suffered on average more vandalism than kiosks elsewhere, i.e. when the 'window effect' was examined separately in relation to council areas and to non-council areas. Table 5:1 shows that in non-council areas, kiosks which were overlooked by relatively many domestic windows suffered less (though marginally less) vandalism than kiosks overlooked by relatively few windows[1]. There

---

[1] t = 2·04; p < ·025; one-tailed test.

Table 5:1
Kiosk vandalism and the effect of overlooking windows

	Non-council areas	Council areas
	Average number of vandal incidents per kiosk	Average number of vandal incidents per kiosk
Less than median number of windows	4·3 (n = 76)	7·1 (n = 36)
More than median number of windows	3·5 (n = 72)	5·6 (n = 33)
All kiosks	3·9 (n = 148)	6·4 (n = 69)

NB: Kiosks in each of the two sectors are divided into two similarly-sized groups according to the number of windows which overlooked them. The split was made at the median number of windows: 19 in the case of kiosks in non-council areas, 28 in the case of the more overlooked kiosks in council areas. (See text for definition of 'council' and 'non-council' areas.)

was a similar result for kiosks in council areas but, perhaps, because of small numbers, it was statistically less significant[1].

The results suggest, then, that kiosk vandals are to some extent deterred by the actual or potential surveillance offered by those who are looking, or might look out of domestic windows. This 'window effect' was not a strong one, and this may be partly because the variance in surveillance has already been reduced by the Post Office who aim to site kiosks to avoid highly secluded areas with little natural oversight.

IMPLICATIONS
The type of 'natural' surveillance by people from within their homes which was measured in this study was shown to have only a small effect on the level of kiosk vandalism. This may reflect the fact that those inside their home pay little attention to public targets when the chance of vandalism - perhaps not considered a serious offence - is still relatively infrequent. Another possible explanation is that people may in fact spend rather little time looking out of their windows and as long as little noise is being made vandals may be relatively safe from being seen.

On the face of it, therefore, the results of the study do not support Newman's (1972) contention that residents can provide a useful function in 'policing' areas outside their homes. To some degree, this may be because telephone kiosks are not often situated in the sort of private or semi-private areas over which offenders think that residents, as Newman claims, adopt proprietary attitudes. Nevertheless, to the extent that public amenities are not usually located in residents'

[1] t = 1·56; p < ·07; one-tailed test.

immediate domain, the present results suggest that casual surveillance of such targets by people from within their homes - at least with respect to minor deviance - may not have a great deal of crime prevention payoff.

The results also appear to suggest that kiosk vandalism is more strongly related to certain characteristics of the population living near individual kiosks than to physical factors pertaining to their siting, and in this respect they are consistent with Newman's later (1976) work which showed that the social make-up of local housing estate inhabitants contributed more to levels of crime and vandalism than housing design. More closely still, they echo a recent Home Office Research Unit study of vandalism on Inner London council estates (see Chaper 4), which showed that the 'defensibility' of the environment mattered relatively little when blocks housed large numbers of boys. However, in the context of the present study at least, the pre-eminence of the social correlates of vandalism should be qualified: first, only one 'physical' factor (the degree to which kiosks were overlooked by domestic windows) was compared with a number of social variables of known explanatory importance; and second, given Post Office siting policy, surveillance was measured on a limited range.

In practical terms, the results of the present study suggest that, taking into account other considerations of convenience and visibility, there is little scope for recommending that more care is taken in siting kiosks as near to domestic properties as possible. A corollary of this is that other 'natural' surveillance (from vehicle traffic, shoppers, etc.) which the Post Office tries to maximise may give no more protection against vandalism than the minimal level provided by overlooking windows. This is likely to be at least as good a 'natural' deterrent as anything similar, as is confirmed by the relatively slight effect of siting in busy areas which Mawby found. Nevertheless, to the extent that this study shows that kiosks in council areas, which characteristically house high densities of boys, are particularly prone to damage, these may merit special consideration. It may be that some very high-risk kiosks should be resited to more overlooked locations. Or - as occasionally happens already with persistently vandalised targets – they may need removing altogether. This usually leads to complaints from users, though in fact they may not be greatly inconvenienced as persistently vandalised kiosks are often left out of order. Furthermore, loss of income to the Post Office is likely to be offset by the savings made in not having to carry out constant repairs.

In view of the fact that there seems little scope for reducing damage through re-siting kiosks, there appears considerable merit in the Post Office's attempts to make kiosks more 'vandal proof'. Notable success has already been achieved in reducing theft by the introduction of steel covers for cash compartments (cash losses in 1976/77 were 4% of the figure for 1971/72). Other 'target hardening' measures such as shatter-proof handsets, recessed dials and reinforced cables may, where they have been used, also have kept in check some of the more serious damage to the telephone mechanism. Moreover, the petty vandalism to the kiosk structure and to directories and notice boards that is currently a problem may be reduced when recent design improvements are more widely introduced. While damage incidents have continued to rise (nationally there were 19% more incidents in 1976/77 than four years before), the target-hardening policy which the Post Office has adopted may well have kept vandalism levels below what they might otherwise have been - between 1972 and 1976 police figures for criminal damage (to all kinds of property but only involving sums of more than £20) rose by 122%[1].

In more general terms, the present results also endorse the provision of alternative telephone facilities less vulnerable to vandalism. For some time, the Post Office has been encouraging the installation of rented call boxes (RCBs) for public use in premises such as pubs, shops and launderettes. Experience suggests that such units sustain minimal damage compared to kiosks, no doubt because they are located in places subject to surveillance by personnel with direct responsibility for the facilities. However, RCBs do not meet the sort of twenty-four hour need served by the 77,000 kiosks now in existence in the United Kingdom, and their merits need to be carefully weighed against the inconvenience and cost of vandalism: the public is usually portrayed as highly concerned about the inconvenience and occasional danger that arises from persistent vandalism in some localities, though the Post Office itself claims that not more than one kiosk in a thousand is out of order on account of vandalism at any one time. Also, it is a point worth bearing in mind that the £1·07 m national cost of kiosk vandalism in 1976/77 represented only 1·8% of kiosk income (*Post Office Report and Accounts, 1976–77*). It seems rather questionable whether these figures would support any more rigorous a policy whereby kiosks are taken out of action when RCB facilities increase.

---

[1] Some of this increase would be accounted for by the effect of inflation.

6 Closed circuit television and crime on the London Underground

John Burrows

In Chapter 1 it was suggested that more use might be made of the surveillance rôle of certain employees who already have a responsibility for the security of their employer's property and for exercising some supervision over public behaviour. One approach which has already enjoyed some popularity in shops has been to provide employees with closed circuit television (CCTV). Such equipment extends the area which can be covered and in theory increases the chances of an arrest. Evidence about the value of CCTV used in this way is not substantial, a little more being known about its usefulness to the police (Hancox and Morgan, 1975). Costs are a severe limitation, of course, and effectiveness, even discounting the possibility of displacement, cannot be taken for granted. For instance, where crime is relatively infrequent the level of vigilance required from those manning a CCTV system may be unrealistic (Young, 1974). There may also be problems in controllers getting a quick enough reaction from other staff or being able to communicate a good enough description of the offender (cf. Home Office, 1973).

The present study assesses the effect - on theft and robbery offences - of equipping staff in the London Underground with CCTV. Some attention was paid in the evaluation to the costs of the system as well as to possible displacement effects. The opportunity for the study was provided by the installation in November 1975 of CCTV in four Underground stations, which were among a number that were particularly vulnerable to what are commonly known as 'muggings'. These comprised attacks on passengers (involving varying degrees of force) for their personal property, committed characteristically by groups of male youths. As the installation of CCTV came after a year's special policing measures in the same vicinity, account also had to be taken of these in assessing the effectiveness of CCTV itself.

THE DATA
The data used in the study came from statistical records of the London Transport (LT) division of the British Transport Police (BTP). With minor exceptions[1], these offences cover all offences reported on Underground stations and trains. The data analysed refer to all incidents of robbery, assault with intent to rob, and theft from the person[2] committed between October 1973 and November 1976.

---

[1] Twenty-nine of the 276 London Underground stations in operation when the study took place were policed by other divisions of the BTP. Offences committed at these stations are not included.

[2] These are referred to throughout as robbery and theft. A person may be found guilty of robbery if either before or at the time of committing an act of theft he subjects another to force or to the threat of force (Section 8, Theft Act 1968). Theft from the person technically involves no force.

The term 'mugging' (which has no definition in law) is most commonly used to refer to robbery or assault with intent to rob. However, particularly in press and popular usage (Hall *et al.*, 1978), it often embraces offences which are probably recorded as theft but which (as in the case of bag-snatching) might involve a measure of force. A distinction is maintained between theft and robbery in the discussion below, not least because despite concern about the supposed problem of violent 'mugging', it serves to show the extent to which the small number of serious offences of robbery are outweighed by the number of thefts.

This said, however, there is little way of knowing how complete a record of offences committed in the Underground is contained in BTP statistics. Inevitably, a proportion of offences will not be reported by victims at all, particularly thefts which are likely to involve less trauma; moreover, though the presence of station staff may faciliate reporting, thefts may not be discovered by passengers until they have left the Underground system. Apart from these omissions (which are probably constant over time), there is some likelihood that for other reasons BTP records underestimate the extent of crime which is reported. A substantial proportion of crime in BTP records is not notified directly by the complainant but is transmitted to the BTP after complaints made to LT staff and police officers of civil forces. Experience suggests that both parties sometimes fail to pass on crime complaints (cf. Crump and Newing, 1974). Furthermore, it seems that where the BTP have difficulty in contacting complainants (as in the case of tourists) to complete and verify details of alleged offences reported to station personnel, these offences are sometimes left unrecorded. The proportion of offences 'lost' in these two ways, however, may be small and is likely again to be fairly constant over the time period analysed. Possibly more theft offences than robberies are omitted from BTP records, one reason being that some of the former might find their way into the records of the civil police if the passenger cannot be certain that the loss occurred in the Underground itself.

DISTRIBUTION OF OFFENCES
In comparison with theft, robbery occurs very infrequently on the Underground, although it has become relatively more common since 1974 (see Table 6:1).

Table 6:1
Number of thefts and robberies on the London Underground system, 1973–1976

Year	Robberies	Thefts	Ratio (R:T)
1973	70	3569	1:51
1974	74	6105	1:82
1975	121	5081	1:42
1976	109	3487	1:32

Although the number of offences on the Underground varies somewhat from year to year, in terms of the very considerable number of users, the risk of being a victim of robbery or theft on the system as a whole is extremely small. Comparing journey figures for 1972 with the average annual offence figures for 1973–76, it appears that only one robbery occurred for each 8·4 million journeys made. With regard to theft offences, one offence occurred for each 173,000 journeys made[1].

Although in general theft and robbery offences occur with the greatest frequency at those stations dealing with the heaviest passenger traffic[2], user levels alone do not explain all the variation in risk figures for theft; certain highly-used stations located in office areas (e.g. Bank/Monument, Liverpool Street) have relatively low levels of theft, while theft levels are high at some stations dealing with fewer passengers but located in shopping or tourist areas (e.g. Knightsbridge, Glouces-ter Road).

The risk of robbery and to a lesser extent theft was disproportionately high in the southern sector of the system (particularly at stations close to the Stockwell interchange) which first attracted attention in 1972 on account of 'muggings' (see Baxter and Nuttall, 1975). As Table 6:2 shows, during 1974–75, the 19 stations

Table 6:2
Risk of robbery and theft on the London Underground system

Stations	Annual users 1972 (000,000s)	Thefts (annual average 1974–1975)	Robberies (annual average 1974–1975)	Risk of theft per million users	Risk of robbery per million users
All southern sector stations (n = 19)	111·3	651	37	5·8	·33
All other stations (n = 228)	1462·9	4942	60·5	3·4	·04
All stations (n = 247)	1574·2	5593	97·5	3·6	·06

(8% of all stations for which data were available) south of the Thames on the Northern, Victoria and Bakerloo lines accounted for 74 reported offences of robbery (38% of the total)[3]. Theft figures also reflect this pattern but much less markedly: 12% of all thefts were committed in the same area. While it may be that stations in the southern sector were genuinely riskier with regard to robbery offences, it is also possible that the attention paid by the media to 'muggings' in this locality resulted in certain marginal offences being inflated in seriousness and defined as robbery. Nevertheless, the vulnerability of southern sector stations with regard to offences against passengers is clear.

---

[1] 'Journeys' refer to journey stages taken; 'user' levels (see Table 6:2) to passenger traffic entering, leaving or interchanging at individual stations.

[2] Over all stations, the correlation between the estimated annual user level (1972 figures) and the theft rate for 1974 was high ($r = 0.85$).

[3] The BTP practice is followed of allocating offences committed between stations to the next station in the direction of travel.

CRIME PREVENTION MEASURES

The concentration of offences in the southern sector led in the first place to the setting up of special police patrols in station areas. These began at the end of 1974. The information available about these patrols is incomplete. Broadly speaking, police effort was concentrated in the vicinity of Stockwell on Friday and Saturday evenings, high-risk times for 'muggings' to occur. It fell into three stages. For an initial period, between the end of September and the beginning of November 1974, the patrols involved both the Metropolitan Police and British Transport Police CID officers. Following this, plainclothes CID officers from the BTP policed the area alone. At the end of March 1975 the CID patrols were replaced by uniformed squads from the BTP which operated until the beginning of December 1975. There is, however, no detailed record of which particular stations were subject to police vigilance, of the numbers of police involved, or of further patrols, additional to those mentioned above, conducted by civil police forces at this time. Because of this, there is some difficulty in interpreting how effective the special patrols were.

As Table 6:3 indicates, the number of thefts recorded in the southern sector during the main period of heightened police activity was 27% less than in the preceding period of normal policing, a fall that was significantly more marked ($p < \cdot001$) than that recorded at other Underground stations. There was a marked *increase* in robberies in the southern area over the same period; this was of greater magnitude than a similar increase at other stations, though the difference was not significant.

Three explanations of these results suggest themselves. First, with regard to the more statistically pronounced trends in relation to thefts, it is possible that the decrease at southern sector stations was the result simply of an atypically high level of theft at these stations prior to special policing (i.e. a regression to the

Table 6:3
The effects of special policing

	Theft		Robbery	
	12 months before special policing	12 months during special policing	12 months before special policing	12 months during special policing
All southern sector stations (n = 19)	778	571	22	49
Other stations (n = 228)	4884	4490	43	67
All stations (n = 247)	5662	5061	65	116

NB: To enable comparison to be made with the figures in Table 6:4, the 'before special policing' figures in this table refer to crimes recorded in the 12 month period October 1973–September 1974. As the police activity continued for 14 months, the 'during special policing' figures represent 12/14 of actual reported crime.

mean effect). A second explanation is that the conflicting trends in relation to robbery and theft are largely spurious: one might assume that the distinction between the two offences is so unreliable that they can only legitimately be considered together. (Doing this, the combined offences fell by 23% in the southern stations during police activity and by 8% elsewhere ($p < \cdot01$.)

Thirdly - and this is a more convincing explanation - it is likely that police action, while effective in deterring thefts committed largely as opportunities present themselves, often in crowds, has considerably less effect on more serious offences involving premeditation and usually taking place in situations where it is clear that the police are not present. This explanation is supported by other research (Chaiken *et al.*, 1974) which showed that additional night patrols in the New York system were more effective in reducing minor crimes that serious offences. In any event, the evidence in this case suggests that the pattern of robbery offences was unaffected by the police initiatives. The presence of the police may even have elicited a higher reporting rate from the public - one which did not apply to thefts because losses are not always discovered in the Underground or its close vicinity.

THE INSTALLATION OF CCTV

Special police patrols operating in the southern sector of the Underground were removed at the end of the first week of December 1975. This decision was taken following the installation of a CCTV monitor control at Stockwell which began to operate on 24 November 1975; the CCTV provided the facility to view from the Stockwell control, station areas at Stockwell, Clapham North, Clapham Common and - a matter of weeks later - at Brixton. The units installed at these stations combined fixed cameras fitted with 35mm lenses with microphones. They were mounted externally at vantage points in each station and provided a view of all principal station areas - platforms, ticket halls, interchange concourses, areas at the foot and head of escalators, together with other high-risk points for crime or vandalism. Where necessary wide-angle lenses were fitted. The cameras were quite conspicious to passengers and notices were also posted in the stations informing the public that CCTV was in operation.

Signals from the equipment are relayed to four 12″ monitor screens[1] and speakers at Stockwell, which are continually manned during passenger traffic hours. The controller can either elect to observe a scene of his choice on these monitors or may switch them to scan all station areas automatically at seven second intervals. The controller has several means of dealing with an incident: contact may be made with station staff or the nearest police room; public address announcements may be made to any station areas selected; and - in the case of incidents on the Victoria line - contact may be made through the line controller,

---

[1] There are now eight monitor screens (arranged in two banks of four) in the Stockwell control room; of the additional four, three provide surveillance of South Wimbledom, Balham, and Tooting Broadway stations. The fourth monitor provides the facility to playback pictures video-recorded by the others.

with train drivers. A further feature of the crime control measures taken in the four stations at this time was the installation of alarms in all ticket collectors' boxes; when pressed these operate sirens on the top of the boxes and hold the camera on the collector's box until such time as the Stockwell operator cancels the signal.

The method used to evaluate the effectiveness of the CCTV installations was to compare the distribution of reported cases of theft and robbery between the four stations subject to surveillance and other stations in the Underground, particularly the remaining stations in the southern sector, during the first year of complete CCTV operation (December 1975–November 1976) and an earlier one-year period before the commencement of police patrols at the end of September 1974.

RESULTS

At those stations subject to CCTV surveillance, recorded thefts were *nearly four times* lower during the period of CCTV compared to the period before police patrols began (see Table 6:4). This reduction was significantly greater than that at the 15 other stations in the southern sector not subject to CCTV surveillance where theft offences were about 1·4 times lower ($p < ·001$). It was also greater than the slightly more pronounced fall at the remaining Underground stations ($p < ·001$). With regard to robbery, the decrease in the small number of such offences at the four stations with CCTV was significantly different from the doubling of robbery offences at the stations not in the southern sector ($p < ·05$), though it was not significantly different from the slight increase in these offences at the other southern sector stations. Taken together these results suggest therefore that CCTV reduced the incidence of both theft and robbery in the four stations where it was installed.

Table 6:4
The effects of CCTV

	Theft		Robbery	
	12 months before special policing and CCTV	First 12 months of CCTV	12 months before special policing and CCTV	First 12 months of CCTV
Stations with CCTV (n = 4)	243	66	9	7
Other southern sector stations (n = 15)	535	393	13	16
Other stations (n = 228)	4884	2962	43	93

NB: The periods compared here comprise the 12 months directly before the introduction of special policing patrols (October 1973–September 1974; as in Table 6:3), and the 12 months directly following the start of CCTV operations (December 1975–November 1976).

Some attempt was made to consider whether any displacement of offences occurred as a result of the CCTV installations. Temporal displacement was unlikely because the CCTV system operated at all times, but some geographical displacement of offences could not be ruled out, either to locales outside the Underground, or to stations within the system not covered by CCTV. There was little possibility of knowing whether any incidents were displaced outside, as such offences were likely to be 'lost' in the greater volume of street offences. However, comparison of crime levels between stations subject to CCTV and other nearby stations in the southern sector provides evidence that is consistent with (though not proof of) some displacement of theft offences. Comparison of the first twelve months of CCTV operations with an equivalent period before special police patrols (see Table 6:4) shows that at the fifteen southern sector stations not subject to CCTV thefts fell by 27%, while in other stations of the Underground they fell by 39% - a significant difference ($p < .01$).

Moreover, closer examination of the pattern of thefts in the southern sector shows that the eight stations furthest away from those with CCTV (to which it might be assumed crime was least likely to be displaced) experienced a drop in thefts (45%) similar to that outside the southern sector. In contrast, at the seven nearer stations (which admittedly had higher levels of crime, more akin to those at stations where CCTV was installed) the drop in thefts was less pronounced at 24%.

Whether or not some thefts were displaced by the CCTV installations, the number of robbery offences is too small to conclude much about any displacement of robbery. In fact, though, the increase in robbery in the southern sector stations without CCTV was less than that at other stations, which does not suggest that displacement occurred.

CONCLUSIONS

This analysis of the effects of equipping station staff with a CCTV system in four relatively high-risk stations in the London Underground suggests that CCTV was useful, at least in the first year of its operation, in reducing the number of thefts and robbery offences at target stations. There is some evidence consistent with the fact that some theft offences might have been displaced to nearby stations, though it cannot be taken as definite proof that displacement occurred. If it did, it may have nullified up to 85% of the savings in theft offences apparently produced by the CCTV installations.

The usefulness of CCTV at the stations where is was installed supports London Transport's view that the cameras have proved effective in combatting vandalism and theft. (Their value for transport operations has been the main factor in the decision to extend CCTV to six central Underground stations, but the anticipated crime prevention benefits have not been ignored.) It would seem that the publicity given to the installations, particularly at the stations where they were located, the visibility of the cameras, and the fact that station users were able to see that monitor controllers could communicate to other staff, all acted as a deterrent to potential thieves. It also seems possible, though there is no evidence available to test this, that a deterrent effect was further realised by improved arrest rates. It is possible, though again untestable, that the installation of alarms in ticket collectors' boxes was additionally useful in preventing crime. There is no reason to think, however, that the change in crime at the four stations studied would have been greatly different had CCTV been the only preventive measure introduced. A caveat that must be made is that the effectiveness of the system might have resulted to some extent from its novelty and that as time goes on offenders may discover that CCTV is less to be feared than they had imagined. This implies that effectiveness should continue to be monitored.

The study has been useful, therefore, in providing some further evidence of the value of CCTV as a surveillance aid for employees. The present results are in line with informal opinion that CCTV in the new Metro system in Washington has been a valuable part of the security measures which were incorporated into the design of the system (see *Nation's Cities, 1977*), though it should be said that detailed information about the part CCTV plays there is not yet available. They also appear to confirm a point which has emerged from retailers' experience with CCTV (Home Office, 1973): namely, the need for sophisticated equipment and communication systems which can be seen to result in action. In this case, camera coverage was extensive and several means were provided of establishing contact with the police or other station personnel. However, whether simpler equipment (perhaps even 'imitation' cameras) can operate as a less costly deterrent to crime, at least in certain circumstances, is a question which cannot be satisfactorily answered at present.

Although this study included an assessment of the effectiveness of extra policing in relation to Underground crime, as well as that of CCTV, it is difficult to draw any conclusions about the relative merits of the two strategies. This is because there is not enough information about the policing measures to decide how any effects were produced. In any case, the result of police action in apparently 'increasing' robbery (theft declined significantly) is particularly difficult to interpret.

Assessing the cost-effectiveness of the two strategies is problematic also, not least because there is virtually no information available on the police resources used. With regard to the CCTV system, installation and operating costs in the first year are known (the four installations studied cost London Transport £128,000 at 1975 prices)[1]. Thus, taking crime figures for the first year only, and assuming that theft and robbery would have followed the trend at other southern stations not covered by CCTV, the cost per prevented theft was about £1140 (discounting any possibly displaced thefts), and per prevented robbery £31,450. (Other assump-

---

[1] This includes the cost of the Stockwell control rooms. To incorporate the facilities necessary to extend surveillance to South Wimbledon, Balham and Tooting Broadway stations, and to video-record events, raised the final cost of the 'Stockwell system' to £200,000.

tions can be made. If theft and robbery had followed the trend for stations outside the southern sector, the cost per prevented theft was £1570 and £10,270 per prevented robbery.) It would be dangerous, however, to place much weight on these figures, the uncertainty of displacement apart. The costs of the system will be written off over a number of years and might be offset by a number of benefits other than reduced robbery and theft offences: as mentioned earlier, London Transport view the installations as useful for crowd control, as a means of reducing vandalism (which it is claimed is now at a lower level), reducing assaults on staff, and promoting a greater willingness on the part of the public to use a 'safer' Underground system. In addition, the reduced rate of robberies and thefts might have led to some saving of police time and of other costs associated with bringing offenders to justice.

7 Police truancy patrols

Paul Ekblom

INTRODUCTION

Much research has shown that truants are particularly likely to come to the attention of the police for juvenile offences (Tyerman, 1968; Tennent, 1971; Belson, 1975; May, 1975; Farrington, forthcoming). Tennent, for example, showed that 25–40% of juvenile court defendants had truanted, but only 2–20% of the total school population. Farrington, studying both teacher-rated and self-reported truants in secondary schools, found that roughly half were delinquents compared with some 15% of the remaining children.

Tyerman (1968) has argued that if a pupil finds he can successfully avoid school, it may be a step to believing that he can just as easily defy authority in other ways. Cohen (1955) is of the opinion that anti-social attitudes are engendered by truancy to the extent that this combines with school failure. Equally likely, though, is the possibility that truancy leads to delinquency by virtue of the greater opportunities the truant would seem to have for getting into trouble (cf. Mannheim, 1965).

Whatever the link between delinquency and truancy, the level of truancy in this country causes concern. Statistics pertaining to truancy[1] which derive from attendance records have several limitations (cf. Williams, 1974), but calculating from a school age population of 11 million (*Annual Abstract of Statistics, 1977*), upwards of a quarter of a million children probably truant on any one day in Great Britain.

POLICE TRUANCY PATROLS

The police endorse the belief that truants are more likely than other children to become delinquent. Furthermore, while some officers in the Metropolitan Police District who have been involved in running truancy patrols now argue that truants avoid offending at times when they would be conspicuous (a view supported by Belson's (1975) self-report study but countered by the present Commissioner (McNee, 1979)), most forces believe that much daytime crime is committed by children who should be in school. In any event, some seven or eight forces in Britain have recently established projects aimed at reducing truancy, the majority of which are special patrols. Apart from patrols which were operated until 1975 in a number of MPD divisions (Devlin, 1974; *Times Educational*

---

[1] Truancy is taken here to mean illegitimate absence from school with or without the knowledge and connivance of parents; it is calculated as the proportion of days lost out of the total possible number of days' attendance at school.

85

Supplement, 18 January 1974), patrols have operated in Gloucestershire, South Wales, Sussex, Avon and Somerset, Northamptonshire, and in a sub-division of the Glasgow force (Haining, 1973).

The more formal patrols have consisted of one or two officers, frequently accompanied by, or co-operating with, education welfare officers (EWOs), and have covered a sub-division, or an area around a large comprehensive school. Unaccompanied children encountered on the streets during school hours are challenged and, if no plausible excuse is presented, are often returned directly to school. Follow-up visits by EWOs are frequently made to the parents of the children deemed to be truanting.

Records have usually been kept of the numbers of children stopped, and occasionally attempts have been made to see whether local crime has fallen during patrol periods. For many patrols for which data are available (not all are adequately documented), large numbers of children were picked up - for example 200 a day in Hackney, mostly aged 13–14. Comparing crime figures during patrol periods with those of the previous year, a 12-day sweep in Brixton and Lambeth, for example, was said to result in autocrime falling by 26% and petty crime by 30%. In Glasgow, during an unusually long patrol of 10 weeks, 53 crimes attributed to juveniles were reported as having been committed during school hours, with 56 apprehensions of juveniles; in the same period the previous year, 115 crimes were reported as committed during school hours, for which 22 children were apprehended. As far as can be judged from school registration figures, the Glasgow patrol seemed to have considerably improved the attendance of persistent as well as casual truants[1].

Whilst previous assessments of truancy patrols have focussed largely on police crime figures, there is a strong case to be made that these are inadequate (even, as in Glasgow, when used in combination with school registration figures). First, crimes known to the police may be neither representative of, nor bear a constant relationship with, the actual level of crime. Second, the use of the previous year's statistics as a comparison figure is less than ideal since the weather, the position of holidays, etc., may vary. Third, police figures do not in most cases show who committed an offence (i.e. child or adult), or its exact timing (i.e. in or out of school hours). Related to this is the uncertainty as to whether offences prevented during school hours by patrols have merely been 'displaced' to other times or places. Finally, whilst the percentage falls in crime seem large the absolute numbers are often small and thus unreliable.

The study reported below was an attempt both to evaluate the need for truancy patrols and their effectiveness in reducing the level of daytime crime by truants. It was judged necessary to examine a patrol set up experimentally rather than to

---

[1] Two truancy patrols conducted in California are discussed by White *et al.* (1975). One two-week patrol in San Bernardino involving nine police officers appeared to reduce daytime burglaries, though from the data given it is not clear whether this was a chance effect. A four-week patrol in Glendale coincided with a somewhat more definite fall in daylight burglaries.

examine one retrospectively, using information additional to that provided by the police. The help was sought of the Avon and Somerset Constabulary, because it had prior experience of truancy patrols and because Bristol was judged fairly representative of a number of moderately urbanised regions in which patrols have been run.

METHOD OF EVALUATION

Design
The study comprised two time series of observations, before and after half-term in the Spring term of 1978 (see Figure 7:1). In each half of the term, observations (comprising various daily counts of children at large during school hours) were taken before, during and after a week's patrolling; these were then considered in relation to a number of crime indices.

Figure 7:1 The Design

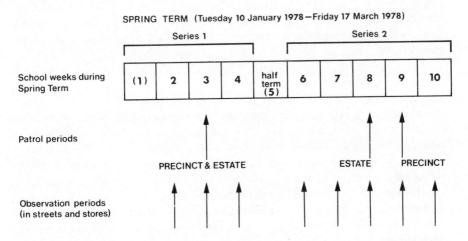

Patrols and observations were conducted in two city divisions - the central shopping precinct and an outlying council estate. To check for displacement the patrols in the second series were staggered such that the patrol in the precinct occurred a week later than that in the estate. In the opinion of the police the precinct was the most likely destination of those displaced from the estate.

The amount of truancy patrolling over the school term (four patrol weeks in all) was greater than that usually provided by the police in the area (two days per term). This reflected a pragmatic decision to seek effects of measurable strength whilst not exceeding by too great a margin the level of resources the police feel able to devote to this activity on a regular basis. (It was judged rather unrealistic in this respect to evaluate a patrol of the length adopted in Glasgow.) Publicity and teacher co-operation (common features of truancy initiatives) were avoided to single out the effect of special police presence. The method of patrolling was

87

typical: a group comprising a male and female police constable (both uniformed) and an EWO covered a given area, interviewing children without adults, and where necessary returning them home or to school. The precinct team worked on foot; the estate team mostly in marked cars.

Several confounding events imposed themselves upon the study, most significant of all being the closure due to snow of all the schools in Bristol for at least one day during week 7 (when it was originally intended that the estate patrol would take place). This resulted in the estate and precinct patrols being shifted to the weeks shown in Figure 7:1, cutting short the post-patrol measurement period and reducing the quality of the week-to-week comparisons.

Data recorded

i. *Police patrol figures*
Patrols were asked to record the age and sex of children stopped, the time any action was taken and their judgement of the validity of any excuses proffered. Unfortunately, a misunderstanding resulted so that in many cases the author had to make the latter judgement himself on the basis of the police description of the excuses given.

ii. *School registration figures*
For each week of the Spring term, the number of absences (for whatever cause) was found for the boys' and girls' comprehensive schools in the estate (there were no schools in the precinct area). This was partly to see whether patrols were directly affecting attendance levels. It was also meant as a way of establishing whether background variations in absence, occurring independently of any patrol effects, might be affecting the principal dependent variable, namely the numbers of children counted on the streets. For this latter purpose it was also necessary to take note of absence figures from two schools similar to those in the estate, situated in a district that was comparable to, but well removed from, the patrol areas.

iii. *Child counts on the street*
Research workers also made counts each day, on regular routes and times, of school age children seen at large between 10 a.m.–12 noon and 2 p.m.–3.30 p.m., who were not obviously on any school activity. For each child details were noted of sex, approximate age and whether he/she was alone, with other children, or with adults. Each morning and afternoon two researchers spent some half an hour together driving round the streets of the estate and walking round the shopping centre there; 30 minutes were also passed walking round the precinct. In the estate only one researcher counted; in the precinct both researchers counted whilst following separate routes. No child was approached by the researchers and assumptions were made about the proportion of children counted who had legitimate reasons for being out of school. In all cases the

change in numbers from week to week was of central interest, rather than the absolute totals counted, since these could depend on arbitrary factors, not least the possibility of some double-counting of children by the two researchers in the precinct. An attempt to allow for this in the analysis of statistical significance is noted in Table 7:2.

iv. *Child counts in a department store*
It was thought possible that truants might attempt to avoid the patrols by going into large stores in the city centre. By arrangement with the management of a large department store in the precinct therefore, the two researchers spent a further 30 minutes each morning and each afternoon counting as inconspicuously as possible the children who entered the store. By judicious positioning most of the main entrances were covered.

v. *Store detectives' records*
Since, according to some sources, shoplifting is the offence most frequently committed by truants, it was arranged that store detectives from about ten large stores in the precinct would keep records of shoplifting by children in school hours. In the event, however, so few kept up their initial enthusiasm that the figures were considered unreliable.

vi. *Police daily crime reports*
Weekly totals were derived of offences reported as taking place within each patrol boundary[1], which *could* have been committed in school hours (not all offences could be precisely located in time) and which by their nature *could* have been committed by children (offences such as cheque frauds, or those where adult suspects were described, were eliminated from the total).

vii. *Juvenile bureau entries*
Since offences which are followed by immediate arrest if they are detected (such as shoplifting) do not appear in daily crime reports, to avoid missing these the weekly totals of all entries in the juvenile bureau records were derived for the respective divisions in which the patrols were located.

RESULTS

Patrol figures

In the first half of the term the patrol in the precinct picked up 32 children virtually all with unacceptable excuses. (For this patrol particularly, it is not known whether the patrol recorded every child approached.) The estate patrol recorded 136, of whom 46 (34%) had excuses judged unacceptable by the author.

---

[1] This is seen as justified in the light of study by Baldwin *et al.* (1976), where the majority of offences by children under 16 appeared to have been committed within a mile of home (Table 12, p. 83).

In the second half of term the precinct patrol picked up 29 children, only 8 (28%) of whom had poor excuses (again judged by the author); the estate patrol interviewed 127, of whom 53 (42%) had poor excuses. The discrepancies in the numbers of children picked up in the two areas (which hold up even when differences between the street count figures from both areas are taken into account) are interesting since they may imply that patrols catch children more easily in the suburbs by car than in the central area on foot. The fact that transporting children to an outlying school took up more time in the precinct than the purely local requirements in the estate could not be considered responsible for the observed differences, because not a great number of children were taken back to school in either division. It seems more likely that children could readily spot the foot patrol and more easily elude them.

School registration figures

An average of 476 children were officially absent from the comprehensive schools in the estate at each registration, of whom national estimates would conservatively suggest that some 100 were truanting. While these figures cannot be meaningfully compared with the street count data, they are useful in assessing the impact of patrols. The average daily number of children of appropriate age and with poor excuses, who were picked up by the estate patrols was 8 - a small proportion, that is, of those at whom the patrols were aimed.

Counts of children

The average daily counts of children without adults were 27 in the precinct, 15 in the store and 26 in the estate. Some of these children are likely to have had legitimate grounds for being out of school, but probably not in so high a proportion as that reported by the patrols (some two-thirds), since it is reasonable to expect that children illegitimately at large would have sought more than their fellows to avoid the police. The corresponding figures for children seen in the three locations *with* adults were 28, 12 and 12 and it is possible that a fair proportion of these, too, were truanting or feigning sickness with the condonement or assistance of their parents[1]. The child counts[2] are presented in weekly totals in Table 7:1. Certain corrections which have been made to the figures are explained in the Appendix to this Chapter, which also describes checks on their reliability.

It would appear at first sight from Table 7:1 that the patrolling resulted in sizeable falls in the numbers of children counted. (Percentage falls are presented in Table 7:2.)

---

[1] In the recent Hastings patrols, roughly half the children recorded as truants had their absence judged as 'condoned by parents'.

[2] Unless otherwise stated the counts refer to children observed alone or in groups without adults, for whom there was considered by the researchers to be no doubt as to whether they were of compulsory school age.

Table 7:1
Corrected weekly totals of child counts

Week	Precinct	Store	Estate	Event
2	174	105	110	—
3	144	93	130	estate and precinct patrol
4	128	56	117	—
5				half-term
6	185	73	150	—
7	164	95	296	snow closure
8	124	60	101	estate patrol
9	78	26	91	precinct patrol
10	94	20	69	—

Table 7:2
Percentage falls in child counts between the week preceding and the week(s) after the patrol periods

Series 1		% fall	Series 2		% fall
Precinct	wks 2–4	26	Precinct	wks 8–10	24*
Store	wks 2–4	47†	Store	wks 8–10	67†
Estate	wks 2–4	4	Estate	wks 6–9	39†
			Estate	wks 6–10	54†

* denotes $p < .05$
† $p < .001$ (Chi-squared)
NB: Week 7 is omitted from all comparisons; the child count scores in the precinct were reduced by one-third when calculating Chi-squared values to correct for possible double-counting.

Significant or near-significant drops occurred in the precinct and the store before half-term (series 1) and in all three locations after half-term (series 2). This most favourable interpretation of the results is further enhanced by the apparent lack of displacement of children in week 8 from the estate to the precinct, although outside events reduced the quality of the test. Similarly there is no indication of displacement from the streets of the precinct to stores, either from the store counts or from store detectives' records (whatever their faults), which showed no rise in shoplifting by children during or after patrols.

There are, however, several good reasons for attributing a large proportion of the observed changes to background influences rather than to the patrols[1].

[1] There were no significant differences for any of the observations (patrol figures, child counts, store detectives' records) as a function of day-to-day changes in rainfall. Breakdown of the observations by sex, by age and by children in groups and alone revealed few consistent differences from the overall trends.

i. More children were picked up by the patrols in the estate, yet the falls appeared stronger in the precinct and the store; the falls were greatest in the store, where the patrols rarely went[1].

ii. The falls in the second series - where the pre-patrol measurement period was longer - appeared to begin immediately after half-term, before the patrols operated. It is unfortunate, however, that the numbers in the precinct and the store in week 6 may have been increased to some extent by private school holidays.

iii. In the estate (in series 2) the observed falls were greater in magnitude in the second week after the patrol. Whilst it is reasonable to expect a fall in children on the streets the week after patrolling, any further drop is difficult to put down to police action; moreover, the falls in the previous weeks also become suspect.

iv. Over the whole term, the absence figures for the schools in the estate tended to mirror those for the control schools outside it. This indicates that a fair proportion of the variance in attendance at the former schools was probably due to extraneous factors. In the second series, the child counts in all locations also tended to follow the same pattern as absence figures in the control schools[2], though the correlations were not large enough to suggest that all the changes in the child counts can be explained as background rather than patrol effects. (In the first series, the weekly changes in street counts *opposed* the pattern of control absences.)

v. Much the strongest evidence arguing against attributing the observed falls to the patrols comes from an examination of the *daily* changes in street counts. In the precinct in the first series, and in all locations in the second, much of the drop occurring in each patrol week took place on the Monday, when patrols would be expected to have least effect. This was generally the reverse of the patterns observed in pre-patrol weeks, where Mondays tended to yield the highest counts of children.

All in all, the child counts when taken in context strongly suggest that background factors played a greater part in determining the numbers of children visible than did the patrols - although it is clearly not possible to provide firmer evidence of their relative influences.

Store detectives' records

Over the eight school weeks of the study period, some nine store detectives in five stores saw only ten definite cases of shoplifting by children in school hours, and 60 suspected cases (many of which may have been unsupported by any concrete observations). The corresponding figures taken separately from the store where researchers counted children (whose detectives maintained good records

---

[1] It is unlikely that the falls were the result of the observers' presence since the drop took two weeks from the start of counting in series 1, but four weeks in series 2.

[2] There are positive but not quite significant rank correlations between them, ranging from precinct male × control male tau = + ·7, to estate female × control female tau = + ·3.

throughout the study) are one definite case and 13 suspected. An estimated total of some 2600 children[1] entered this store during school hours over the eight-week period, giving a minimum proportion of 1/186 of these children being probable shoplifters who were sighted by store detectives. The number who were shop-lifting but who were not spotted remains unknown but, as the children them-selves were probably aware, the store detectives paid them special attention if they entered during school hours (cf. May, 1978).

Daily crime reports and juvenile bureau entries
Combining the patrol areas' scores for precinct and estate in the first series resulted in weekly crime totals of 13, 9 (the week when the patrols operated) and 14 - a statistically insignificant fall in the patrol week. The figures from the second series are even less clearcut. There were no significant differences to these patterns when various offences were considered separately - no evidence, that is, that street crimes (e.g. car theft) fell as a result of patrols whilst off-street crimes (e.g. burglary) rose.

As regards the juvenile bureau entries, in neither series and in neither division is there any evidence to suggest that patrols reduced crime - indeed in the precinct the number of entries rose throughout the first series.

CONCLUSIONS

The effectiveness of patrols
It is not easy to draw clearcut conclusions from this research. The results were obscured by an unexpectedly low rate of daytime offending by truants, and by unkind background variations and coincident events. These included the fact that the counts of children in the streets and the store in the week after half-term were probably inflated by children legitimately away from private schools, and - more important - that all the Bristol schools were closed for part of one week due to snow. However, the results make it hard to attribute much of the observed falls in the numbers of children on the streets and in the store to the activity of the Bristol patrols. The most generous assessment possible is that the patrols may have played a small contributory part, lasting up to two weeks after each single week of patrolling.

Clearly, the patrols may have influenced the behaviour of some children, if only those picked up and found to have poor excuses for being absent from school. The present study cannot show whether the attendance of these children subse-quently improved (as was claimed in Glasgow), or indeed whether the patrols caused any *other* children to return to school or perhaps stay inside their homes. The lack of any clear effect of the patrol may be because the patrols posed little threat to truants; this is strongly suggested by the likelihood that only a small proportion of truants at large were stopped.

---

[1] This figure in fact refers to the number of entries made by children. Some children may have entered the store more than once.

93

In terms of the consequences for a child of being picked up, his or her experience at the hands of the patrol is unlikely to be unpleasant in itself (for first-timers, fear of the unknown perhaps being more aversive than the real thing); and further action by the school or by EWOs in follow-up visits may or may not constitute a threat.

The extent to which children in the relevant area became aware of patrolling is unknown; it is of course possible that a patrol run on a routine basis (and accompanied by more publicity, a point returned to later) could deter more children from truancy than the practice adopted for the present study; alternatively, truants could become more familiar with the threat, and more skilled at, or concerned with, escaping apprehension. Issues such as the extent of deterrence achieved or the degree of awareness of patrols might have been clarified by interviewing children in the patrol areas, but this was judged impractical on several grounds, not least of which was resources. It was also felt that interviewing during the study period might have interfered with the effects of patrols, while retrospective interviews (of necessity carried out after the three-week Easter break) would have overtaxed the memory (if not the imagination) of the children concerned.

In relation to the effect of patrols on crime, the child count had been intended to serve as a sensitive but indirect indicator relating to the *opportunity* of children to offend. As the fall in numbers of children observed can at best be attributed only in a small degree to the patrols, it cannot be concluded that these would have been responsible for a reduction in crime as a result of fewer children being at large. In fact, there was no direct evidence from police or store detectives' records that crime went down during or after the patrolling period, though there is a small possibility that some fall in crime *not* reflected in the records examined resulted from the fact that fewer numbers of children were to be seen.

Advice to the police
Advice to the police on the effectiveness of truancy patrols in achieving immediate cuts in crime cannot, however, consist of a categorical rejection generalised from the Bristol experience. Though it is difficult to assess how rigorous the evaluations of patrols conducted by other forces were, it has been claimed that they were more successful. If their evaluations can be relied upon, the relatively strong effects on numbers of children who truanted and committed offences during school hours reported by the Glasgow and the several London patrols may be attributed to a number of factors. Differing circumstances (e.g. higher child density) may have been responsible, together with longer patrol periods and greater publicity for the projects. It may also have been possible that any publicity given, or any involvement of school staff in providing records of truants' attendance (neither of which occurred in the present study), may have led teachers and parents to make greater efforts to keep children in school. This would have given a false picture of the effectiveness of patrolling.

Each police force must of course make its own decision concerning truancy patrols, based on knowledge of local conditions. One important fact that emerged during the study was the apparently diminutive size of the problem posed by truants in Bristol. In the estate area there were, as mentioned before, some 500 absences at each registration in the two comprehensive schools and perhaps 100 truants among them. Yet it emerged during the study that *only half a dozen crimes were reported per week which might, or might not, have been committed by children in school time.* Admittedly, the majority of petty offences are probably not reported to the police but even allowing for this there would appear to be little reason for the police (in Bristol, at least) to devote special attention to truants with a view to achieving immediate and significant cuts in crime. The amount of school-time shoplifting by children in the city centre (a statistic that merits separate scrutiny) would equally seem to constitute no major source of trouble, *with some ten children recorded as offending in five major stores over eight weeks.* All this underlines the general need for the police (and the various bodies which seek to influence their activities) to assess carefully the case for committing special resources to deal with a perceived problem: as Belson (1975) found, truants probably tend to break the law outside school hours, which runs counter to the conventional police wisdom.

If a police force has judged crime committed by truants to be worthy of special action it is important that any trial innovation includes some means of evaluating its effectiveness. (Outside research staff cannot of course be relied on to investigate each diverse case.) For truancy patrols it is still felt that counts of children on the street (conducted by plain clothes officers other than those concerned with the patrols - possibly by cadets) are perhaps the best index of the effect of patrolling, being more sensitive indicators than police crime figures, and enabling the influence of background factors to be taken more easily into account.

On the evidence of this study it seems that for truancy patrols to be effective they may require more resources than many forces are willing or able to provide; certainly a week's patrolling does not seem adequate. In the current situation of financial stringency this further augments the need to see whether action against truants is warranted and whether any truancy patrol that is conducted is effective.

With this caution in mind, the present study can offer some guidance to police forces who consider that their local circumstances merit the operation of truancy patrols. Foot patrols may be more effective in central shopping areas, car patrols in suburbs. The wearing of uniforms on patrol appears to have advantages in all contexts. Although easier for children to spot, they may serve to emphasise the presence of the police and allay fears the public could have on seeing strangers leading off children. (It is fair to note, though, that where plain clothes have been worn on truancy patrols no problems have arisen.) The extent to which truancy work is popular with the police officers taking part remains unclear, but it is probable that officers who have had some experience in juvenile liaison work would be more willing and better able to carry out the duties.

95

Also, truancy patrols almost certainly benefit from the involvement of EWOs. The legal basis for apprehending children and conducting them back home or to school remains somewhat vague, but the position of patrols operating without EWOs seems legally weaker[1]. These are, moreover, less likely to be effective both in assessing the excuses of children encountered, and in keeping the returned children in school on a long-term basis. Whilst the patrols whose activities have been reported seem to have given rise to little in the way of complaints by children, school staff or parents (indeed, most parents seem to have been grateful for the action taken), it is felt that the presence of an EWO in or working closely with[2] the patrol team is useful at least until the police officers involved have gained experience of situations which require considerable tact and skill.

Patrols in a wider context

Relevant to the police decision of whether or not to conduct patrols are a number of issues additional to the central one of achieving an immediate cut in daytime crime by truants. For one thing, it might be argued that the officers engaged on truancy patrol duty are just as effective in deterring adults from crime as they might be when patrolling the streets on normal beat duty. Another advantage that has figured in several of the police reports on patrols is that they pick up absconders from various juvenile institutions. In relation to truants themselves, patrolling may serve to reduce crime in that a child's truancy, offending and associated social problems come earlier to the attention of parents, school and social workers. While some patrols have been established with this longer-term objective in view, the present study can throw little light on it. Additionally, while under some circumstances truancy patrols may be counter-productive (they may dramatise truancy, or if clumsily conducted antagonise truants further), it is equally likely that they can serve to increase general police-pupil-teacher contacts, in line with the aims of the police juvenile liaison bureaux established over the past few years. From a public relations point of view, truancy patrolling on an occasional basis may yet be valuable to the police as an exercise to show the community their involvement in alleviating the problems posed by juveniles.

If suitably lengthy patrols do manage to keep children in school, they may have educational benefits additional to crime preventive ones. Again, it must be noted that the present study has done little to evaluate these. Some patrols (Glasgow and Sussex, for example) have been run, however, at least partly with educational goals in mind.

To conclude, it remains a moot point how much use truancy patrols can be unless

---

[1] The Metropolitan Police when operating truancy patrols relied on Section 28 of the Children and Young Persons Act 1969, which empowers a constable to take to a place of safety a child who appears to be at risk in a number of defined ways. It was subsequently established, it seems, that Section 28 did not cover truanting children and patrols were therefore stopped in 1975. Other forces, however, have not made this interpretation; further, the EWOs with whom they cooperate have the power of *loco parentis* vested in the local education authority.

[2] In some patrols operated by other forces the EWO was based at a local police station and dealt with children as the police brought them in.

accompanied by an increased parental interest in and commitment to their children's attendance at school. Relevant to this was the noticeable presence in Bristol during the study of school age children out shopping with their parents in school hours. The greater effectiveness of truancy patrols may sometimes also require improvements in the security routines in the schools themselves - tighter registration procedures, spot checks, monitoring of exits and so forth (cf. Boyson, 1974). In the current study, for example, two girls were able to play truant again not long after being taken back there by the estate patrol. It should also be borne in mind, however, that although short-term tactical measures (such as truancy patrols) may be of value in some circumstances, many educationalists and others would argue[1] that it is even more important to consider whether the goal of producing educated, relatively law-abiding citizens may ultimately best be served by capturing the interest and motivation of children, rather than simply by capturing their persons.

---

[1] Some useful discussions of the relationship between truancy and educational processes may be found in Tyerman, 1968; Turner, 1974; and Carroll, 1977.

Appendix Corrections to, and reliability checks on the child counts

Some sort of representative figure for the week in which schools were closed down for one day because of snow was obtained by multiplying the sum of the days on which schools were open by 5/4. This still probably gives an inflated figure and as a consequence week 6 was preferred as the comparison pre-patrol week for the estate in series 2.

Figures for the last week (in all three locations) were amended by subtracting the last day's scores (which were high due to the end of term) and multiplying by 5/4. Although this may have removed a Friday peak (which appeared only infrequently in the study), the somewhat swollen figures for the last Thursday suffice to remedy this.

A number of different observers assisted the author for about a week each. As a check on inter-observer reliability, counts in the precinct by the author and the other researchers grouped together were compared for 20 randomly-selected days from both series. The only significant difference was that the author recorded fewer numbers of children under 10.

Eight immediate re-counts were conducted at various random days in the second series (a repeat of the drive round the estate), yielding a significant test-retest correlation of $r = +\cdot73$.

8 Police car security campaigns

John Burrows and Kevin Heal

INTRODUCTION

Many police forces meet their responsibility for crime prevention by mounting publicity campaigns designed to inform people about the risk of crime and the steps that can be taken to prevent it. The study described here examines the effectiveness of a publicity campaign designed to encourage car drivers to lock up their vehicles.

Two basic assumptions underlie car security campaigns: first, that drivers who leave their vehicles unlocked invite theft, and second, that by disseminating information about the risk of theft, drivers can be persuaded to take more care to protect their vehicles. If publicity is to continue to play a central role in a bid to prevent crime it is clearly important to consider the validity of these assumptions.

Car security publicity is disseminated from two sources: from the police, and from the Home Office. Campaigns conducted by the police are typically local events, organised on relatively low budgets, but taking considerable advantage of the willingness of local authorities, firms, and news media to disseminate public service advice at little or no cost. With obvious reason, evaluations of police campaigns - mostly carried out by crime prevention officers themselves - have looked at the effect of publicity on levels of reported crime, though sometimes changes in drivers' car-locking behaviour have been monitored. Home Office campaigns, in contrast, are conducted by professional advertising agents at considerably greater cost; the task of evaluation here generally falls to market research organisations. The evaluation of the 1976 Home Office national campaign, unlike those undertaken by the police, was concerned primarily with the impact of publicity on drivers' attitudes and their knowledge of the risk of vehicles theft.

A considerable number of police campaigns are reported to have been successful in reducing autocrime[1], for example, those in Sunderland (Sunderland Crime Prevention Panel, 1975), Southampton (Home Office, 1974a), Bolton (Home Office 1975a) and the West Midlands (Home Office, 1976a) are said to have reduced vehicle theft by varying degrees. However, in those instances where changes in drivers' locking behaviour have been evaluated as a measure of effectiveness, the evidence is conflicting. A short campaign of intensive publicity in Sheffield failed to raise the number of locked cars (Bright, 1967), whereas campaigns in Nottingham (Home Office, 1974b) and Bath (Home Office, 1975b) are reported to have met some success in achieving this objective.

A central difficulty in attempting to evaluate publicity in terms of its effect on

---

[1] Autocrime is defined in this report as taking and driving away, and theft from and of vehicles.

crime arises from the need to predict normal variations in crime during a campaign, so that changes occurring outside this range can be attributed to the police activity in question. Few evaluations of police campaigns recognise the complexity of this problem: as a result, campaigns are conducted without controlling or taking into account extraneous influences on crime. Moreover, autocrime statistics are analysed without reference either to the changing pattern of another property offences in the vicinity, or to the incidence of car crime in comparable non-campaign areas.

Those studies which have investigated the influence of campaigns on drivers' propensity to lock their vehicles when leaving them unattended have similar drawbacks. From the information available, it appears that most police checks are made without any considered decision about either what sampling techniques are to be employed, or what steps are required to ensure comparability between samples. Nor is there evidence regarding the precautions taken to reduce the visibility of those carrying out checks, and so avoid the likelihood that these measure the public response to the checks themselves in preference to the publicity[1], Bright's Sheffield evaluation, though in other respects a careful study, was based on an uncommonly low level of pre-campaign insecurity (6%)[2], probably arrived at because in place of a single 'snapshot', security was determined by a large series of conspicuous police checks in the same area. Furthermore, few evaluations encompass a series of checks designed to identify how rapidly car drivers respond to police advice and the duration of this effect.

The results of previous evaluative efforts, therefore, offer no clear indication as to the effectiveness of police advertising campaigns. Similarly, the results of the 1976 national campaign have been subject to various interpretations. There is evidence that this campaign, conducted at a cost of some £250,000, led to an improvement in drivers' attitudes to car locking, and to drivers' knowledge of the risk of car theft (Research Bureau Limited, 1977), but, from the relatively small-scale survey of vehicles carried out, it appears that this desired improvement in attitude was not translated into improved locking behaviour. There is, moreover, no clear evidence that car theft was reduced as a result of the campaign: there was a minor fall in the incidence of offences of theft and unauthorised taking during 1976, but there is no strong evidence to support the view that this should be attributed to the campaign. The fact that some comparable property crimes remained stable in 1976, and that vehicle thefts were higher during the campaign quarter than in the preceding quarters, seems rather to contradict this explanation.

The study reported below seeks to explore the same questions as these previous

---

[1] Of course the police may use vehicle checks to publicise the extent of vehicle insecurity; reference here is to checks carried out purely for evaluative purposes.

[2] This was certainly lower than any level recorded by campaign evaluators in similar pre-campaign daylight checks: Research Bureau Limited (1977) found 35% of the vehicles they checked insecure in some way, and the police in the Nottingham area showed "an average as high as 37 to 40% vehicles were left insecure" prior to the campaign in this area (Home Office, 1974b).

evaluative efforts, but under more rigorous research conditions. Its aim was to examine, by means of controlled experiment, the effectiveness of a typical police campaign both in reducing car crime and in improving drivers' locking habits. It was thought necessary to take account of crime statistics as well as levels of security since, even if the latter did not improve, crime levels might have declined as a result of potential offenders being deterred by the attention given to autocrime.

EXPERIMENTAL CAMPAIGNS
The value of the controlled experiment has been widely discussed by both criminological (e.g. Clarke and Cornish, 1972) and advertising research authorities (e.g. Bloom and Twyman, 1978). The experiment described here shares many of the characteristics, and the difficulties, associated with this type of research, above all the need to control for extraneous variables likely to influence the results obtained; in contrast, however, there has been little need to come to terms with many of the critical issues of design and methodology particular to more complex experiments. Thus, to take an example, while penologists have to consider the variety of aims served by penal treatments, the police aim in mounting security publicity is not so diffuse, the behavioural response of the public quite easily monitored, and – in place of the more intractable ethical and practical problems involved in allocating offenders to different treatment – the research has to face the less complicated task of randomly sampling vehicles during checks carried out in the campain area.

The controlled experiment has, of course, been used a great deal to measure the effect of advertising campaigns (see Caffyn, 1977). It has been pointed out, nonetheless, that it is inappropriate to undertake short-term evaluations in certain circumstances, for such studies are not a reliable means of measuring long-term effects (particularly in the case of campaigns dealing with themes of sustained public concern, such as smoking), or of effects apparent only after a lapse of time (the 'sleeper' effect).

For a number of reasons, these arguments were thought to carry less weight with regard to police campaigns designed to promote car security. Although campaigns of this nature may be an enduring aspect of the crime prevention officer's work, in any one area this matter is only publicised occasionally; the issue, therefore, receives only irregular publicity that is unlikely to produce a gradual change in public attitudes. There appears, moreover, to be little reason why any effects of these campaigns should be delayed; whereas the smoker, when short of money or ill, may have cause to reconsider his initial negative reactions to publicity, the car driver is passed only a simple message, and is likely only to reconsider his initial negative reaction after he or an acquaintance become victims of theft themselves.

The most common charge, however, to be made against publicity experiments of any type is that general implications cannot be drawn from the findings of any one study, for the response of the public is largely dictated by the creative content of advertising material and campaign expenditure levels. Although the apparently contradictory results of research on other social persuasion campaigns stand witness to the validity of this assertion, it is held here that in the case of car security campaigns it has less force. Notwithstanding the occasional publicity gimmick produced by the police to highlight the issue, most campaigns conducted by the police vary little either in the media sources used or in the message transmitted, and in the majority of cases forces use the same publicity material provided free by the Home Office. The principal objective of the experiment described here was to evaluate a police campaign conducted along these conventional lines.

CHARACTERISTICS OF THE CAMPAIGN
The campaign was conducted in Plymouth (population 300,000, approximately) over a five week period between mid-November and mid-December 1977). Although not excessive by the standards of some other cities of comparable size, its level of autocrime was seen by the police to be one of its more pressing problems[1]. Several features of the city made it an excellent site for the experiment: it coincides with a single police division with an active crime prevention department, and-possessing an independent radio station together with two daily and two weekly newspapers, each enthusiastic to assist police efforts-it offered a wide range of outlets by which the campaign message could be disseminated.

In order to satisfy the requirements of the sampling design (discussed below), a great deal of the campaign publicity was concentrated within the high-risk areas for autocrime offences. These were identified by an analysis of autocrime in the area carried out before the campaign; the areas selected comprised approximately one third of the city, and included the whole of the city centre; within the selected areas the police distributed posters and handbills. In addition, extensive coverage of the campaign was provided by the press, the local radio station, and television, by which means the campaign message was disseminated well outside the city boundaries. It was assumed that those resident in the central area, subject to the publicity from each of these sources, would be those most aware of the existence of the campaign.

Publicity material from all these sources was devised with a view to gaining maximum impact of the campaign message; it referred to the level of crime in the locality, the high risk points, the types of vehicle at risk, notable instances of car crime recently reported to the police, and to the negligence of many victims. The publicity generated by both the media and the police was considerable: total press coverage for the campaign comprised 109 column inches, much of it headline space, and radio/TV coverage ranged from short mentions in news bulletins to a 'talk-in' programme involving crime preven-

---

[1] In 1977, 1,035 unauthorised takings and thefts of vehicles, and 973 thefts from vehicles, came to the notice of the police in the city division.

tion officers. A total of 5,000 handbills were distributed (outlets ranging from garages and motorists' spare parts shops to clubs and post offices); over 140 posters were placed at strategic points in central car parks (particularly close to payment meters) and garages; and the 'talking car', a vehicle used by the police to publicise crime prevention advice[1], toured central areas on five occasions.

The cost of the campaign is difficult to assess. The local media offered extensive editorial and programme support free of charge[2], on condition that the information was newsworthy. The direct cost of the campaign to the police was therefore nominal, and was restricted primarily to charges made for the printing of posters and handbills. Indirect costs, of police time engaged in making arrangements for publicity, distributing advertising material, or manning the 'talking car', were undoubtedly the principal component of the total cost incurred. Four divisional crime prevention officers were engaged in varying degrees for the duration of the campaign, as was–to a lesser extent–the time of crime prevention officers and press officers at the police headquarters.

METHOD OF EVALUATION
Two measures were used to monitor the impact of the campaign: levels of car security, and autocrime statistics. These are discussed in turn.

Security levels
In order to measure changes in the level of car security, checks were carried out at various stages of the campaign. These were made by four teams comprising one uniformed policeman and one researcher; they were carried out:

i. on the day preceding the start of the campaign[3];

ii. at the close of the second week;

iii. at the close of the fourth week; and

iv. at the end of the campaign.

Each check was conducted along the same route in the high risk central area of

---

[1] The 'talking car' is fitted with most available security devices, and a public address system. Manned by a police officer, it is generally employed in busy shopping or office areas to provide the public with security advice.

[2] This is not always the case in the metropolitan areas primarily because of the increased cost of news space and the fact that other local news is likely to be more sensational. The 1977/78 Metropolitan Police security campaign, for example, incurred a bill of £96,000 (direct cost alone).

[3] Despite careful briefing of the police, two newspapers and the local radio station gave premature notice that the police intended to conduct a campaign. The police were able to prevent further publication, and the amount published amounted to little more than a routine reminder to the public of the dangers of leaving their cars unlocked.

the city and covered 1,000 cars or non-commercial light vans parked there, an estimated 5% of those in the area[4].

For a number of reasons - not least that the majority of autocrime offences are carried out under cover of darkness - these checks were conducted in the evening between the hours of 6 and 10 p.m. This reduced the visibility of the police officers carrying out the checks and the impact their activity might have had on drivers' behaviour. Each police/researcher team was allocated a fixed route measuring approximately four miles, along which they checked the doors, windows and boots of 250 vehicles. In the absence of detailed local authority plans showing the distribution of vehicles in the evening period, each pair was directed to make a random selection of the vehicles checked. There were two constraints on this selection: a predetermined number of vehicles were to be selected from designated car parks along the route (the capacity of the park dictating the numbers chosen), and each route was divided into five equal sections, from each of which 50 vehicles were to be checked. Teams finding vehicles insecure were directed to record the make, model and registration details of that vehicle, the source of insecurity, and its parking location.

On the third check the teams recorded these details for all the vehicles checked (whether insecure or not). The information gathered enabled the researchers to distinguish the respects in which vehicles left insecure differed from those locked. In addition, by this means it was possible to confirm that the vehicle sample covered a representative cross section of cars in the area.

Autocrime statistics
The crime statistics analysed were principally drawn from the records of offences known to the police. The incidence of autocrime committed in the city division during the time of the campaign was compared with that in the preceding year. The incidence of burglary was then examined as a suitable indicator of the general pattern of crime in the area, and, as a further control, the pattern of autocrime in the campaign division was compared with that in two otherwise similar towns completely removed from the influence of the campaign.

In order to examine the possibility that there was either physical or temporal displacement of autocrime during the campaign period, a detailed analysis of crime complaint forms was necessary. To this end, information was extracted about the physical and temporal distribution of autocrime between September 1976 and February 1977, and compared with similar data extracted for offences committed during the campaign.

---

[4] There are an estimated 60,000 vehicles registered in the city (Department of Environment statistics); the checks were carried out on weekday evenings in the high risk central area where publicity disseminated by police effort (as distinct from that of the media) was focussed, which comprised approximately one third of the city area. Given the relatively low vehicle ownership in this area, the number of cars owned by residents was probably well below a third of the city total (20,000), but the presence of additional cars whose owners were enjoying central entertainment facilities probably brought the estimated area total close to this figure.

RESULTS

Security levels

There was no statistically significant change in the level of vehicle security recorded during the campaign. The security check made prior to the start of the campaign shows 19·0% of vehicles to be insecure - a proportion close to that revealed in previous security checks under similar conditions[1] - and checks during and after the campaign revealed levels of insecurity of 20·9%, 21·7% and 19·2%. In 51% of the cases of insecurity discovered, this was caused by an unlocked door, in 10% by an open window, and in 39% by an unlocked boot, or - in the case of estate cars - the tailgate to the vehicle; 17% of the insecure vehicles had more than one source of insecurity. The four checks were carried out under similar cold but dry conditions and the weather is unlikely to have prejudiced the results obtained.

These results suggest that the campaign had no measurable impact on the level of car security, and other data seem to support this inference. No relationship was found between insecurity levels and the parking location of vehicles, though the proximity of police posters in the central car parks would suggest that those parking there would be more likely to be aware of the campaign than other motorists. Furthermore, an analysis (carried out by using records held at Swansea to trace owners) of where the owners of the vehicles lived showed that those living within the campaign area were no more likely to have secured their vehicles than those from outside the city boundaries.

Autocrime statistics

No significant change in the level of autocrime was recorded either during or after the campaign. The total number of offences committed (195) during the campaign weeks represented a 38% increase on that recorded (141) for the corresponding weeks in the previous year; this pattern was also found in the control areas where autocrime increased 32% on the previous year's total. The difference between the campaign area and the two control towns in this respect was not statistically significant. Although the level of autocrime fell during the opening weeks of advertising, this downturn was in progress before the start of the exercise, and was not dissimilar from the pattern of burglary offences recorded at this time.

A substantial part of the general rise in autocrime during the campaign was the result of high level of 'taking' offences[2], these reached a peak during the final

---

[1] In 1971, six urban forces carried out security checks in co-operation with 'Drive' magazine. The checks were carried out on Friday evenings in April and - across the forces - revealed a 22% level of insecurity (Automobile Association, 1971). It should be noted that the daytime level of insecurity is - for a variety of reasons - likely to be higher (Research Bureau Limited, 1977).

[2] Police records maintain the distinction between the unauthorised taking and theft of vehicles, all offences being recorded in the latter category until such time as the vehicle is recovered. Because other forces make this distinction upon different criteria, and in many cases there is no doubt a failure to amend records to the effect that the vehicle in question has been recovered, these offences were treated as one.

week of the campaign higher than any other weekly figure recorded during 1977. None of the weekly totals recorded, however, fell outside the range of normal fluctuations that would be expected for this crime.

There is evidence that during the campaign autocrime offences were more likely to be committed under cover of darkness than in daylight. Despite the difficulties of estimating when many offences occur[1], it is clear that - by comparison with the same weeks in the previous year - there was a statistically significant shift in the temporal distribution of these crimes during the campaign weeks ($p < 001$), to the effect that more offences were committed in the early hours of the morning (see Table 8.1).

Table 8:1
Autocrime: time of day at which offences occurred during the 5 campaign weeks and during the same 5 weeks in the previous year

Time period	Preceding year*	Campaign†
0600–1200	22·1%	7·3%
1200–1800	17·9%	11·2%
1800–2400	35·0%	32·0%
2400–0600	25·0%	49·5%

* 15 November to 20 December 1976
† 15 November to 20 December 1977

This change in the temporal distribution of crime may be attributed to the effect of the campaign itself, which could have persuaded offenders to act with more caution (cf. the response of car radio thieves to increased police activity reported in Parker, 1974) perhaps by fostering the expectation that the police were directing more attention to this form of criminality.

Alternatively, victims of autocrime aware of the publicity may have preferred to report that their vehicle had been stolen in the early hours of the morning, even if this was not so, rather than suffer the embarrassment of admitting that they had left their cars insecure or with expensive objects on display during the daytime. On the other hand, it is of course possible that the increase in offending during the campaign year led, at least in part, to the observed change in the temporal distribution of autocrime. It is conceivable that the higher proportion of crime committed between the hours of 2400 and 0600 was accounted for, say, by the activities of a gang of youths (possibly from an outlying suburb) who might have begun to frequent the city in the evenings during the year of the campaign.

Other features of car crime seemed unaffected by the campaign. There was no

[1] For the purpose of this comparison if the police or victim could not identify the exact time of the offence, this was treated as the mid-point between when the victim left the vehicle parked, and returned to discover that an offence had been committed.

evidence of the geographical displacement of offences outside the campaign area, nor did cars parked in different parking locations (such as streets, car parks, waste land etc.) become more or less vulnerable.

INTERPRETATION OF THE RESULTS

The findings of the present study are largely negative: first, during the campaign studied, police publicity proved to have no effect on drivers' locking behaviour; and second, its effect on autocrime was not to reduce it, but possibly to modify its form[1].

It would be simplistic to attribute evidence of the ineffectiveness of the campaign solely to the standard of its publicity. Set against the expenditure levels of larger commercial concerns, the direct costs incurred by the police in the conduct of these campaigns are low; but in this instance there is no reason to believe that by spending more on publicity the police could have achieved better results (though this possibility cannot be entirely ruled out). Small interview surveys[2] were carried out on two occasions during the campaign; both these surveys recorded encouraging levels of public awareness, established at 67% and 71% of all local drivers. This compares extremely favourably with the levels of awareness achieved in the 1976 national campaign (Research Bureau Limited, 1977). Clearly a substantial number of car drivers do not comply with the advice given them by the police. This is generally construed by the police to be a sign of public complacency, but the explanation is probably more complex. This study, with others, provides evidence that not all insecurity arises from driver negligence; indeed, it suggests that drivers take into account a number of considerations when leaving their vehicles unlocked. It seems, for example, that the value of the vehicle driven may affect this judgement: evidence accrued in the experimental campaign shows that older vehicles are more likely to be left open. The perceived risk of theft over different lengths of time is doubtless another influence: several researchers (Bright, 1967; Research Bureau Limited, 1977) have noted that drivers intending to leave their vehicles for long periods are more careful to secure them. Similarly, the increased probability of car windows being left open during hot weather (Research Bureau Limited, 1977) is probably the result of drivers preferring to face the risk of theft rather than the discomfort of entering a hot vehicle.

Underlying these considerations is possibly the driver's judgement of whether locking will reduce the risk of car theft. Attitude research has borne out the view that many drivers, expecially the young, are sceptical of the protection afforded

---

[1] Though it was noted on page 103 that the principal cost of the campaign was that of police manpower, the question of cost-effectiveness has not been closely examined. Nevertheless, the results of this research clearly suggest that little is to be gained from crime prevention officers conducting campaigns of this sort.

[2] These were carried out at random locations in the central shopping area. Having established that the respondent was a driver, the interviewer asked respondents whether they were aware the police were conducting a campaign, to describe the publicity material they had seen or heard (in order to distinguish the current impact from that of previous campaigns) and to state whether or not they lived in the city. Each survey covered 200 drivers, equally grouped by age and sex characteristics.

by locking up their cars (Research Bureau Limited, 1977). To some extent these drivers are correct in recognising that car locking does not totally remove the risk of theft. Parker's (1974) account of the activities of car radio thieves in Liverpool, for example, suggests that many offenders do not regard conventional locks as any impediment. Several police reports have illustrated this point more forcefully by examining the ways in which those apprehended for theft and unauthorised taking offences gained access to vehicles: for example, Hampshire Constabulary (1977) and Sunderland (Sunderland Crime Prevention Panel, 1975) have demonstrated the widespread use of duplicate keys as a means of gaining access to vehicles.

A more likely explanation for drivers' failure to lock their cars may be that they probably do not share the authorities' view of the seriousness of autocrime. It is likely that most drivers are aware that the risk of having their car stolen is low; even the owners of older vehicles probably appreciate this fact[1]. Many drivers may also believe that the loss of their car will generally constitute only a temporary inconvenience (72% of vehicles stolen during 1977 in the Metropolitan Police District, for example, were retrieved within 30 days), and that if this is not the case the loss will be borne by insurance. To the extent that car - owners view autocrime from this perspective - and fail to consider the costs borne by the wider community in tracing and retrieving lost vehicles, or in paying increased insurance premiums - police appeals are unlikely to succeed.

IMPLICATIONS FOR CRIME PREVENTION

One important point to emerge from the various studies of autocrime is that it is not simply the 'professional' who will take a secure vehicle. Though it is conventional to distinguish the opportunist, or casual, thief from his professional counterpart, it is questionable whether there are many opportunists who will take a car simply because they notice one unlocked. It is probably more useful to distinguish three types of offender: those who will take a particular vehicle whether it is insecure or not (the professional falls in this category), those who will look for insecure vehicles, but break into a car if an unlocked vehicle is not found, and those who steal only unlocked vehicles. Various police reports show that the size of this latter group is often exaggerated; arguably, most autocrime offences are committed by fairly determined individuals who will not be deterred if they fail to find an unlocked vehicle. The fact that most thieves steal a car with a particular aim in mind (most frequently, as a means of transport, cf. McCaghy et al., 1977) would seem to support this view. So also does the fact that some makes of vehicle face an exaggerated risk of theft regardless of whether or not they are

---

[1] In the area of the experimental campaign, 85% of the theft and unauthorised taking offences recorded between September 1977 and February 1978 were directed at vehicles produced before 1971. If the life expectancy of these vehicles is set aside, and it is assumed that older vehicles throughout the country are equally as vulnerable, then the owners of such vehicles can expect to have their cars stolen once every 18 years (i.e. it can be calculated that during 1977 5·4% of the pre-1971 vehicles registered were subject to theft or unauthorised taking).

locked by their owners. Evidence from this study shows that although vehicles manufactured by Ford are less likely (given the numbers at risk) to be left insecure[1] than those of a number of other manufacturers, they are more likely to be subject to theft than others (see Table 8:2).

Table 8:2
Proportion of vehicles subject to autocrime and proportion of vehicles found insecure, by make

Manufacturer	Autocrime	Insecurity
Ford	42·0%	20·9%
British Leyland	39·0%	47·0%
Chrysler	6·2%	9·4%
Vauxhall (GM)	5·9%	8·4%
Other British	4·1%	2·4%
Foreign	2·8%	11·9%
	100%	100%

NB: For various reasons, the figures in the columns of Table 8:2 are not directly comparable. The figures in the first column refer to all autocrime offences committed in the campaign division (between September 1977 and February 1978). In contrast the insecurity figures, which represent the cumulative total of all vehicles found insecure in the four campaign checks, refer to insecurity in a particular area and at a particular time. While these points cannot be ignored, it is unlikely that they can account for the differences observed in the levels of insecurity from one make of vehicle to the next, particularly since the sample of cars on which the insecurity figures were based was representative of vehicles in the campaign division.

Common models of car appear generally to face exaggerated risks; it may be that these are attractive to thieves (particularly if fitted with comparatively unsophisticated door locks), but also these cars are less likely to attract police attention if stolen. Between September 1977 and February 1978, for example, the Ford Cortina accounted for 19·7% of all thefts in the study area.

If most autocrime offences are committed by fairly determined individuals, there is little prospect that the police can reduce autocrime simply by persuading drivers to lock their vehicles. Those who do comply with police advice are likely to reduce their chances of having their car broken into or stolen[2]. But, given that a comparatively large pool of unprotected vehicles will remain even after the most forceful police campaign, it is likely that offenders will instead turn to these

---

[1] One explanation for this is that recent models of Ford have been fitted with 'automatic' boot locks (i.e. the catch can only be operated by key).

[2] Baldwin (1974) has shown, from an examination of police crime records in Sheffield, that victims of autocrime offences were more likely to be careless in protecting their property than car drivers in general. Baldwin is, however, likely to have exaggerated the risk taken by those who fail to lock their vehicles. On the one hand his calculations were based on Bright's (1967) finding that 'typical' insecurity in Sheffield was of the order of 6% of vehicles, an improbably low estimate (see Introduction). On the other, his finding that about 34% of autocrime victims had left their vehicles insecure is much higher than the 16% found in similar exercise in Plymouth prior to the campaign. Nonetheless, because many may be unwilling to admit leaving their vehicles insecure, both these figures probably constitute minimum estimates of victim liability.

more vulnerable targets, and that overall levels of autocrime will probably remain unchanged. The probability that autocrime offences would be displaced in this manner has been argued by Riccio (1974) in the United States, and strong supportive evidence supplied by Mayhew et al. (see Chapter 2) who demonstrated that the effect of fitting steering column locks in this country has simply been to displace crime from protected vehicles (now an estimated 71% of the private cars and vans in Great Britain) to those unprotected.

Another drawback is that even in the unlikely event that the police achieved total compliance from the public (thus removing any risk of displacement) car thieves would probably respond by adopting more forceful means of entering vehicles and, again, any significant reduction in autocrime would be unlikely. Given the high proportion of offenders presently using duplicate keys as a means of entry to vehicles, the probability that others would operate in this way seems high. This itself is a problem amenable to technical solution, for more sophisticated door locks, which are not so simple to break, are available at relatively low cost (Birmingham Crime Prevention Panel, 1977). But, without legislative requirement, it would be necessary to gain manufacturers' approval, and whatever the means used, the police would continue to be faced with the task of persuading motorists to use the locking devices fitted to their cars.

One solution to the problem of displacement and the need to ensure public compliance has been the development of 'automatic' locking devices such as the steering column lock. Although not able to prevent offenders breaking into cars, devices of this type have proved an effective means of preventing the unauthorised theft of vehicles fitted with them, and - when all vehicles have been equipped as in West Germany in 1963 (Bundeskriminalamt, 1973)- this benefit has extended to reducing overall levels of unauthorised taking. In addition more sophisticated locking devices such as these do not appear to be so susceptible to changes in offenders' methods of operation, though there have been some claims (e.g. Birmingham Crime Prevention Panel, 1977), as yet unsupported by firm evidence, that the initial impact of the steering column lock has diminished as ways of overcoming them become known[1]. There appear, therefore, to be some grounds for the optimism expressed in official circles that - though to date the level of unauthorised taking offences has not declined, and has instead been sustained by a dwindling pool of older, unprotected vehicles - as these vehicles are scrapped and replaced by vehicles fitted with steering locks so these offences will occur less frequently (cf. Chapter 2).

SUMMARY
The study reported above examines the efficacy of police crime prevention

---

[1] If this proves correct, it may become necessary to rely on some of the increasingly sophisticated devices available (like microprocessors) to protect new cars (see Ekblom, 1979) for a discussion of such devices). For the present generation of vehicles, the solution may lie – insofar as 'breaking' is facilitated by lock wear – in including a check of the steering column lock among the requirements of the annual MOT check.

publicity as a means of reducing autocrime. The campaign evaluated did not succeed in persuading a greater proportion of drivers to lock their cars, nor did the campaign effect a reduction in autocrime. It was argued that part of the reason for this public intransigence may be that many drivers do not perceive the risk and the consequences of having a car stolen as that serious.

While the individual driver who locks his car when leaving it unattended may reduce the risk of it being stolen, the conclusion is reached that publicity campaigns in any circumstances are unlikely to result in a noticeable reduction in the level of autocrime. Most autocrime offences are committed, not merely in response to the opportunity offered by an unlocked vehicle, but by more determined offenders. Thus even in the event of a campaign reducing the number of unlocked cars, offenders are likely to counteract this either by directing their attention to those vehicles left unlocked, or by changing their modes of operation.

9 An evaluation of a campaign to reduce car thefts

D. Riley

Reference was made in Riley and Mayhew (1980, Chapter 1) to a number of car theft advertising campaigns run in the United Kingdom over the past few years, the most important of which was the 1976 national press and poster campaign sponsored by the Home Office and organised by the Central Office of Information (C.O.I.). There is little reason to think that this campaign produced savings in the number of offences the police had to deal with, despite the fact that autocrime (the term used throughout this chapter to refer to thefts of and from motor vehicles) increased to a smaller extent in 1976 than in previous years. The limited impact of the 1976 campaign is matched by the results of the study conducted by the Home Office Research Unit (see Chapter 8), which assessed the effect on car-locking behaviour of a specially-mounted police autocrime campaign run in Plymouth at the end of 1977. Other local and generally smaller-scale initiatives also fail to provide any sound evidence of positive campaign effects on car-locking or vehicle thefts, though a number of claims have been made to the contrary on the basis of apparently inadequate analyses of variations in the level of autocrime offences known to the police.

Despite this somewhat negative picture, growing concern over the amount of police resources taken up with dealing with thefts of and from vehicles (together accounting for 25% of all the indictable offences known to the police in 1978)[1] provided the grounds for a fresh Home Office initiative in the early part of 1979, again organised by C.O.I. This campaign has been the subject of two evaluations. One of which - dealt with in this chapter - was conducted within the Home Office Research Unit and assessed the impact of the campaign on police autocrime statistics, as well as on the extent to which parked vehicles were left secure by their owners. In a separate study, conducted by N.O.P. Market Research Limited for C.O.I., the effectiveness of the campaign was further evaluated in terms of changes in motorists' attitudes to car theft, their beliefs about the risks involved and their reported car-locking behaviour. The results of this survey are discussed briefly later.

THE CAMPAIGN
The campaign took the form of two separate advertising projects. Both were

---

[1] The average amount of police time spent in dealing with a reported theft of a motor vehicle including the prosecution of offenders has been estimated to be approximately six man-hours. Costing this conservatively, and taking into account the number of reported incidents of vehicle theft in England and Wales in 1978, the 'cost' to the police of thefts of motor vehicles alone is in excess of £8 million a year. The cost of dealing with incidents of theft of property from cars may be less than this, but still substantial.

directed mainly at the owners of older cars without steering column locks, although the main recommendation never to leave one's car unlocked was relevant to all motorists. The first used television advertisements on Tyne-Tees Television in north-east England; the second used the more usual form of autocrime publicity - press and poster advertisements - in north-west England. It was anticipated that differing degrees of effectiveness might be apparent from the two media, which would provide some useful pointers for future campaigns. Both campaigns ran for eight weeks starting on 28 February 1979 and together cost in the region of £100,000, equivalent to a national campaign costing £2 million at 1980 prices. The main aim of the campaign was to reduce the number of stolen vehicles (a rather optimistic reduction of 10% in the number of stolen vehicles in the campaign areas during 1979 was hoped for, calculated to provide a saving of some £200,000). Although more secure vehicles might also be expected to reduce the incidence of thefts of property from cars (virtually the same in number as thefts of cars), this was not a factor which featured in the advertising content.

Television campaign
The television publicity took the form of two different advertisments both on a humorous theme in which a motorist, apparently unconcerned about locking his car, leaves it with a 'Please steal me' sign on the roof. The commentary ran as follows:

"If you don't lock your car you might as well put a big sign on top of it. Especially if you've got an older model. Of the hundreds of cars stolen each day, 80% are 'J' registration or earlier. Remember, an unlocked car is an open invitation. LOCK IT."

The television advertisements also showed a simple anti-theft device being used to secure the steering wheel of a car with the clear implication that this was a further way in which motorists without steering column locks on their cars could protect their vehicles.

The press and poster campaign
A number of national newspapers print different regional editions and these were used to restrict the display of the campaign press material to the target area in north-west England. The newspaper advertising took the form of rather more detailed advice to motorists than was given in the television commercials. A typical press advertisement read as follows:

"It only takes two seconds to lock a car, and not much longer to steal an unlocked one. Every day a thousand cars are stolen. So if you're not locking your car you might as well place a sign on the roof. Many cars are stolen from car parks, or when the owner was 'only gone a minute'. 80% of stolen cars are over 7 years old, and cars of that age don't usually have steering locks. If your car doesn't have a steering lock, you can buy a simple but effective anti-theft

114

device for a few pounds. It won't cost as much as your no-claims bonus. But the most basic form of security still consists of remembering to wind up all your windows and lock all your doors when you leave your car. Then when you get back there'll be more than just an empty parking space. AN UN-LOCKED CAR IS AN OPEN INVITATION. LOCK IT."

The newspaper publicity was additionally supported by displays on poster sites and buses.

THE STUDY

It was considered that the most direct way of measuring the success of the 1979 campaign - given the emphasis of the advertising on vehicle security - was to examine directly whether drivers were more careful after the campaign than before it about locking their cars. This involved physical checks on a total of over 25,000 vehicles. In addition, account was taken of the number of thefts of[1] and from vehicles recorded by the police[2], as the campaign also had the objective of reducing police workload, and as potential offenders might be deterred by the attention given to autocrime even if drivers' security behaviour was not improved.

In order to take account of the fact that any observed changes in the campaign areas may have been due to factors operating independently of the publicity, police statistics and vehicle security were also examined in a 'control' area not exposed to any publicity.

For the two types of police records examined (see below), a comparison was made between February and March 1979 when the advertising was shown and the following month of April - together referred to as the *campaign period* - and the same period of 1978 - referred to as the *pre-campaign period*. For the physical checks on cars, observations were made immediately before and at the end of the campaign.

In detail, the three measures of campaign effectiveness which were used in the present evaluation were as follows:

i. Criminal statistics

Firstly, the number of recorded offences of thefts of and from motor vehicles were obtained for police forces within the campaign and control areas, for the campaign and pre-campaign periods. Also, since changes in the overall tendency to crime in a given area might be expected to influence the number of autocrime

---

[1] The term 'thefts of', which is used throughout, includes the police categories of vehicles 'stolen' (which are not recovered within a set period of time) and those 'taken without authority' (which are).

[2] While statistics may have some limitations in measuring changes in the level of autocrime, figures of thefts of cars in particular are much more reliable than some other police data as far as the reporting of offences is concerned because of the requirement that the police are notified when an insurance claim for theft is made and because of the owner's dependence on the police to help recover the vehicle.

offences independently of any publicity, the total numbers of indictable offences other than autocrime were analysed. In the press and poster campaign area these data were obtained for the police forces of Greater Manchester, Lancashire and Merseyside; in the T.V. campaign area for the Durham, Cleveland and Northumbria forces; and in the control area for the Nottinghamshire, South Yorkshire, West Midlands and West Yorkshire forces.

ii. Police crime reports

A second measure was derived from detailed information on police crime reports recording the theft of a motor vehicle[1] (thefts from vehicles were not considered). Since the campaign was directed specifically at the owners of older vehicles not fitted with integral steering column locks, it might have been expected to influence these owners more than those with newer vehicles. To take this into account, the vehicle registration suffix letter appearing on each police crime report was used to obtain the year of registration of stolen vehicles[2]. For the press and poster campaign area, details of crime reports relating to stolen vehicles were obtained for the Greater Manchester and Merseyside forces, and for the T.V. area for the Durham and Northumbria forces. The control area was the same as that used in the analysis of criminal statistics.

iii. Police checks on parked cars

Vehicle security checks were carried out by police officers on parked cars in January 1979 before the campaign began and in March 1979 at the end of the campaign. The cars checked were those parked in suburban streets where there was little or no garaging of cars. Checks were carried out in suburban areas since it was felt that this would maximise the proportion of vehicles included in both stages of the exercise. The streets in which cars were checked were selected by the co-operating police forces. The checks were made after midnight in order to reduce the chance of motorists locking cars because they had observed the police checking vehicles. The registration number of each vehicle checked was recorded in addition to the number of doors (including the boot) or windows left insecure;

---

[1] Crime reports relating to thefts of motor cycles, mopeds and heavy goods vehicles were excluded from the analysis.

[2] The registration suffix letter indicates the 12-month period (1 August–31 July of the following year) in which the vehicle was first registered for use. Older vehicles were taken to be those with a registration suffix letter of 'H' or earlier, indicating that the vehicle was registered prior to 1 August 1970. Newer vehicles were taken as those with a suffix letter of 'J' to 'R' indicating that the vehicles were registered between 1 August 1970 and 31 July 1977. As steering column locks were made compulsory on all cars manufactured in and imported to this country from January 1971, it is possible that some 'J' registered vehicles were without steering column locks. The numbers of these, however, may not be very great as manufacturers were fitting improved locks on cars for some time before the 1971 measure, in anticipation of it. Since for the period February–April 1978, 'S' registrations were still continuing and, of course, there were no 'T' vehicles, comparisons of the vehicle 'populations' in 1978 and 1979 omit consideration of 'S' and 'T' registered vehicles. In addition, there are a number of instances when the registration suffix will not correspond with the age of the vehicle - for instance, in the case of second-hand imported vehicles and 'personalised' registrations. There is no reason, however, to suppose that these (infrequent) exceptions would have differed between the test and control areas, or over time.

it was also noted whether the vehicle was fitted with an anti-theft device other than an integral steering column lock. On the basis of the car registration suffix, separate quotas were established for the checks on older (pre-'J' registration) and newer vehicles, permitting an assessment of the effect of the campaign on each group of vehicles. In the press and poster campaign area, the police checks on vehicles were carried out by the Greater Manchester force, in the T.V. campaign area by the Northumbria force, and in a control area by the West Midlands and West Yorkshire forces. In all, over 25,000 vehicles were checked by the four forces involved which each carried out approximately 3,000 checks both before the campaign and at the end of it.

RESULTS

i. Autocrime offences recorded by the police

Table 9:1 shows, for each of the campaign areas and the control area, the number of recorded offences during February–April 1978 and in the same period in 1979, relating to (i) theft of a motor vehicle, (ii) theft from a motor vehicle, and (iii) the total number of other indictable offences.

In relation to both thefts of motor vehicles and thefts from motor vehicles, the number of recorded offences showed the largest decrease in the *control* area rather than in either of the test areas. Taking the two test areas together, thefts of vehicles fell by less than 1% and thefts from vehicles by less than 2%, compared with decreases in the control area of over 13% and 10% respectively.

However, since the recorded number of autocrime offences may be expected to be related to overall changes in the level of crime independently of any advertising campaign, account must also be taken in each of the three areas of changes in the level of other indictable crime. The changes in the number of autocrime offences in each test area expressed as a percentage of the total number of other, non-autocrime offences were compared with those in the control area. This indicated that in the press and poster campaign area, changes in both thefts of and thefts from motor vehicles were not statistically significantly different from the corresponding changes in the control area. In the T.V. campaign area, while the change in thefts from motor vehicles was not significantly different from that in the control area, recorded thefts of vehicles relative to the control area constituted a significantly higher proportion of all indictable offences during the campaign period than during the same period in 1978. Thus, it would not seem that publicity directed at autocrime served to produce any gains for the police.

ii. Police crime reports relating to thefts of 'old' and 'new' motor vehicles

The number of police crime reports recording the theft of a motor vehicle assumed to be with ('new') and without ('old') steering column locks are presented in Table 9:2 for the test and control areas, in each of the campaign and pre-campaign periods. In this table the number of vehicles 'on the road' in the old

Table 9:1
The effect of the campaign on the number of autocrime offences recorded by the police*

	Theft of a motor vehicle			Theft from a motor vehicle			Total of other indictable offences		
	February–April 1978	February–April 1979	Change	February–April 1978	February–April 1979	Change	February–April 1978	February–April 1979	Change
Press and poster campaign area	14173	13321	−6·0%	9273	9039	−2·5%	60863	63570	+4·4%
T.V. campaign area	4697	5439	+15·8%	4476	4487	0·2%	32506	32761	+0·8%
Control area	15324	13306	−13·2%	11353	10193	−10·2%	82596	79331	−4·0%

* Recorded offences also include those relating to motor cycles, mopeds and heavy goods vehicles.

118

Table 9:2
The effect of the campaign on the theft of 'old' and 'new' vehicles

	'Old' vehicles*			'New' vehicles		
	February–April 1978	February–April 1979	Change	February–April 1978	February–April 1979	Change
Press and poster campaign area	7075	5965	$-15.7\%^a$	3444	4064	$+18.0\%^b$
T.V. campaign area	1561	1572	$+0.7\%^c$	790	1185	$+50.0\%^d$
Control area	6822	6073	$-11.0\%^{a,c}$	2585	2785	$+7.7\%^{b,d}$

* Note: The classification of 'old' and 'new' vehicles is explained in footnote 2, page 116.
a. $\chi^2 = 4.71$, 1 d.f., $p < .05$; b. $\chi^2 = 6.37$, 1 d.f., $p < .025$; c. $\chi^2 = 9.46$, 1 d.f., $p < .005$; d. $\chi^2 = 38.18$, 1 d.f., $p < .001$.

and new age-groups has been taken into consideration by adjusting theft figures in each area by the percentage change in the number of registered older and newer vehicles between the pre-campaign and the campaign period.[1]

Table 9:2 shows that, in the press and poster campaign area relative to the control area, there was a statistically significant decrease (-15.7%) in thefts of older vehicles but a significant increase ($+18\%$) in thefts of newer vehicles.

In the T.V. area, relative to the control area, there were significant increases in thefts of both newer and older vehicles and, thus, apparently no evidence that the campaign was successful. As may be seen in Table 9:1, there was an increase in overall crime levels relative to the control area. Whilst this may go some way toward accounting for the increase in thefts of older vehicles in the T.V. campaign area relative to the control area, it is clearly insufficient to account for the much larger percentage increase in the number of thefts of newer vehicles.

Analysis of police crime reports suggests at first sight, then, that in the press and poster campaign area the autocrime advertising may have had some success in reducing the number of thefts of older vehicles. This finding can be contrasted with statistically significant increases in thefts of newer vehicles in that area and with significant increases in thefts of both older and newer vehicles in the T.V. area. However, just as attributing the observed *increases* in motor vehicle thefts to the campaign would seem to be counter-intuitive and unlikely to be justified, it may be similarly unwise, in view of the overall evidence here, to attribute the reduction in thefts of older vehicles in the press and poster campaign area to the effects of the advertising. In addition, such selectivity in the effects of the

---

[1] This information was obtained from the Department of the Environment motor vehicle census in June 1978 and in December 1978. The changes over this six-month period were doubled to provide an estimate of the annual changes between June 1978 and June 1979, an interval approximating to that between the campaign period in 1979 and the corresponding period in 1978. Decreases in registrations over this interval were taken into account by increasing the actual number of recorded offences by the annual percentage change, and vice-versa.

advertising is arguably improbable. Rather, the decrease in thefts of older vehicles in the press and poster area may simply represent an unsystematic seasonal variation in the thefts of older cars in that region, although in the absence of relevant data this remains untested. The suggestion derives some support, however, from the results of vehicle security checks reported in the following section which, to anticipate their presentation, fail to show any consistent evidence of a change in motorists' actual car-locking behaviour.

iii. Police checks on parked vehicles

The results of the vehicle checks were analysed in a number of different ways, for older and newer vehicles separately[1]. The analyses were based on:

a. the numbers of completely secure vehicles;
b. the total number of points of insecurity;
c. the number of vehicles with secure driver's doors;
d. the number of vehicles fitted with an additional anti-theft device (that is, a device other than an integral steering column lock).

In addition, since two vehicle security surveys were conducted, both in the same general area, there were a number of vehicles which were examined by the police twice. Analysis of the checks on this subset of vehicles, presented later, provides an opportunity to assess the effects of the advertising campaigns minimising the problems of sampling variations.

a. The numbers of completely secure vehicles

Table 9:3 presents the proportions of both older and newer vehicles found to be *completely* secure (i.e. with no doors or windows insecure) in the two surveys in the two campaign areas and in the control area.

Table 9:3
The percentage of vehicles found to be completely secure

	'Old' vehicles		'New' vehicles	
	Before campaign	End of campaign	Before campaign	End of campaign
Press and poster campaign area	84·7% (1487)	81·1% (1525)	88·4% (1752)	87·0% (1789)
T.V. campaign area	81·3% (1777)	80·7% (1555)	86·2% (1990)	88·1% (1863)
Control area	78·0% (2350)	77·3% (2283)	86·2% (3882)	86·4% (2956)

NB: The number of vehicles involved in each check is given in parentheses.

---

[1] Older vehicles are taken to be those with a registration suffix of 'H' or earlier. Newer vehicles are those with a suffix of 'H' or earlier. Newer vehicles are those with a suffix letter from 'J' to 'T'.

It can be seen that in neither the press and poster campaign area nor in the T.V. area was there any statistically significant increase in the proportion of vehicles found completely secure in the second check[1]. The proportions of vehicles which were secure, incidentally, compares well with the security levels observed in the Plymouth study (see Chapter 8); older vehicles were less secure and the slightly higher overall number of secure vehicles in the present exercise (83·9%) than in Plymouth (79·8%) can probably be explained by the fact that owners leaving their cars parked overnight are more likely to secure them than owners parking in the late evening.[2]

b. *Number of points of insecurity*
An analysis of changes in the numbers of points of insecurity found in the vehicle surveys was included to allow for the possibility that, while the proportions of secure and insecure vehicles might remain unaltered by the advertising, the total number of points of insecurity might decrease[3].

In the press and poster campaign area, there were statistically significant reductions at the end of the campaign period in the number of points of insecurity for both older vehicles (falling from 386 to 285 compared with a decrease from 826 to 790 in the control area) and newer vehicles (falling from 419 to 311 compared to a decrease from 681 to 677 in the control area). In the T.V. area, there was also a significant decrease in the case of newer vehicles (falling from 356 to 286 compared to the decrease from 681 to 677 in the control area), but not for older ones. These apparently positive effects of the advertising are not, however, consistent with the result of an additional analysis, discussed below, on the subset of vehicles which were checked by the police in both surveys.

c. *Number of vehicles with an insecure driver's door*
As the advertising may have been expected to have had maximum impact on the number of vehicle owners locking the driver's door - the most likely point of unauthorised entry - a check was made on the proportions of vehicles with a secure driver's door in the two surveys. There were, however, no statistically significant changes in either test area, the proportion of cars with secure driver's doors remaining fairly high at around 93%.

---

[1] Vehicle security may be expected to be affected to some extent by weather extremes in that cars may be unused for longer intervals during periods of adverse road conditions. The change, however, in the weather in the test and control areas was roughly comparable between the two stages of the vehicle survey and is unlikely to have exerted a significant bias on the extent to which owners locked their cars.

[2] A few other surveys involving checks on cars parked during the *daytime* (e.g. R.B.L., 1977) have shown security levels to be between 60% and 65%.

[3] Account was taken, of course, of differences in the number of vehicles checked by the police in each survey; and a check was also made that the proportion of two- and four-door vehicles checked did not differ significantly in the two surveys.

d. *Additional anti-theft devices*

Although the advertising was designed to encourage motorists owning vehicles without an integral steering column lock to fit extra security devices, the proportion of older vehicles found to be protected by such a device varied remarkably little between the two surveys in both the campaign areas and in the control area. In the press and poster area, about 8% of older vehicles had security devices in the two surveys; in the T.V. and control areas the figure was about 11%. For newer vehicles in the T.V. and control area, about 6% had extra devices in the two surveys. In the press and poster areas, 5·3% of newer cars were found to have additional protection at the end of the campaign compared to 11·5% at the beginning. This is more likely to represent a sampling difference in the vehicles checked in the two surveys rather than an actual decrease in the use of security devices.

CARS CHECKED TWICE

The analysis of checks on vehicles involved in both security surveys[1] provided an additional measure of the effects of the publicity in which sampling variations between the two groups of vehicles were completely controlled.

Vehicles checked twice can be placed in one of four categories:

a. Completely secure on both checks.

b. Insecure on both checks.

c. Insecure on first check but secure on the second.

d. Secure on the first check but insecure on the second.

If the campaign had been successful, there would have been a significantly greater number of vehicles falling into the third category than into the fourth. Table 9:4 below, indicates that this was not the case for either older or newer vehicles in either the press and poster campaign area or the T.V. area. (The result for older

Table 9:4
The security of vehicles checked twice

	Number of 'old' vehicles				Number of 'new' vehicles			
	Secure both checks	Insecure both checks	Insecure first check, secure second	Secure first check, insecure second	Secure both checks	Insecure both checks	Insecure first check, secure second	Secure first check, insecure second
Press and poster campaign area	318	25	45	61	399	18	47	60
T.V. campaign area	308	25	64	58	284	9	23	29

[1] For the four forces carrying out the surveys the average number of vehicles which were checked twice was 445.

vehicles in the T.V. area is not statistically significant.) These findings confirm the conclusion, based on the results of the complete set of vehicle checks, that the advertising was not successful in increasing the number of vehicles which were found by the police to have all doors and windows secure.

The apparent decrease in the number of points of insecurity for both vehicle groups in the press and poster campaign area and for newer vehicles in the T.V. campaign area is not supported by the corresponding analysis on vehicles checked twice. The numbers of vehicles with fewer points of insecurity on the second check than on the first were compared with the numbers of vehicles with a greater number of points of insecurity on the second check than on the first. Clearly, if the publicity has been successful in reducing the number of points of insecurity, the number of vehicles in the first category would have been *greater than* the number of the second. In the press and poster campaign area, the corresponding figures were 49 vs. 72 for older vehicles and 55 vs. 65 for newer ones. Similarly, in the T.V. area the numbers were 70 vs. 65 for older vehicles and 25 vs. 31 for newer ones. None of these four differences indicates a statistically significant *decrease* in vehicle insecurity. A similar analysis for vehicles checked twice of the use of additional anti-theft devices indicated no increase in the use of such devices for older cars in either of the campaign areas. This again reinforces the earlier result based on the complete sets of vehicle checks.

CONCLUSION

In summary, none of the three measures used to evaluate the 1979 autocrime campaign showed that there were any benefits which could be unequivocally attributed to the advertising. In the first place, while the number of recorded autocrime offences fell somewhat in the press and poster campaign area, this was less than in the control area and has to be set against an increase in offences in the T.V. area.

Secondly, the analysis of crime reports relating to stolen vehicles, which examined the effects of the advertising on older and newer vehicles separately indicated that, in the press and poster campaign area relative to the control area, there was a significant decrease in thefts of older vehicles but a significant increase in thefts of newer vehicles. This latter finding may be partly attributable perhaps to the greater increase in the rate of other indictable offences in the test area. The reduction in thefts of older vehicles, which may have reflected an unsystematic seasonal variation in the number of offences relating to such vehicles, was contrasted with the negative results of the police security checks on parked cars. In the T.V. campaign area, relative to the control area, there was no apparent reduction in thefts of either older or newer cars.

The security checks on parked cars, thirdly, produced no consistent evidence that the autocrime advertising encouraged car owners in either of the campaign areas to be more conscientious about locking their vehicles. In the press and poster area, certainly, there was a decrease for both older and newer vehicles in the number of points of insecurity at the end of the campaign period. Set against this, however, is the apparent failure of the press and poster advertising to effect any improvement in vehicle security as measured by the percentage of completely secure vehicles, the percentage of vehicles with secure driver's doors, or the percentage of vehicles fitted with an additional security device. Further, the results of checks on vehicles which came to be included in both the police surveys in the press and poster area do not provide any indication of an increase in security. The results of the checks in the T.V. area indicated that only for newer vehicles was there a decrease in the number of points of insecurity at the end of the campaign period. Again, however, the security checks in the T.V. area showed that the advertising had no measurable effect on the percentage of completely secure vehicles, the percentage with a secure driver's door, or the percentage of vehicles fitted with an extra anti-theft device. Nor was there any indication from newer (or older) vehicles checked twice by the police in the TV area of an increase in vehicle security.

N.O.P. Survey

Fieldwork by N.O.P. Market Research Limited was carried out on behalf of C.O.I. before and after the campaign was run in both the press and poster and the T.V. areas (see N.O.P., 1979). Different samples of respondents at the two stages were asked about how they behaved with respect to securing their vehicle. In addition, a series of attitude statements (for example, 'A car is reasonably safe unlocked if it's only left for a minute') were read to respondents who were asked how far they agreed or disagreed with each statement. Those interviewed also indicated how likely they thought it was that their car would be stolen.

In brief, the N.O.P. surveys found no statistically significant improvements in claimed car security behaviour, perceived risk of car theft, or in any of the attitude measures taken singly. However, N.O.P. were prepared to conclude on the basis of the data for the complete set of attitude statements that, in both campaign regions, attitudes registered a 'very slight but fairly consistent shift' in a positive direction.

In conclusion, then, the findings of the evaluation reported in this chapter suggest that the 1979 autocrime campaign met with little success either in achieving improvements in car-locking behaviour or in reducing the number of recorded car thefts. This finding is in close agreement with the results of other victim-oriented campaigns on residential burglary and autocrime discussed by Riley and Mayhew (1980, Chapter 1) insofar as these have measured direct changes in behaviour on the part of victims. Following the arguments laid out there, it is suggested that the present campaign failed to produce discernible improvements in vehicle security for two main reasons. Firstly, security habits appear to reflect subjective perceptions of the overall risk of car theft and the risk faced in particular situations (for example, when a car is parked for a short time or in a seemingly 'secure' condition - cf. R.B.L. 1977). In this respect, the present campaign may not have improved security behaviour because it failed to produce large enough changes in perceptions of risk either generally or in relation to specific parking situations, a point confirmed by the results of the N.O.P. survey. While the campaign pointed out that secure locking (particularly for 'older' cars without steering column locks) reduces the chance of having one's car stolen, the advertising was not designed to promote the idea that an individual motorist stood a greater chance of having his vehicle stolen after the campaign than before it if he left his security habits unchanged. Secondly, the advertising may have done little to overcome other beliefs supporting non-compliance with the campaign recommendations. Personal views about the ineffectiveness of car-locking may not be much altered simply by the expression of a contrary position: many motorists, for instance, feel that thieves will resort to duplicate keys even if a car is locked (cf. Chapter 8). Moreover, the advertising in this case may not have upset the feeling that the consequences of theft are often minimised by insurance protection, or more important perhaps, that the risk of autocrime is remote in any case - a view no doubt well-based on personal experience in most cases.

10 An evaluation of a campaign to reduce vandalism

D. Riley

This chapter describes an evaluation of an anti-vandalism television campaign conducted in north-west England early in 1978 as a preliminary to a possible national campaign. The campaign was funded by the Home Office at a cost in excess of £200,000, equivalent to a national campaign costing £1·3 million at 1980 prices. As a topic for crime prevention publicity, vandalism is somewhat unusual, the only previous initiatives being locally-based ones involving press and poster coverage. The present campaign was also notable in being double-edged, aimed at both deterring youngsters from vandalism through emphasising the risk of being caught, and at instilling in parents the need for closer supervision of their children. For these reasons, it was of particular interest to see whether the 1978 television vandalism campaign appeared any more effective in changing behaviour than other publicity initiatives (see Riley and Mayhew, 1980, Chapter 1) aimed at reducing crime either through encouraging potential victims (of car theft, for instance) to be more security conscious, or through deterring people from breaking the law.

The campaign, transmitted by Granada Television, took the form of two television 'advertisements' each lasting approximately 45 seconds. The first of these was known as *Police Visit* and was aimed at boys aged between 9 and 13 years. The film was intended to highlight the serious consequences of being 'found out' for damaging property and featured the nervous reaction of a young boy to an unexpected visit by the police to his home. The 'voice over' on the film ran as follows:

> "If you are a young lad and you spent the afternoon with your mates breaking windows and smashing telephone boxes . . . then you will know what it's like to dread every knock on the door . . . but one of these nights it really is going to be the police . . . so if you've been out damaging property today, remember, it could be your turn tonight."

The second film, known as *Front Room*, was aimed at the parents of young boys and attempted to increase the extent to which parents controlled what their children did outside the home. The advertisement featured a group of young boys vandalising the interior of one of their homes. The 'voice over' ran as follows:

> "Most of us think that vandalism in the streets has nothing to do with us. But just for a minute imagine if it happened in our own home. Spraying our walls, ripping our phones out . . . and generally smashing up our things. Well, this is exactly what our children are doing out in the streets. And it's up to us to make them understand, and to stop them. They're our children."

Although the campaign was originally scheduled to run for a continuous period of eight weeks, there was a three-week break in the broadcasts due to an industrial dispute at Granada. The advertising was in fact transmitted in two 'bursts': one of three weeks from 1 February to 20 February and one of five weeks from 27 March to 30 April. In total, *Police Visit* was transmitted on 69 occasions and *Front Room* on 57 occasions making the campaign a comparatively heavy one. This is borne out by the findings of a survey for the Central Office of Information (C.O.I.) by Research Bureau Limited (R.B.L., 1978) in which 96% of parents interviewed claimed to have seen one or the other advertisement at least once.

The effectiveness of the Granada campaign was assessed in three studies. The Home Office Research Unit evaluation reported here examined a number of measures to see whether the publicity had any effect on the level of vandalism in the campaign area. The other two studies, which were conducted for C.O.I. at the request of the Home Office by outside research organisations, are discussed briefly later. The more extensive of the two examined whether the publicity changed parents' attitudes to vandalism and their claimed control over their children's leisure activities.

THE STUDY

The basic design of the study was a comparison between the levels of four measures of vandalism during the campaign period (1 February 1978–30 April 1978) and those during the equivalent period in 1977, attention also being paid to the monthly levels of vandalism in the interval between these two periods. This comparison was made for selected places in north-west England where the publicity was transmitted ('test area') as well as for a 'control' area in north-east England (where Granada television is not transmitted) to take account of factors (such as the weather) which might have influenced the level of vandalism in the north of England independently of the publicity in the north-west. It was assumed that if the campaign was effective, there would be a proportionately smaller increase (or greater decrease) in vandalism in the test area compared to the control area.

Four measures of damage were taken to examine the effect of the publicity. The two principal ones were based on local authority repairs of damage, recorded as vandalism[1], to (i) schools and (ii) council housing. These covered the number of

---

[1] The issue of the reliability of vandalism records kept by public bodies has been taken up by Clarke (1978). There is no doubt that there are a number of difficulties in distinguishing between vandalism (as wilful acts of damage) and damage due to wear and tear or boisterous play. However, whilst there is no way of knowing for certain the extent to which the local authority and Post Office records examined in this study accurately portrayed the level of deliberate damage, there is no reason to think that inaccuracy or mis-recording would vary substantially over time, or that significant reductions in vandalism would not be reflected in such records.

repair visits made and the costs of repair carried out[1]. Together council housing and school vandalism repairs probably account for over 90% of local authority spending on vandalism[2]. Post Office data on repairs for vandalism to telephone kiosks were examined as a third measure[3]. Both campaign films mentioned damage to telephones (*Front Room* highlighting damage to telephones in the home, and *Police Visit* featuring damage to telephone kiosks) and, as it has been suggested (e.g. Home Office, 1975c) that publicity aimed at youngsters might encourage imitative behaviour, it was felt that Post Office records might be particularly useful in assessing whether the 1978 campaign had any such counter-productive effect. Finally, an examination was made of police statistics for the number of offences of criminal damage recorded by the police[4,5]. Although Sturman's (1978) study revealed that less than 7% of incidents of vandalism committed in a local area found their way into police records, they were nevertheless included for completeness.

In the case of local authority data, the test and control areas were Manchester and Bradford respectively. The selection of these areas was dictated largely by the fact that the vandalism records kept by these local authorities were more suitable than those kept elsewhere in the north-west region or in the Yorkshire region where the controls for the R.B.L. evaluation referred to later were chosen. Also, there was some anticipated advantage in paralleling the Marplan study, also referred to later, which had been commissioned in Manchester and Bradford. On the incidence of damage to telephone kiosks, figures were readily available from the Post Office for the whole of the north-west region (the campaign area) and for the north-east region (taken here as the control). For the number of offences of criminal damage recorded by the police, data were obtained for the forces of Greater Manchester and Merseyside within the campaign area and for the South Yorkshire and West Yorkshire forces which were taken as controls.

---

[1] In both Manchester and Bradford local authorities (the test and control areas respectively), it is the policy of the council to repair vandalism damage as quickly as possible on the grounds that such damage often invites further attack and causes considerable inconvenience to users of the property concerned. Accordingly, since each incident is dealt with as it arises, it was felt reasonable to assume that local authority repair documents would tend to relate to separate incidents of vandalism.

[2] It was recognised that there would inevitably be a small number of repairs carried out in the three-month period from February to April which related to vandalism incidents committed before the beginning of the period. However, it was clear from an early examination of the repairing systems in Manchester and Bradford that at least 90% of repairs related to vandalism committed in the 'target' period.

[3] Again, there is reason to think that most of the repairs for vandalism carried out by the Post Office in the 'target' periods relate to vandalism incidents committed in these periods.

[4] There is no statutory offece of 'vandalism', but most of the deliberate or malicious damage to property commonly referred to as vandalism could be prosecuted under Section 1 of the Criminal Damage Act, 1971 and would appear in the *Criminal Statistics* under 'criminal damage'.

[5] The figures examined in plice records exclude the very small proportion of criminal damage offences involving arson, criminal damage endangering life, or threat to commit criminal damage.

RESULTS

i. School vandalism

The data concerning school vandalism repairs do not provide any indication that the number of vandalism incidents was influenced by the publicity campaign. Although the number of repairs fell by $7 \cdot 1\%$ in the test area, a similar reduction ($8 \cdot 5\%$) took place in the control area (see Table 10:1). That this result is not 'masking' a difference in the actual amount of damage repaired is indicated by a broadly similar change in the total expenditure on school vandalism in Manchester and Bradford. In addition, analysis of the vandalism data relating to the months between January 1977 and January 1978 indicated that the changing patterns of vandalism in Manchester and Bradford were similar.

Table 10:1

The effect of the campaign on vandalism to schools

	Test area (Manchester)			Control area (Bradford)		
	February–April 1977	February–April 1978	Change	February–April 1977	February–April 1978	Change
Number of repair documents issued	1133	1052	$-7 \cdot 1\%^{a}$	667	610	$-8 \cdot 5\%^{a}$
Total expenditure on school vandalism	£49020	£58777	$+19 \cdot 9\%$	£29967	£36086	$+20 \cdot 4\%$
Average expenditure per repair	£43·27	£55·87	$+21 \cdot 9\%$	£44·93	£59·16	$+31 \cdot 7\%$

a. $\chi^2 = \cdot 03$; 1 df; ns.

ii. Housing vandalism

The interpretation of the housing data is rather more complex, as can be seen from Table 10:2.

The number of vandalism repairs to local authority dwellings and surrounding property decreased in the test area during the campaign period by 29%, whereas in the control area it increased by 30%. Whilst this is consistent with a campaign effect, analysis of the vandalism repairs over the period February 1977 to January 1978 reveals that there was a tendency ($p < 0 \cdot 02$) for the number of repairs in Manchester to decrease over the period, the level of repairs in the campaign period continuing the overall trend (see Figure 10:1). In Bradford over the same period, there was no consistent trend in the level of repairs: monthly figures over the year preceding the campaign suggest that the apparently large percentage increase in vandalism during the campaign is a reflection of the unusually low level of damage during the control period in 1977 rather than an exceptionally high level during the campaign period in 1978. Taking both these factors into account, there is no reliable evidence that the advertising campaign influenced the level of housing vandalism repairs in Manchester.

130

Table 10:2
The effect of the campaign on vandalism to council housing

	Test area (Manchester)			Control area (Bradford)		
	February–April 1977	February–April 1978	Change	February–April 1977	February–April 1978	Change
Number of repair documents issued	2787	1968	−29·4%[a]	358	466	+30·2%[a]
Total expenditure on housing vandalism	£86715	£94243	+8·7%	£5689	£6648	+16·9%
Average expenditure per repair	£31.11	£47.89	+53·9%	£15.89	£14.27	−10·2%

a. $\chi^2 = 65·06$; 1 df; $p < ·001$.

In addition, there were rather different changes in the average expenditure per repair in Bradford and Manchester. In Bradford, an analysis of the distribution of actual repair costs (which was not practicable in the case of the Manchester data) indicated that the unexpected decrease in the average repair cost resulted from a considerable reduction in the proportion of very expensive repairs. The 54% increase in the average repair cost to Manchester may have been due in part to the effects of inflation on maintenance costs (estimated from the schools data to be about 30%). In additon, however, the decrease in repair documents issued in Manchester may indicate some 'bunching' of the amount of work appearing on a single repair document, which would also have increased the average amount spent per repair. Unfortunately, the nature of the repair data kept in the local authority records did not allow this possibility to be checked directly.

iii. Telephone kiosk vandalism
In the case of acts of 'wilful damage' (the Post Office classification of vandalism), the change in kiosk damage (shown in Table 10:3) can be seen to be comparable

Table 10:3
The effect of the campaign on telephone kiosk vandalism

	Total number of incidents of 'wilful damage'		
	February–April 1977	February–April 1978	Change
Test area (North-west)	8683	7552	−13·0%
Control area (North-east)	7480	6537	−12·6%

$\chi^2 = ·04$; 1 df; ns.

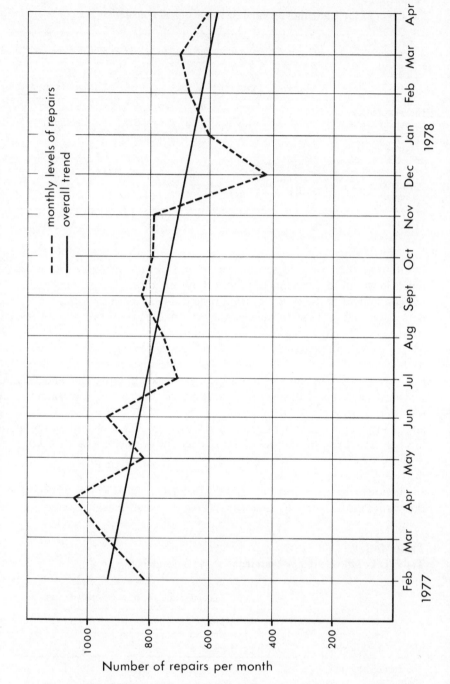

Figure 10:1 Manchester housing vandalism: number of repairs per month

for the test and control areas; this provides no evidence that the campaign had any impact on telephone kiosk damage.

iv. Recorded offences of criminal damage

Police data on the number of recorded offences of criminal damage are shown in Table 10:4[1].

Comparing the campaign period with the equivalent period a year earlier, it can be seen that in the test area recorded offences fell by 5·7%, whereas in the control area offences rose by 4·7%. Although at first sight this suggests a campaign effect, the general trends in the data in the year preceding the campaign cast some doubt on this. Analysing the number of recorded offences of criminal damage on a monthly basis from January 1977 to January 1978 reveals that, in addition to a marked seasonal pattern in both the test and control areas, there was a significant tendency ($p < 0.005$) for the difference in the monthly figures between the test area and the control to decrease (see Figure 10:2). While it is not clear whether such variations reflect changes in the reporting of such incidents, the implication here is that the number of recorded offences in the two areas during the campaign period compared with the same period a year earlier reflect this statistically significant trend rather than any effect of the campaign.

In retrospect, the different underlying trends in the test and control areas in the data relating to housing vandalism and offences of criminal damage may have important implications for the interpretation of changes in vandalism rates during the campaign. Against a background of apparently falling levels in the test area relative to the control area, the effect of a campaign, if any, would not readily be discriminated from such a general trend and would, in consequence, probably fail to be detected using analyses limited in scope by the data available. Nevertheless, given the lack of a campaign effect apparent in the school vandalism and Post Office data, there is little reason to think that there would have been a discernible campaign effect even if the general trends in the test and control areas had been comparable.

Table 10:4
The effect of the campaign on the number of offences of criminal damage recorded by the police

	February–April 1977	*February–April 1978*	*Change*
Test area (Greater Manchester + Merseyside)	7002	6603	−5·7%
Control area (South Yorkshire + West Yorkshire)	5694	5961	+4·7%

$\chi^2 = 17.02$; 1 df; $p < .001$.

[1] See footnote 5 on page 129

Figure 10:2 Recorded offences of criminal damage in the test and control areas

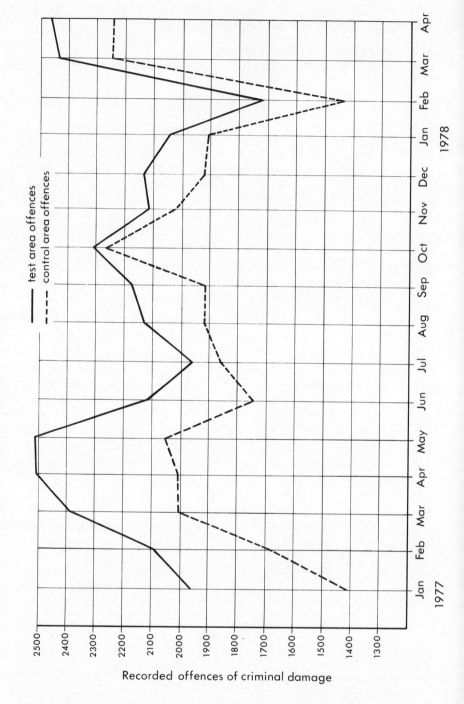

— test area offences
--- control area offences

Recorded offences of criminal damage

134

EVALUATIONS BY MARPLAN AND RESEARCH BUREAU LIMITED

In addition to the present evaluation, two other campaign assessments were carried out for the Home Office, co-ordinated by C.O.I. The first of these, by Marplan, was an observational exercise using householders to record the number of new items of vandalism that were observed in their local area over the campaign period (see Marplan, 1978).

In the Marplan study, one area (Manchester) from the test region was matched with a control area (Bradford). Two wards were selected from within each of these cities and 38 observers were recruited from within each ward. These observers covered individual groupings of 3–4 streets and were instructed to note such incidents of vandalism as broken milk bottles and graffiti in their assigned areas on a regular weekly basis. The focus of the Marplan evaluation was a comparison of the rate of new incidents of vandalism in the nine weeks following the commencement of the campaign[1]. This comparison showed that in both Manchester and Bradford the incident levels remained fairly constant throughout the campaign period, although no statistical analysis was carried out on this data by Marplan who were of the opinion that their survey data were insufficiently reliable. Subsequent analysis of the Marplan data (such as it was) by the present author showed that there was not a statistically significant difference between vandalism levels in Manchester and Bradford.

The second study, by Research Bureau Limited, focussed mainly on claimed supervision of, and expressed interest in, children's leisure activities by parents in social classes C1, C2, D and E (R.B.L., 1978). The pre- and post-campaign surveys closely bracketed the actual campaign, being conducted in January and May 1978 respectively. The surveys in the test area were conducted in Greater Manchester and Merseyside and those in control areas in South and West Yorkshire; there were approximately 300 interviews in each of these four Metropolitan counties at each stage of the two-part survey. In interpreting their results, R.B.L. considered the difference, before and after the publicity campaign, between the test and control areas in terms of the percentage of parents who, for example, claimed to be aware of their sons' activities outside the home or to have discussed vandalism with their sons.

Parents were asked, amongst other things, how often there was an adult at home when their son returned from school and how often the son was left alone without an adult. In response to both questions, parents in the test area showed a significantly greater tendency after the campaign to leave children on their own. This, on the face of it, is a particularly unexpected finding in view of the fact that the *Front Room* commercial was typically interpreted by parents as showing the consequences of leaving children alone. In addition, the campaign did not appear to influence the extent to which boys were allowed to go out alone after getting

---

[1] Although the Marplan study was initially scheduled to cover the whole of campaign period, because of certain operational difficulties, the evaluation was not extended to allow for the three-week break in transmission. The Marplan observations, therefore, terminated about three weeks before the campaign ended.

home from school, though it seems to have increased the extent to which parents claimed to know where their son was going. In terms of what parents in the test area claimed to have discussed with their sons, there was also a significant increase in discussions of damage to bus and train seats, hanging around with gangs and breaking into empty houses. The apparent increase in vandalism-related discussions is somewhat unexpected in view of the finding that 94% of parents interviewed at the pre-campaign stage agreed with the statement 'I'm sure my son behaves himself when he's out of the house'. In addition, there were increases in discussions of truancy and ringing 999 as a joke, which were unrelated to the advertising.

The interpretation of this rather inconsistent set of findings is not immediately obvious. The significant *net* shifts detected by R.B.L. typically rested on minimal changes between the pre-and post-campaign surveys in the test area being compared with much larger changes, frequently in contrary directions, in the control area. This suggests that many of the positive effects attributed to the campaign by R.B.L. may simply reflect variations between the parents sampled in the pre- and post-campaign surveys in the control area. There is the additional possibility that, since the R.B.L. questionnaire involved a relatively large number of items on which conclusions about the campaign might be based, it could be expected that, on average, about five of the questions would show a campaign effect purely by chance alone (assuming a significance level of 0.05 and a one-tailed test). Thus, neither at the levels of attitudes nor claimed behaviours was there any unequivocal evidence of a campaign effect.

CONCLUSION

None of the three publicity campaign evaluations discussed above provides any reliable evidence that the advertising in the Granada Television area had a significant effect on parents' attitudes to vandalism or on the amount of vandalism committed. In the present evaluation, the data relating to schools and telephone kiosks showed clearly that there were comparable decreases in the level of vandalism in both the test and control regions. In the case of the housing data, the large variation in the average cost per repair between Manchester and Bradford meant that the changes in the number of repairs could not be directly compared. However, on the basis of an analysis of the trends in the data, it was concluded that the evidence did not support the idea that housing vandalism in Manchester had been influenced by the campaign. Similarly, although the level of criminal damage recorded by the police appeared to be lower where the publicity was televised than where it was not, this was interpreted in terms of the trend, pre-dating the campaign, towards decreasing numbers of recorded offences in the test area relative to the control.

The present campaign is the first one on vandalism conducted by the Home Office. Its largely negative results in changing behaviour are consistent with the findings of other offender-oriented advertising campaigns, discussed by Riley and

Mayhew (1980, Chapter 1) which have relied on persuasion to deter potential wrongdoers, unaccompanied by changes in legislation or law enforcement. Two reasons were suggested to account for the failure of purely persuasive offender-oriented campaigns: firstly, that potential offenders are unlikely to be moved by exhortation or generalised threats unless they have reason to believe that the actual risks and consequences of detection are worsened; and, secondly, that remote advertising messages may stand little chance of competing with the immediate pressures operating at the time an offence is being considered.

In relation to the present campaign, it may have been that the risks and undefined consequences of contact with the police over an act of vandalism emphasised in *Police Visit* did little to convince young boys that their vandalism days were numbered. In contrast, the claimed success of a series of vandalism campaigns mounted by the Devon and Cornwall Constabulary in 1975 (Home Office, 1976b), which urged parents and teachers to warn children of the installation of intruder alarms in a number of schools, is consistent with children believing that the odds involved in damaging schools property had changed against them. In relation to competing influences on behaviour, the fact that the present campaign failed to influence children's behaviour may be understandable to the extent that vandalism amongst young boys arises out of easy opportunities for damage (see Clarke, 1978) and takes place in a group situation where there are strong pressures to demonstrate toughness and masculinity in destructive behaviour (Opie and Opie, 1969; Gladstone, 1978). The ease and rewards of vandalism, in other words, win the day.

11 Co-ordinating crime prevention efforts

F. J. Gladstone

Editors' Note:
In this printing, part of the introductory discussion in Co-ordinating Crime Prevention Efforts *(HORS No. 62) has been omitted because of overlap with the ideas presented in the early part of Chapter 1 of this book. In brief, the part which has been omitted describes the increasing awareness on the part of criminologists and policy-makers of the limited potential for controlling crime through criminal justice strategies focussing on 'treatment' and deterrence, though some discussion of the role of the police in crime prevention highlights the work of crime prevention officers and the increasing emphasis on 'community policing'. Mr Gladstone draws attention next to the way in which government departments outside the Home Office, and other agencies, are coming to appreciate the crime prevention implications of their policies, though he concludes that there is still considerable scope for more to be done, as well as a need for more systematic evaluation of the effectiveness of various current activities. At this point, reference is made to the setting up within the Home Office of the Working Group on Crime Prevention (with representation from the Crime Policy Planning Unit, the former Economic Planning Unit, the Research Unit, Her Majesty's Inspectorate of Constabulary, the Probation and After-Care Inspectorate, the former Urban Deprivation Unit and Community Programmes Department), the brief of which was to examine '. . . the scope for progress in influencing social policy for crime prevention purposes and for articulating the crime prevention dimension to other departments'. Attention is drawn to the available evidence, considered by the Working Group, on three approaches to crime prevention:* opportunity reduction *which attempts to reduce opportunities for offending;* social prevention *which tries to counteract criminal motivation; and* legislative prevention *which aims to reduce crime by reinforcing legal prohibitions. It is at this point that the text of the report is taken up.*

The need for a co-ordinated approach

Clearly none of these three approaches to crime prevention offers a panacea yet each has something to offer. Which is most relevant would depend on the specific crime under consideration as well as on the circumstances peculiar to the various localities in which it occurs. All three need to be considered and the Working Group's report concluded that rather than starting from targets in general, or criminals in general, as is generally the case at present, it would be more helpful to begin at the nexus of the criminal act itself, that is the circumstances surrounding the commission of a particular offence. This implies a need for increased liaison and co-ordination of effort because knowledge, skills and responsibility for decision making with respect to each approach are frequently divided between several agencies.

The need for systematic decision-making

The Working Group's report argued that a more systematic approach to decision-making is also needed:

> 'A considerable amount of information is available about the social conditions in which offenders have been brought up and now live and about the physical targets of crime. But in the development of broader crime prevention measures what has tended to be lacking has been the coherent and systematic marshalling of that information in respect of the circumstances surrounding particular types of offence. An examination of the situation in which a particular type of offence takes place can reveal the conditions necessary for or conducive to its commission and can suggest preventive measures which relate directly to these conditions.'

To meet this lack the Working Group devised a simple decision-making procedure which could be applied to any offence, noting that in practice it might often be best applied to a fairly narrowly-defined offence such as theft from supermarkets rather than theft or shoplifting in general. (Measures which are effective in preventing theft from supermarkets are unlikely to be effective against thefts from a small corner shop.)

The procedure involves

 i. a thorough analysis of the situation in which the offence occurs in order to establish the conditions (opportunities, motivation and legislation) that need to be met for the offence to be committed;

 ii. the identification of measures which would make it more difficult or impossible to fulfil each of these conditions;

iii. an assessment of the practicability, likely effectiveness and costs of each of these measures; and

iv. selection of the most promising measures.

The procedure is not in itself a method of preventing crime, but rather a decision-making tool to facilitate a more co-ordinated and systematic approach to the organisation of crime prevention activity; as the Working Group's report pointed out, it:

> 'should not be seen as providing new and certain answers on how to prevent crime or necessarily as supplying any fresh individual techniques. Rather it is intended to make up for the limited ability of the traditional approaches to meet the need for a broader-based crime prevention initiative. It would facilitate the more systematic and coherent application of existing techniques, and would provide the framework in which present knowledge could be exploited and empirically tested, and the foundation on which new knowledge may be built up'.

THE FEASIBILITY STUDY

The report of the Working Party provided a theoretical basis for a new approach to the organisation and co-ordination of crime prevention activity. In order to ascertain how well the approach worked in practice it was decided to mount a feasibility study in which the recommended approach would be applied to a concrete problem and carried through, if possible, to the implementation and evaluation of suitable preventive measures.

In choosing a specific crime problem for the study, various possibilities were considered (including cheque frauds, violence on buses and drunken driving), but in the event school vandalism was chosen. This was partly because a considerable amount of information on the subject was readily available, including a recently completed programme of research by the Home Office Research Unit (see Clarke, 1978). Equally important, however, was the desirability of selecting an offence which was the subject of public concern and which would use to the full police expertise and involvement in crime prevention but also be suitable for involving bodies from outside the criminal justice system in the preventive effort.

Aims and objectives

A project group was established to co-ordinate work on the feasibility study which included, under the aegis of the Crime Policy Planning Unit, police officers, social scientists from the Home Office Research Unit and an operational researcher. The group started by setting out the aims of the project. These were:

'i. to assist the Home Office in broadening the focus of its work on crime prevention, so that it can develop the means for providing wider assistance to other departments and agencies, both nationally and locally, on the crime prevention aspects of their policies;

ii. to test the recommended new approach to crime prevention, in relation to the practicability of applying it to a specific crime and to its effectiveness in identifying viable crime prevention measures;

iii. to evaluate specific measures for reducing the incidence of vandalism of schools; and

iv. to facilitate improved co-operation on crime prevention between local authorities, the police and other local agencies; and, in particular, to involve school authorities in tackling the problem of vandalism'.

Preliminary analysis

Before involving local authorities, however, it was thought advisable to collate the many strands of information available about school vandalism and analyse this material along the lines proposed by the Working Group on Crime Prevention. It was recognised that this would be a somewhat theoretical exercise, which could need considerable modification in the light of local circumstances, but it seemed important, in approaching localised problems, to take advantage of the

141

full range of research and practical experience on the subject. Several months were devoted to this task and a systematic review was prepared in the Home Office Research Unit summarising what was then known about the circumstances conducive to school vandalism and the many remedies which might be applied to the problem.

In broad outline the conclusions reached were that a wide variety of conditions affected whether or not a school was vandalised and that the possible remedies were correspondingly diverse, including both social prevention and opportunity reduction measures, though probably not legislative prevention. It was also apparent that, although some of the measures proposed could be rejected more or less out of hand, there was little hard evidence of the efficacy of virtually any of them, although optimistic claims were often encountered.

Once this preliminary analysis was completed it was decided to study vandalism at the local level. With the help of the Department of Education and Science discussions were held with a few local authorities and police forces, as the result of which the City of Manchester and the Greater Manchester Police were invited, and agreed, to collaborate in a limited action-research project. There are almost 300 schools in Greater Manchester in a compact area of about 10 square miles, and vandalism in these schools presented a serious problem which the local education authority, and in particular the Buildings Branch, were concerned to tackle. The Greater Manchester Police have a crime prevention department headed by a chief inspector, with a crime prevention section in each police division. This department already had some experience in advising schools on crime prevention. Another factor that made Manchester particularly suitable for the feasibility study was the comparative sophistication of its records of damage, which were computerised. This provided easy access to information about individual schools and seemed likely to assist in any later evaluation of the study.

The project was developed in three stages. A pilot study involved discussions with local government officers, the local police and other interested parties, visits to schools and detailed analysis of records of vandalism, in order to find suitable schools to participate in the project. This work was undertaken by a small research team provided by the Home Office. A research and planning phase followed in which eleven schools were invited to take part and a steering group for the project established which included representatives from the Education Department, the police, the Home Office and the Crime Prevention Centre. The research team, with the help of those involved locally, then proceeded to adapt the 'desk' analysis of school vandalism already undertaken to take into account local circumstances, and prepared a dossier for each participating school including an analysis of its problems and an assessment of possible remedies.

Thirdly, there was a decision-making and implementation phase, which involved the convening of a meeting for each of the schools at which representatives from the schools, the local authority and the police considered the dossier and formulated recommendations for preventive action. Much of the liaison required in this phase was undertaken by a part-time project co-ordinator paid for by the Home Office. The Steering Group then prepared a report incorporating these recommendations, together with others concerned with the improvement of the monitoring of vandalism and with inter-agency liaison. The Education Committee, to which the report was submitted, agreed to the recommendations, and the process of implementation then began. The final stage of the project will involve an evaluation of the measures taken, to be conducted by the Home Office Research Unit. This has yet to be undertaken because the measures cannot be expected to have an immediate effect and even if they did this might not be sustained: to allow for the possibility of ephemeral effects, chance fluctuations and so forth, it will be necessary for a period of up to a year to elapse before an evaluation can be mounted.

MONITORING VANDALISM

Before attempting to devise possible means of preventing vandalism and other problems suffered by schools it is necessary to identify the schools which suffer worst, since effective prevention is likely to require resources to be concentrated where the greatest gains can be made. In short, some sort of system for monitoring the incidence of vandalism is an essential prerequisite for any systematic preventive activity.

As mentioned above, by comparison with many local authorities, the system of recording vandalism used in Manchester was found to be unusually sophisticated. It formed part of the City's integrated accounting system, but its primary purpose was for financial control and auditing rather than for crime prevention and in practice the wealth of detailed information potentially available was largely unused. The Education Department relied instead on a much simpler parallel system, which supplied each month a list of schools where more than one 'incident' of vandalism had occurred. Each 'incident' listed represented in reality one visit to a school by maintenance staff: this might not amount to more than the reglazing of a single window but where a backlog of work had accumulated an 'incident' might correspond with the repair of as many as 50 windows. The system actually in use, therefore, did not appear to yield any very reliable indication of the extent of damage at individual schools. Nor did it provide any indication of the type or cost of damage.

Moreover, by no means everything which was labelled vandalism really qualified for that description. At five out of the eleven premises selected for the project it was found that a significant amount of the damage labelled 'vandalism' occurred accidentally, a typical example being a football through a window. In some cases accidental damage was called 'vandalism' because the headmaster or caretaker believed (erroneously, it is said) that vandalism was repaired more quickly than wear and tear. At other times it was the repair men or the clerk at the local depot of the Direct Works Department (the agency responsible for school maintenance) who misattributed damage. Furthermore, by no means every incident labelled vandalism came to the notice of the Education Department - one of the schools participating in the project had suffered £1,000 worth of broken windows, none of which appeared in the monthly list. In short, the Education Department did not seem to be in a position to identify, in any systematic way, which of its schools were the main recipients of the nearly £200,000 spent annually on 'vandalism' at that time.

The need for modification of the monitoring system

Given the shortcomings of the vandalism monitoring system used by the Education Department and the existence of an alternative, more reliable source of information, it seemed worth considering the possibility of developing a more satisfactory system. An extensive commitment of resources was not needed because the City's computerised financial accounting system already collated detailed records of vandalism. All that seemed necessary was to improve the quality of the input to the system and to prepare a computer programme which could sift the raw material and draw out the essential information needed to pinpoint vandalism 'black spots'.

The development of a more adequate monitoring system was seen as having several advantages. First, it would eliminate the need for the monthly compilation of lists of 'incidents', currently used by the Education Department, which would represent a significant saving in manpower. Secondly, it would supply the Education Department with much more reliable and informative evidence of the incidence of vandalism in schools, thus enabling a more systematic approach to preventive activity. Finally, it could provide a better basis for the evaluation of the effectiveness of future preventive measures. In the absence of such information *ad hoc* research projects are needed to evaluate preventive efforts; these are so costly that it is doubtful whether they could provide the basis of an extensive body of knowledge about the effectiveness of different strategies. At the very least the more or less automatic production of reliable information about vandalism should obviate most of the routine clerical fieldwork necessary at present in such evaluation research.

Monitoring systems and evaluation research

Evaluation research usually has to make do with patchy and imperfect data which are costly to extract. One of the more useful lessons of the Manchester feasibility study may turn out to be that more adequate monitoring systems can be developed and that such a strategy is, in the long run, a more productive use of resources. This argument can be applied, of course, to a much wider field than vandalism or, for that matter, crime prevention in general, but it will often be resisted; researchers and their customers often want quick results, while those who control monitoring systems may be reluctant to change them even when the information provided is of dubious value. Nevertheless, if these objections can be overcome, an approach of this kind seems to hold out more hope than more traditional modes of research of making progress with problems, such as vandalism, where there is a wide range of preventive measures of unknown effectiveness, the separate evaluation of which is likely to be a lengthy process. On the

144

other hand it is important not to set up elaborate information systems which are not in the event used because they do not provide the data of the kind or in the form that are subsequently found to be required.

Development of a new system
Once the Education Committee had agreed, in principle, to the modification of the existing financial information system, outline proposals for its revision were prepared. Bringing about such a change was a complex task as the responsibility for the system was divided between three different departments of the authority: the Direct Works Department (responsible for the input to the system), the City Treasurer's Department (responsible for the computer system) and the Education Department (responsible for the various uses made of the system's output). This illustrates the importance, for effective crime prevention, of co-ordination and liaison work.

A meeting of the three departments was held, at which they agreed to collaborate in a feasibility study to be undertaken by an operational researcher from the Scientific Advisory Branch of the Home Office. On the basis of this study (which involved about six weeks' work) detailed proposals for a new monitoring system were prepared. The details of these proposals need not be described here; briefly what was suggested was that the Direct Works Department should introduce (and train its staff to use) new codes in filling in repair records, while the City Treasurer's Department was asked to adapt the computer system so as to incorporate the new monitoring programme. These proposals were agreed at a second meeting of the interested parties.

The choice of monitoring indices
One aspect of the new system that calls for special mention is the nature of the indices adopted. The important issue here is whether it is better to continue to attempt to identify vandalism as such or whether it would be more sensible to focus on damage in general. Obviously there are advantages in being able to identify vandalism as such but in practice there are a number of obstacles to doing so. Following extensive consultations, it was concluded that the nature of the problem and the way in which repairs were carried out did not permit the adequate discrimination of vandalism from other kinds of damage such as wear and tear and that to attempt to do so was counter-productive on account of the inaccuracy and unreliability of the resulting information.[1]

The main difficulty was deciding what caused a particular incident of damage. The most obvious source of information on this score was the school requesting the repair of damage. However, even at the school itself it might not be clear whether the damage was caused accidentally or not, and a subjective judgment

---

[1] Although the existing monitoring system in Manchester did not seem adequate for the purpose of ascertaining patterns of trends at individual schools, the overall trends for Manchester over the years are probably more reliable since no evidence was found to suggest that the proportion of the bill attributable to accidental damage had changed for Manchester as a whole.

was involved which made it difficult to ensure consistency between schools. Moreover, for a number of reasons some headmasters might prefer not to reveal that damage was caused by vandals, while others might report accidental damage as vandalism in the hope of a more rapid response. Even if these difficulties were ignored, it would still be necessary to ensure that all requests for work arising from vandalism were correctly identified by the coders at the Direct Works Department. Some special device would be required to draw to their attention requests for work arising from vandalism, which might involve special forms pre-printed with an appropriate code, or the use of coloured paper. This would, however, introduce further complications in form-filling at schools, a task which is seldom popular. For these reasons, it seemed unwise to rely on schools to report vandalism for the monitoring system.

Alternatively, the workman who performed the repair might be required to decide when the damage was caused by vandalism. But there was no reason to believe that the workman would be more accurate or a more reliable informant than the staff of the school and by the time the repair note or order for work reached the workman it had (in the existing system) already been assigned a cost code which might have been copied over to other forms for cross-referencing. To alter codes at this stage would involve considerable disruption to current procedures.

In short, it did not seem that there was any reliable way of identifying vandalism as such and it was therefore decided that the nature of the damage itself, as recorded on the request for work, should be used for monitoring, rather than attempting to use any subjective judgment of the cause of the damage. If the damage associated with vandalism is classified into groups according to type, the largest groups appear to be:

i. broken glass;

ii. painted slogans;

iii. damage to basins, cisterns, lavatory pans and seats and urinals;

iv. broken fencing.

Other types of damage are caused by vandalism, but they are either difficult to identify (leaking roofs, for example, may or may not be caused by vandalism), or they are too varied to be formed into reasonably sized groups. It is true that the above groups, particularly broken glass, will include some accidental damage but, provided that this is taken into account in considering the results obtained from monitoring, this system should give a more accurate and reliable analysis of the changing patterns of vandalism and should be comparatively simple to operate.

To use indices of damage in general rather than of vandalism is not without drawbacks: simply knowing that a school suffers a relatively high rate of broken windows, for example, provides an inadequate guide to precisely what action should be taken. From the point of view of an Education Department, however, this is not a major shortcoming since, whatever the cause of damage may be, it

146

must be repaired and the possibility of its recurrence reduced; the prevention of accidental damage may sometimes even prove more important, at least in terms of cost, than the prevention of deliberate damage.

Although the work in Manchester suggested that in the circumstances obtaining there it was better to attempt to monitor damage rather than vandalism, this may not apply where the system for recording and repairing damage is different. Nor does it mean that monitoring systems which do not have a vandalism code are necessarily satisfactory but rather that there is a case for monitoring vandalism by starting from records of damage in general and only attempting to ascertain the cause (by informal enquiry) at schools where levels of damage are disproportionately high. Nor is it clear how far it would be appropriate to adopt the 'damage-in-general' approach for targets other than schools; in some cases it may be possible to identify vandalism unequivocally - telephone kiosks might be such a case.

Besides the question of whether to measure vandalism or damage in general there are other measurement problems. In particular it is important to recognise that the size of a school may affect the level of vandalism. The data available in Manchester do not at present provide a particularly accurate basis on which to reach conclusions but the available evidence suggests that levels of damage are greatly affected by a school's size. This may be simply because a large school offers more targets, but other factors may also be involved, such as the greater difficulty in a large school of exercising adequate supervision and controlling access to the premises.

'Distributional analysis'
Accurate records of damage alone do not go far towards providing an adequate monitoring system; some way of collating and condensing what is likely to be a very large amount of data is needed. It is not possible here, however, to give a detailed account of the new computer programme in Manchester as this is still at a development stage. (A report by the Home Office Scientific Advisory Branch on the monitoring system will include a full description of the computer programme.) Essentially, however, the programme will produce a summary of where damage is worst, and how the current position at all schools compares with the recent past. This will include the specification of those schools where levels of damage provide the basis of the routine evaluation of preventive measures.

ANALYSIS IN CRIME PREVENTION
The Working Group's report highlighted the need for systematic and comprehensive analysis of the circumstances surrounding the crime problem being studied, and the questions how and to what extent this might be achieved were given special attention in the feasibility study. The ground was prepared, as will probably usually be necessary, by the 'theoretical' analysis described on page 142, however, this exercise could not take into account circumstances peculiar to individual localities, nor did it anticipate the prior need to ascertain the exact

nature of the problem. This latter point is particularly important for, as was mentioned in the last section, in nearly half the schools participating in the project the main problem turned out to be accidental damage rather than vandalism.

It was not thought appropriate that the local analysis should be the responsibility of the Home Office research team because the aim for the longer-term was a technique which could be applied locally with minimal assistance from central Government; it would obviously be impracticable to provide extensive research resources to every school that suffered from vandalism and wanted help. It was resolved, therefore, not to undertake work which could not be repeated later on a wider scale but rather to develop 'do-it-yourself' methods and materials which would not require high-level professional skills.

The role of the police crime prevention officer

At the local level there is already the service provided by the police crime prevention branch: one of the main tasks of crime prevention officers is the preparation of surveys (including surveys of schools) and any new approach needs to draw on that experience and expertise. At the outset of the research and planning phase of the project a brief study of their approach was undertaken by the Home Office Research Unit. This looked at the 25 school surveys carried out in the Manchester area over a period of six months in 1977. From an analysis of these reports and from discussions with crime prevention officers two problems became apparent.

In the first place crime prevention officers appear to accord burglary a much higher priority than vandalism, largely no doubt because burglary is the more serious offence and prevention of breaking-in provides the bulk of their work and predominates in their training. As a result few of the measures recommended were specifically concerned with preventing vandalism (toughened glass, for example, was rarely suggested); most measures, for example strengthening doors, were aimed at preventing entry. Preventing entry has, of course, an indirect effect on vandalism that is associated with break-ins, and on the theft of school equipment (which in 1976/77 cost £12,000 to replace). In practice, however, only a small proportion of the damage to schools (which cost about £180,000 to repair in 1976/77) is of this kind.

Another point raised by this work was the nature and level of the crime prevention officers' contacts with the schools. In practice it seems that the extent of their contact with headmasters and other staff is very limited so that their approach begins not so much from the actual problems suffered by the school as from a repertoire of anti-burglary measures which, however valuable in principle, may not meet the current needs of the school. There is thus a need for crime prevention officers to obtain complete support from headmasters and to be prepared to evaluate priorities when surveying school premises. It would be appropriate for these points to be brought out in the training given to crime prevention officers. But it is also incumbent on schools themselves to work towards better communications with crime prevention officers; headmasters are busy people, of course, but an hour spent in properly briefing a crime prevention officer could do much to aid active prevention.

The contribution of crime prevention officers should not be under-estimated: their knowledge of target-hardening is often extensive and the fact that their primary concern has been with school burglary does not mean that their efforts are in vain: although the relatively low level of school burglaries in Manchester raises a question about their current priorities, it may well be that the burglary rate would be much higher were it not for their expertise.

A 'diagnostic package'

It seems unlikely that these problems are confined to Manchester and on the basis of the Home Office Research Unit's study it was decided that the preparation of guidelines for a more analytic approach to the diagnosis of vandalism problems might be helpful. With the help of the Home Office Research Unit a prototype 'diagnostic package' was designed; this took the form of a structured questionnaire for use by crime prevention officers and others. This was divided into two parts. The first part consisted of an interview schedule designed to elicit from the heads of schools precise details of the types of problems encountered, where and when they occurred, which problem caused a school most trouble, and so forth. The second part of the package was intended to facilitate systematic survey of the school site in the light of information obtained in the interview and to suggest suitable preventive measures. The aim was to supply a procedure which would guide the user from a precise definition of the problems experienced by the school, through a systematic analysis of those problems, to appropriate recommendations for action.

The prototype was tested at the schools participating in the project by four crime prevention officers and the results formed the basis of the dossiers already mentioned. This process revealed, however, a number of shortcomings; it showed the desirability, for example, of interviewing the school caretaker as well as the head because each of them was likely to know of some aspects of the problem of which the other was unaware. (One headmaster, for example, was surprised to be told that in the previous 12 months breakages of glass at his school had cost £1,000 to repair; he was unaware of the damage because it occurred gradually.) Despite these shortcomings, however, it was generally agreed that the use of the package helped to uncover a number of important factors that might otherwise have been overlooked. A revised version of the 'diagnostic package' has been prepared* and the Greater Manchester Police have already shown some interest in using it more generally in the Manchester area. It can also be used by the schools themselves. The development of materials of this kind, however, requires

---

* **Editors' Note**: *Reproduced in Appendix A of Home Office Research Study No. 62.*

repeated testing, feed-back and re-design, and further revision may well prove necessary in the light of experience in the field.

Other contributions to analysis

Crime prevention officers are in the best position to undertake the precise specification of the problems suffered by the schools and consideration of possible opportunity-reducing measures. But there are other analytical needs, which it might be more appropriate to meet in other ways; these lie primarily in the sphere of social prevention. In particular, there is the evidence that the level and quality of leisure provision may affect the amount of vandalism to schools. For the Manchester project some helpful information was provided by the City Planning Department, relating to the leisure provision in the area surrounding each school, compared with that for the city as a whole. The sample (11 schools) was too small to permit any firm generalizations from this evidence but it was interesting to find that the areas surrounding the two worst-hit schools were particularly poorly provided for and this conclusion proved useful at a later stage. The Planning Department also provided useful information about plans for development for recreational purposes of waste land in the immediate vicinity of two schools, which could have been relevant to prevention efforts: the possibility of bringing forward the plans was considered but for various reasons was not practicable.

Local authority planning departments may often have a useful contribution to make but they cannot do this unless they are aware of the possibility and this is unlikely in the absence of deliberate liaison activity; in some parts of the country liaison has been successfully established between planning departments and crime prevention officers, and there is a need for such liaison to be developed further.

Other agencies and individuals, such as the local youth service or community development workers, may also have a contribution to make. The limited resources available for the project did not, however, permit liaison with the whole range of possible contributors.

APPROACHES TO DECISION MAKING

The results of the research and planning stage were collated and a dossier on each of the schools prepared. The next step was to convene the interested parties in order to produce recommendations for preventive action. The aim was to keep decision-making at a 'grass-roots' level, as far as possible, so as to maximise the participation of those involved with the school. To this end a series of half-day meetings were arranged to consider the information assembled on each of the schools and formulate recommendations for preventive action. Representatives of various interests were invited including, as appropriate, the schools themselves, the Education Department (Buildings Branch, Schools Branch, Schools Inspectorate and Community Education), the Direct Works Department, the Greater Manchester Police (Crime Prevention, Community Contact and divisional uniformed branch), the Social Services Department (Community Development Branch) and the City Planning Department.

Discussion at these meetings, which was often lively, sometimes shed new light on the problems, and in every case it proved possible to arrive at agreed recommendations for action. But it is doubtful whether this is the most effective way of formulating recommendations since it may not be possible for all the relevant people to attend. In particular, attending every meeting would represent a considerable burden for agencies with a general interest, such as those responsible for leisure provisions or community development, who were not well represented as a result; this inevitably limited consideration of preventive strategies in these areas. Most of the necessary consultations could be done more informally but the question arises of who could perform this task. Given the right person (who would need to have the necessary public relations skills) this might be either a crime prevention officer or someone from the local authority. In some areas force crime prevention officers already fulfil this function.

In either case, however, there is a considerable burden of administrative and liaison work. In the feasibility study it was found that arranging meetings, encouraging the various interests to attend and assembling the necessary papers amounted to a substantial task, even though only 11 of Manchester's 300 schools were involved. Nor did the work end once decisions were taken; monitoring the implementation of preventive measures was also an important task. Whoever is responsible for this work needs to have access to the various departments and support from a senior officer in the Education Department who can help to ensure that co-operation is forthcoming. Such staff may not readily be available: in Manchester the problem was solved by appointing a part-time project co-ordinator paid for by the Home Office and based in the headquarters of Buildings Branch. Successful as the appointment proved to be, it was made with some reluctance since the need for such a post indicated the difficulty of undertaking a project of this kind without additional resources.

Measures recommended for schools

No attempt will be made here to discuss in detail problems at the schools participating in the project or the recommendations made by the local consultative groups. The situation can be summarised, very broadly, as follows:

i. At five schools what initially appeared to be vandalism was found to be mainly accidental breakage of glass, in the course of ball games or boisterous play (a couple of medium-sized windows broken each week can add up to £1,000 in a year). At these schools the use of toughened glass to replace windows when broken was recommended.

ii. At four schools the problem, though not severe, seemed to consist of deliberate damage to windows, sanitary fittings, fencing and roofs. Here the main recommendations were a mixture of target-hardening measures (including wire mesh grilles over selected windows, some use of glass substitutes and attempts to limit access to hidden areas).

151

iii. One school (school 'X') had a moderately severe problem of vandalism and break-ins. This seemed to be associated with the fact that, because there was little provision of public open space in the neighbourhood, the school-grounds were officially open to youngsters out of school hours. It did not appear to be practical to attempt to exclude them but previously the school had been protected by a park warden provided by recreational services. During his time there the problems had been much reduced but after his death he was not replaced and the problem worsened again. It was recommended that this arrangement should be revived or, failing that, that glass substitutes should be used.

iv. Finally, one school (school 'Y') suffered severely from vandalism and break-ins. At the time of the study the bill was often of the order of £1,000 per month and the school was clearly rather demoralised by its state of siege. Here again, part of the problem was that the school is surrounded by large grounds which are open to the public. The main recommendations were to fence off part of the school ground as a play area, close the rest of the school ground to the public and erect a caretaker's bungalow on site. In the meantime it was recommended that a security guard be provided.[1]

It will be noted that, despite the inclusion in a 'diagnostic package' of a range of social preventive measures aimed at reducing propensity to offend, virtually all the measures selected were of the opportunity-reducing kind. This was partly because social measures often did not seem particularly relevant to the schools concerned, and because their role in reducing vandalism was often indirect and hypothetical whereas the potential effectiveness of the opportunity-reducing measures was clear; another factor was the attitudes of head-teachers who were generally rather suspicious of the social approach which many of them seemed to fear would erode their autonomy *vis-à-vis* the local authority.

Social prevention initiatives
This demonstrates neither that social prevention is impracticable nor that the approach recommended by the Working Group on Crime Prevention is at fault but that grass-roots decision-making does not provide a particularly suitable strategy for promoting social prevention.

A report on the project incorporating the consultative groups' recommendations was submitted to the Manchester Education Committee, which welcomed the submission and accepted its recommendations. Misgivings were expressed, however, at the absence of much in the way of 'social' preventive measures and it was made clear that the Education Department would like to redress the imbalance.

Attention was therefore given to developing social prevention measures which

---

[1] In the event it proved impossible to employ a security guard for the summer holidays when the school was expected to be particularly vulnerable. The Education Department arranged instead for caretaking staff to be present in the buildings throughout this period, and for a sports programme for local children, which lasted several weeks. There appears to have been a substantial reduction in vandalism; the details will be given in due course in a separate Home Office Research Unit report.

would affect two of the schools participating in the project. At school 'X' the Education Department Inspectorate was keen to see some kind of evening and holiday play scheme set up, and given that the temporary provision of a park-attendant appeared to have substantially reduced vandalism in the past and that the area was relatively poorly provided with leisure facilities, this approach seemed promising. However, the headmaster, although not against the idea in principle, was clearly concerned that anything undertaken should be integrated into the existing education programme. A pilot 'extended day' scheme is now being planned.

The other school where social prevention may eventually be applied is school 'Y'. This school, which is situated in an area which is almost a text-book case of planning 'blight', was much the worst hit of the schools in the project. Work undertaken for the Manchester Inner City partnership had led to the conclusion that vandalism should be one of the key issues tackled by the partnership and that it was in the area surrounding school 'Y' where action was most needed although other areas might also be included. An area-based anti-vandalism project, funded by the Inner City Programme, is currently under consideration and it seems likely that some broadly-based social prevention programme will be mounted there although it is difficult, as yet, to know exactly what form this might take.

Lack of information
Two major obstacles to effective crime prevention identified in the preceding pages are the lack of co-ordination between different agencies and institutions and the shortcomings of the arrangements for monitoring vandalism. A further stumbling block disclosed by the project is the lack of information available to the police and others about preventive measures. For example, detailed information about the varying properties of different kinds of strengthened glass was available to few of the crime prevention officers involved in the project. The relevant information can be set out on a single sheet of paper, but as far as could be ascertained this had never been done, and for the purposes of the project it proved necessary to collate information from a number of sources. In addition, some further investigation into the design of window frames and discussions with manufacturers have suggested that break-in resistant windows could be produced by only minor modification to existing products. The Stafford Crime Prevention Centre does what it can in this field with the limited resources it has, but there seems to be a clear need for increased efforts to collate and disseminate information on existing materials and techniques and stimulate the research and development of new products.*

Implementation
In Manchester, building and maintenance work is usually undertaken by the Direct Works Department and once the consultative groups' recommendations

---

* **Editors' Note:** *A more detailed account of the work undertaken in this area is set out in appendices B and C of Home Office Research Study No 62.*

had been agreed by the Education Committee they were referred to the Direct Works Department for the preparation of estimates. This task was delayed because both the Education and Direct Works Departments were under considerable pressure as a result of the combined effects of widespread industrial action and an unusually severe winter. The need to consult the Fire Brigade over many of the measures also delayed progress. In all, scarcely any measures had been implemented within six months, and a year is likely to be required before the majority are complete. Since this delay occurred in a situation where there was some pressure to expedite implementation it seems possible that delays could be even longer for more routine crime prevention activity, and the cost of vandalism that might have been prevented could be considerable. If this is to be avoided there is a need to ensure that implementation procedures contain regular checks on whether progress is up to schedule; in Manchester this was undertaken by the project co-ordinator, but it is desirable for a sufficiently senior officer to take a personal interest as well.

The role of non-statutory organisations

Little attempt was made to involve non-statutory organisations directly in the project. Ideally, however, their possible contributions should be borne in mind. The existence of a Direct Works Department in Manchester greatly reduced the scope for involvement of commercial firms, but even in this situation they may have a part to play where they can provide a service that is difficult for the Direct Works Department to undertake. One example of this is the use of toughened glass. This substance, though unable to resist determined attack, has four or five times the strength of ordinary glass, costs little more, and can be particularly useful in preventing accidental damage, for example caused by footballs. Its use is complicated, however, by the fact that it cannot be cut to size once it has been toughened. This can cause delays of a month or more since toughening equipment is expensive and confined to a handful of commercial firms. Few schools are happy to have windows boarded up for long periods-apart from anything else there is some evidence that failure to repair breakages quickly can prompt new attacks - and as a result the use of toughened glass is relatively rare. It is possible that considerable sums could be saved if, in collaboration with commercial firms, new procedures could be devised to reduce delays.

Voluntary organisations may also have a role to play; the successful detached youth work project described by Smith et al. (1972) was undertaken by a voluntary organisation and there is increasing interest in crime prevention from the voluntary sector. In the Manchester study the limited resources for liaison work were concentrated on inter-agency co-operation within the statutory sector; ideally, however, the possibility of voluntary involvement in prevention should be explored. A good starting point for liaison work may be the local Council for Voluntary Service or Community Councils; the National Association for the Care and Resettlement of Offenders, which has some local branches, may also be able to suggest suitable contacts.

PRACTICAL LESSONS

A number of insights into good practice have been gained in the course of the Manchester project. Various obstacles to the effective organisation of preventive activity have been identified and possible solutions explored. A considerable amount has also been learnt about a variety of possible preventive measures which had not emerged from a systematic review of published reports.

Obstacles to effective crime prevention

Four major obstacles to effective prevention at the local level were detected. The first of these was the lack of a satisfactory system for *monitoring* the incidence of vandalism, without which it is difficult to concentrate effort where it is most needed. Clearly the existence of an information system is no guarantee that the data it provides are reliable or accurate. The lesson is that there is a need to check that methods of monitoring crime provide meaningful information and where, as may often be the case, they do not, to secure their redesign.

Secondly, it appears that much could be done to improve inter-agency *co-ordination*. Various bodies may be liable to provide assistance of one kind or another but a certain amount of liaison work is necessary if they are to be aware of their potential contributions. It may well be unrealistic to expect that such work can be undertaken by existing staff. For the purposes of the feasibility study a part-time project co-ordinator was employed and some liaison work was also undertaken by the research team. Even so it was not possible to liaise with everybody with a potential contribution to make. The possibility of employing permanent crime prevention liaison officers deserves serious consideration; such a job would demand a variety of skills, however, and thought may need to be given to how suitable candidates might be trained.

In addition to the difficulty of finding suitable staff it would be necessary to justify the creation of an additional post. In this connection it may be worth remembering, however, that a liaison officer may pay his way even if his impact is only marginal. In Manchester, for example, the combined cost of school vandalism, accidental damage and break-ins is currently in excess of £200,000; a competent liaison officer could facilitate a much more concerted attack on these problems and his costs would be covered if the total bill were reduced by as little as 3%.

Two further obstacles to effective prevention were highlighted by the project; the lack of *systematic analysis* of the varying problems at different schools and the lack of information about preventive measures. To help meet these needs a 'diagnostic package' was developed. It seems likely that similar needs exist for many other crime problems and that similar work along these lines could be of assistance. What is needed is the collation and analysis of available information and the preparation of guidelines for good practice. If duplication of effort is to be avoided such work might best be undertaken by a centralised body.

155

Strategic lessons

It became apparent that, although vandalism was a considerable problem at existing schools in Manchester, no machinery existed for consulting the police when planning new buildings. Crime prevention advice may conflict, from time to time, with educational needs or cost considerations, but the police are aware of a range of design and planning points which, if taken into account at the design stage, can save expense when a school is in use. Indeed the feasibility study itself highlighted the shortcomings of the 'inner quadrangle' design common in Manchester which leaves a large proportion of the outside fabric of the school unobserved, and the benefits of side-hung windows with small panes.

Tactical lessons

A detailed account cannot be given here of the many insights into a variety of preventive measures yielded by the project; but three examples may illustrate the lessons learnt. First, a number of tactics were found to have unsuspected shortcomings. There are, for example, a number of glass substitutes available but all have disadvantages. The difficulties of utilising toughened glass have already been discussed (see page 153) while polycarbonate, which is virtually unbreakable, is not without problems - it is easily scratched, for instance, and requires the modification of window frames. Another example is 'anti-climb' paint. This is a non-drying viscous substance which, applied to drainpipes, is supposed to prevent access to roofs etc. At most of the schools visited during the project, however, it had been applied much too thinly; it quickly dried out and hence was of little value. The reason appears to be that painters are trained to apply paint as thinly as possible.

Dual use of school premises

A more substantial lesson concerned the use of school premises out of hours. An approach to the prevention of school vandalism which has been widely advocated in recent years is 'dual use', in accordance with which schools are opened in the evenings or at weekends for use by outsiders. This may prevent vandalism by providing vandals with more constructive opportunities, or simply because an occupied building is less liable to attack. (On the other hand, if the premises are not properly supervised, dual use may provide additional opportunities for vandalism.) And dual use is attractive to local authorities because it provides a better return on the community's investment in buildings and equipment. But although there is little doubt that dual use can be, in some circumstances, an effective way of tackling vandalism, it suffers from a number of disadvantages. Most of these arise from the division of responsibility for the management of premises. The interests of the parties involved will rarely coincide exactly leading to a variety of conflicts; schools often complain, for instance, that they have to clear up after the evening users. Knowledge of such problems has so jaundiced the view in many schools where dual use is not practised that they were reluctant to agree to its introduction.

Extended use

Making greater use of school premises remains an attractive idea, however, so that what seems to be needed are alternative schemes which avoid the division of responsibility entailed by dual use. Essentially this means that evening and weekend programmes need to be under the control of existing management and such an arrangement could be described as 'extended use'. Many 'community schools' are examples of this but other approaches could also be explored.

OTHER ASPECTS OF VANDALISM

The main purpose of the feasibility study was to assess the value of the more systematic approach to the organisation of crime prevention activity advocated by the Working Group on Crime Prevention. However, the work also highlighted some general aspects of vandalism which may be of interest.

The cost of vandalism

Between 1969 and 1977 the cost of repairing damage identified as vandalism in Manchester schools more than quadrupled, rising from £41,869 to £179,056 (see Figure 11:1). But, of course, over that period prices have risen considerably and where costs are adjusted for inflation,[1] it becomes apparent that the real cost has risen little if at all (see Figure 11:2). It is possible that less 'vandalism' is repaired now than formerly, but the evidence for Manchester is that this is not the case. The *prima facie* conclusion would appear to be that, across the city as a whole, the problem is not getting worse. This is not necessarily the case for individual schools however; some appear to have got worse and others to have improved although the absence of reliable data at the school level makes it difficult to reach any firm conclusions. There are 'success stories' of schools where the cost of 'vandalism' has steadily fallen from thousands of pounds (at current prices) to next to nothing, while at others there is some evidence of a steadily worsening problem. In other cases the pattern is erratic with high costs in some years and low costs in others.

At first sight this evidence may appear to conflict with the official *Criminal Statistics*, which show that the number of offences of criminal damage recorded by the police increased some ten-fold between 1969 and 1977. But these figures exclude offences where damage was valued at £20 and under and, as the Manchester evidence shows, the cost of repairing damage has more than quadrupled over the period in question so that a much higher proportion of offences now involve costs of over £20. Thus the effects of inflation need to be taken into account in interpreting *Criminal Statistics* as well.

Not only is vandalism stabilising in Manchester's schools: by no means everything which is labelled vandalism really qualifies for that description. As men-

---

[1] This is achieved by dividing a year's raw cost by the routine maintenance costs (excluding vandalism for that year and multiplying by the routine maintenance costs for 1976/7). Not dissimilar results are obtained by applying the National Building Costs Price Index, but it is thought that the former method is more accurate.

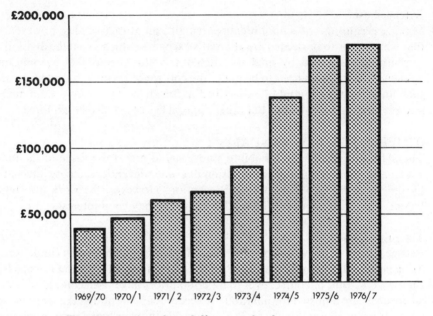

Figure 11:1 The rising price of vandalism to schools

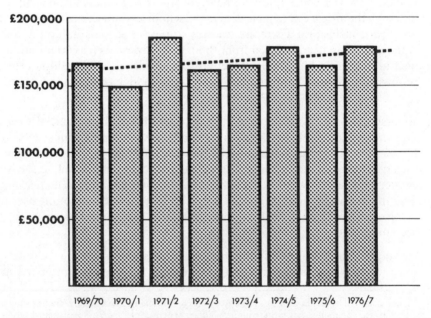

Figure 11:2 Total cost of school vandalism adjusted for inflation
(all at 1976/77 prices)

tioned earlier, at five out of the eleven schools studied it was found that a significant amount of the damage labelled 'vandalism' occurred in reality accidentally. Of course schools collaborating with the project are not necessarily typical of all schools in Manchester. Nevertheless it seems likely that a proportion of so-called vandalism is not in fact deliberate damage at all.

In short, detailed analysis suggests that vandalism in Manchester schools is not as acute a problem as it appears at first sight. And certainly it could not be said that vandalism is regarded as a particularly urgent problem by very many of the schools participating in the project. But it would be wrong, however, to dismiss the problem; as mentioned earlier, one of the schools (school 'Y') seemed to suffer from a level of attack quite outside the experience of the rest, and for the teachers there vandalism is a source of almost daily worry.

Two views of vandalism
These tentative conclusions raise some interesting questions about the significance of vandalism. In particular, they do not lend support, perhaps, to that school of thought which sees vandalism primarily in terms of a drain on the ratepayer's pocket, although there is no doubt that vandalism is a matter of widespread public concern and is offensive aesthetically and environmentally. However, if the object of preventive activity is to save unnecessary expenditure, vandalism may not always be the best place to begin. Accidental damage may be equally important or, for that matter, it might be better to look at quite different areas of spending. It may well be that the development of more sophisticated 'loss-accounting' systems would reveal unnecessary expenditure which had little or nothing to do with criminal activity, and which, once identified, would be easier to eliminate. One might look, for instance, at the way heating costs varied between different schools.

The alternative school of thought sees vandalism primarily as a symptom of other problems - unsatisfactory human relations in schools, for example, or lack of leisure opportunities in a neighbourhood. On this view, which is particularly prevalent among educationalists and educational administrators, the objective of focussing on vandalism is not so much to reduce costs as to identify underlying problems which may have other expressions besides vandalism - such as truancy, theft or low academic performance. Seen in this way, the significance of vandalism is to guide localised compensatory action which goes rather wider than crime prevention; and when such action has been taken, to provide evidence (in terms of the effect on levels of vandalism) of how successful such action has been. In this context the prevention of crime becomes only one goal amongst several.

Both approaches doubtless have their place; and it is essential that the proponents of each work closely together if duplication of effort is to be avoided. And both require reliable monitoring systems, careful analysis of problems and up-to-date information about different ways of tackling them.

CONCLUSIONS

The more systematic approach to the organisation of crime prevention activity recommended by the Working Group on Crime Prevention has been tested in the field by application to a particular offence. There is no doubt that it encouraged a more coherent and informed approach to crime prevention than hitherto, and led to the selection of preventive measures based on a broader range of experience, particularly of the schools concerned, than would otherwise have been the case. To this extent, therefore, the approach may be judged to have been successful. This success must be qualified in several respects: first, while the approach did produce better recommendations for preventive measures, it did so in part by discouraging the use of inefficient measures rather than the adoption of new ones; it also led primarily to the adoption of physical opportunity-reducing measures rather than social measures for which the supporting evidence is weaker (although this may, in part, have been the result of the choice of offence for the study). This suggests that the approach may not encourage innovation to the extent that the Working Group hoped.

The second qualification concerns the initial analysis of the offence. This is an essential step in the procedure, and it must be thorough if it is to be effective. In the feasibility study, however, this work took a considerable time to complete and is relevant to only one aspect of a particular crime. There are obvious resource implications here for the Home Office in its attempts to encourage wider application of this approach to crime prevention. Thirdly, while the approach was successful in encouraging inter-agency co-operation, the particular decision-making model adopted for the feasibility study proved extremely time-consuming for those whose interest was indirect, but whose assistance was necessary when considering some of the more broadly-based possibilities. The liaison task and the need to monitor the implementation of recommendations adopted were also underestimated and these factors suggest that it would be difficult to use the approach with existing staff resources.

Vandalism in schools was chosen as the subject for the feasibility study because of its prevalence, the high level of public concern about vandalism, and the existence of a body of relevant research evidence. These factors undoubtedly increased the relevance of the study and improved the quality of the decision making, but the choice of offence also gave rise to difficulties. Definitional problems made the collection of information about vandalism difficult and this may hinder effective evaluation of the measures implemented. The choice and implementation of the measures was also complicated by the independent position of the headmasters. This applied in particular to social measures. Nevertheless the approach met the Education Department's need for a structure to guide its attempts at prevention of vandalism, and it is hoped that the guidelines to good practice which have been developed following the feasibility study will be of wider value.

Comparatively little was learned in Manchester about those who vandalise schools but considerable knowledge was gained about the offence itself. The apparent stability of the cost of repairing damage to schools in Manchester, and the proportion of this cost which arose from accidental damage, were unexpected results and suggest that a narrow concentration on vandalism alone may not be the best way of saving money, if that is the primary objective. Before the study began Manchester had employed physical defensive measures to prevent damage, some of which were not particularly relevant to that task: most of the measures selected as a result of the study were also of the target-hardening variety. It is too early to attempt to assess the effectiveness of these measures, although it is reasonable to expect that those directed towards accidental damage are likely to be effective against the kind of activity that caused damage in the past. The Home Office hopes to undertake further work at a later date to evaluate the measures introduced.

References

Adams, B. & Conway, J. 1974. *The Social Effects of Living off the Ground.* Housing Development Directorate Occasional Paper 1/75. London: Department of the Environment.

Aronson, E. & Mettee, O. R. 1968. 'Dishonest behaviour as a function of differential levels of induced self-esteem'. *Journal of Personality and Social Psychology*, **9**, 121–127.

Automobile Association. 1971, 'When did you last see your car?' *Drive Magazine*, No. 18, Summer 1971.

Baldwin, J. 1974. 'The role of the victim in certain property offences'. *Criminal Law Review*, June, 353–358.

Baldwin, J., Bottoms, A. E. & Walker, M. A. 1976. *The Urban Criminal.* London: Tavistock.

Ball, J., Chester, L. & Perrott, R. 1978: *Cops and Robbers: an Investigation into Armed Bank Robbery.* London: André Deutsch.

Baxter, R. & Nuttall, C. P. 1975. 'Severe sentences no deterrent to crime'. *New Society*, 2 January, 11–13.

Becker, H. 1962. *Outsiders: Studies in the Sociology of Deviance.* Glencoe, Illinois: The Free Press.

Belson, W. A. 1975. *Juvenile Theft: the Causal Factors.* London: Harper and Row.

Beyleveld, D. 1979. 'Deterrence research as a basis for deterrence policies'. *Howard Journal of Penology and Crime Prevention*, **18**, 135–149.

Birmingham Crime Prevention Panel. 1977. *How Safe in Your Car?* Report of a Working Party on the Security of Vehicles.

Bloom, D. & Twyman, T. 1978. 'The impact of economic change on the evaluation of advertising campaigns'. *Journal of Market Research Society*, **2**, 73–85.

Bottoms, A. E. 1974. Review of *Defensible Space* by Newman, O. *British Journal of Criminology*, **14**, 203–206.

Boyson, R. 1974. 'The need for realism'. In: Turner, B. (Ed.), *Truancy.* London: Word Lock.

Bright, J. A. 1967. *An Evaluation of Crime Cut Sheffield.* Police Research and Planning Branch Report No. 14/67 (official use only).

Brody, S. R. 1976. *The Effectiveness of Sentencing.* Home Office Research Study No. 35. London: H.M.S.O.

Brody, S. R. & Tarling, R. 1980. *Taking Offenders out of Circulation.* Home Office Research Study No. 64. London: H.M.S.O.

Brown, J.H. 1979. 'Suicide in Britain: more attempts, fewer deaths, lessons for public policy'. *Archives of General Psychiatry*, **36**, 119–124.

Bundeskriminalamt. 1973. *Tagungsbericht der Arbeitstagung 'Kraftfahrzeugdiebstahl' beim Weisbaden.*

Burbidge, M, 1973. *Vandalism: a Constructive Approach.* Housing Development Directorate Occasional Paper 3/73. London: Department of the Environment.

Burbidge, M. 1975. 'Some current British research'. In: *Architecture, Planning and Urban Crime.* Report of a N.A.C.R.O. Conference held on 6 December 1974. London: War on Want.

Caffyn, J. M. 1977. 'Measuring effects of advertising campaigns'. Proceedings of the 12th Annual Conference of the Market Research Society, 35–46.

Carroll, H. C. M. (Ed.). 1977. *Absenteeism in South Wales.* University College Swansea: Faculty of Education.

Chaiken, J. Lawless, M. & Stephenson, K. 1974. *The Impact of Police Activity on Crime: Robberies on the New York City Subway System.* Report No. R-1424-N.Y.C. Santa Monica, Calif.: Rand Corporation.

Clarke, R. V. G. 1977. 'Psychology and Crime'. *Bulletin of the British Psychological Society*, **27**, 19–22.

Clarke, R. V. G. (Ed.). 1978. *Tackling Vandalism.* Home Office Research Study No. 47. London: H.M.S.O.

Clarke, R. V. G. 1980. '"Situational' crime prevention: theory and practice'. *British Journal of Criminology*, **20**, 136–147.

Clarke, R. V. G. & Cornish, D. B. 1972. *The Controlled Trial in Institutional Research—Paradigm or Pitfall for Penal Evaluators?* Home Office Research Study No. 15. London: H.M.S.O.

Clarke, R. V. G. & Hough, J. M. (Eds.). 1980. *The Effectiveness of Policing.* Farnborough, Hants: Gower.

Clinard, M. B. & Wade, A. L. 1957. 'Towards the delineation of vandalism as a sub-type in juvenile delinquency'. *Journal of Criminal Law and Criminology*, **48**, 493–499.

Cloward, R. A. & Ohlin, L. E. 1961. *Delinquency and Opportunity.* London: Routledge and Kegan Paul.

Cohen, A. K. 1955. *Delinquent Boys: the Culture of the Gang.* Glencoe, Illinois: The Free Press.

Crump, R. R. & Newing, J. F. 1974. *Footpad Crime and its Community Effect in Lambeth.* Unpublished report of A7 Division, New Scotland Yard.

Decker, J. F. 1972. 'Curbside deterrence: an analysis of the effect of a slug rejector device, coin view window and warning labels on slug usage in New York City parking meters'. *Criminology*, August, 127–142.

Department of the Environment. 1973. *Children at Play.* Design Bulletin 27. London: H.M.S.O.

Department of the Environment. 1977. *Housing Management and Design.* Lambeth Inner Area Study. IAS/IA/18. London: Department of the Environment.

Devlin, T. 1974. 'Truants who are pushing up London's crime rate'. *The Times*, 28 June.

Duffala, P. C. 1976. 'Convenience stores, armed robbery, and physical environment features'. *American Behavioural Scientist*, **21**, 495–497.

Ekblom, P. 1979. 'A crime-free car?'. *Research Bulletin No. 7*, 28–30. London: Home Office Research Unit.

Engstad, P. & Evans, J. L. 1980. 'Responsibility, competence and police effectiveness in crime control'. In: Clarke, R. V. G. and Hough, J. M. (Eds.), *The Effectiveness of Policing.* Farnborough, Hants: Gower.

Farrington, D. P. (in press). 'Truancy, delinquency, the home and the school'. In: Hersov, L. and Berg, I. (Eds.), *Out of School.* London: Wiley.

Gibbons, D. C. 1971. 'Observations on the study of crime causation'. *American Journal of Sociology*, **77**, 262–278.

Gladstone, F. J. 1978. 'Vandalism among adolescent schoolboys'. In Clarke, R. V. G. (Ed.), *Tackling Vandalism.* Home Office Research Study No. 47. London: H.M.S.O.

Gould, L.C. 1969. 'The changing structure of property crime in an affluent society'. *Social Forces*, **48**, 50–59.

Haining, Supt. W. 1973. 'Glasgow's truancy patrol, 24 April–28 June 1973'. *Police Review*, 18/4219, 1629.

Hall, S. Critcher, C., Jefferson, T., Clarke, J. & Roberts, B. 1978. *Policing the Crisis: Mugging, the State, and Law and Order.* London: Macmillan.

Hampshire Constabulary. 1977. *Wheel Watch '77.* Crime Prevention Department.

Hancox, P.D. & Morgan, J. B. 1975. 'The use of C.C.T.V. for police control at football matches'. *Police Research Bulletin*, No. 25, 41–44.

Hartshorne, H. & May, M.A. 1928. *Studies in the Nature of Character (Vol. 1):* *Studies in Deceit.* New York: Macmillan.

Hassall, C. & Trethowan, W. H. 1972. 'Suicide in Birmingham'. *British Medical Journal*, **1**, 717–718.

Heller, N. B., Stenzel, W. W., Gill, A. D., Kolde, R. A. & Schimerman, S. R. 1975. *Operation Identification- An Assessment of Effectiveness. National Evaluation Program-Phase I Summary Report.* National Institute of Criminal Justice, Law Enforcement Assistance Administration, U.S. Department of Justice. Washington D.C.: Government Printing Office.

Herbert, D. 1977. 'Crime, delinquency and the urban environment'. *Progress in Human Geography*, **1**, 208–239.

Home Office. 1973. *Shoplifting and Thefts by Shop Staff.* Report of a Working Party on Internal Shop Security. London: H.M.S.O.

Home Office. 1974a. 'Southampton car security week 1974'. *Crime Prevention News*, No. 24.

Home Office. 1974b. 'Nottinghamshire Constabulary lock it (vehicle security campaign'. *Crime Prevention News*, No. 22.

Home Office. 1975a. 'Short concentrated campaigns beat crime'. *Crime Prevention News*, No. 26.

Home Office. 1975b. 'Bath car campaign'. *Crime Prevention News*, Nos. 25 and 26.

Home Office. 1975c. *Protection Against Vandalism.* Report of the Home Office Standing Committee on Crime Prevention. London: H.M.S.O.

Home Office 1976a. 'Road to riches'. *Crime Prevention News*, No. 32.

Home Office. 1976b. 'School vandalism - a successful campaign'. *Crime Prevention News*, No. 29.

Jacobs, Jane 1961. *The Death and Life of Great American Cities.* New York: Random House. (Published by Penguin Books Ltd., Harmondsworth in 1965).

Jeffery, C. Ray 1971. *Crime Prevention Through Environmental Design.* Beverly Hills: Sage Publications.

Law Enforcement Assistance Administration (L.E.A.A.). 1979. *What Happened: an Examination of Recently Terminated Anti-Fencing Operations.* Washington D.C.: U.S. Department of Justice.

Lerman, P. 1975. *Community Treatment and Social Control.* Chicago: University of Chicago Press.

Mannheim, H. 1965. *Comparative Criminology.* London: Routledge and Kegan Paul.

Manning, P. K. 1977. *Police Work: the Social Organisation of Policing.* London: M.I.T. Press.

Mansfield, R., Gould, L. C. & Namenwirth, J. Z. 1974. 'A socioeconomic model for the prediction of societal rates of property theft'. *Social Forces,* **52,** 462–472.

Marplan Limited. 1978. *An Experimental Research Study to Evaluate an Anti-Vandalism Advertising Campaign: Measurement of Behavioural Change.* R. 51447.

Martinson, R. 1974. 'What works? - questions and answers about prison reform'. *The Public Interest,* No. 35, Spring issue, 22–54.

Matza, D. 1964. *Delinquency and Drift.* New York: Wiley.

Mawby, R. I. 1977: 'Kiosk vandalism: a Sheffield study'. *British Journal of Criminology,* **17,** 30–46.

May, D. 1975. 'Truancy, school absenteeism and delinquency'. *Scottish Educational Studies,* **7,** 97–107.

May, D. 1978. 'Juvenile shoplifters and the organisation of store security: a case study in the social construction of delinquency'. *International Journal of Criminology and Penology,* **6,** 137–160.

Mayhew, P., Clarke, R. V. G., Burrows, J. N., Hough, J. M. & Winchester, S. W. C. 1979. *Crime in Public View.* Home Office Research Study No. 49. London: H.M.S.O.

Mayhew, P. 1979. 'Defensible space: the current status of a crime prevention theory'. *The Howard Journal of Penology and Crime Prevention,* **18,** 150–159.

McCaghy, C. H., Giordano, P. C. & Henson, T. K. 1977. 'Auto theft - offender and offence characteristics'. *Criminology,* **15,** 367–385.

McNee, Sir D. 1979. 'Crime and the young'. *Police Journal,* **52,** 5–14.

Medinnus, G. R. 1966. 'Age and sex differences in conscience development'. *Journal of Genetic Psychology,* **109,** 117–118.

Miller, A. 1973: 'Vandalism and the architect'. In: Ward, C. (Ed.), *Vandalism.* London: Architectural Press.

Mischel, W. & Gilligan, C. 1964. 'Delay of gratification, motivation for the prohibited gratification, and responses to temptation'. *Journal of Abnormal and Social Psychology,* **69,** 411–417.

Molumby, T. 1976. 'Patterns of crime in a university housing project'. *American Behavioural Scientist,* **20,** 247–259.

Morris, N. & Hawkins, G. 1970. *The Honest Politician's Guide to Crime Control.* Chicago: University of Chicago Press.

Nation's Cities. 1977. 'Crime prevention through environmental design - a special report'. In: *Nation's Cities*, December, 13–28. National League of Cities.

Newman, O. 1972. *Defensible Space: Crime Prevention Through Urban Design.* New York: MacMillan. (Published by Architectural Press, London, in 1973.)

Newman, O. 1975. 'Community of interest - design for community control'. In: *Architecture, Planning and Urban Crime.* Report of N.A.C.R.O. Conference held on 6 December 1974. London: War on Want.

Newman, O. 1976. *Design Guidelines for Creating Defensible Space.* National Institute of Law Enforcement and Criminal Justice, Law Enforcement Assistance Administration, U.S. Department of Justice. Washington D.C.: Government Printing Office.

Newman, O. 1980. *Community of Interest.* New York: Anchor Press/Doubleday.

N.O.P. Market Research Limited. 1979. *Car Security Advertising. Pre and Post-Stage Research.* NOP/4100.

Ohlin, L. E. 1970. *A Situational Approach to Delinquency Prevention.* Youth Development and Delinquency Prevention Administration. U.S. Department of Health, Education and Welfare.

Opie, I. & Opie, P. 1969. *Children's Games in Street and Playground.* London: Oxford University Press.

Parker, H. J. 1974. *View from the Boys. A Sociology of Down-Town Adolescents.* Newton Abbot: David and Charles.

Pease, K. 1979. *Reflections on the Development of Crime Prevention Strategies and Techniques in Western Europe, Excluding Roman Law Countries.* Report to the United Nations Centre for Social Development and Humanitarian Affairs (mimeo). Department of Social Administration, University of Manchester.

Peterson, M. A. & Braiker, H. B. 1980. *Doing Crime: a Survey of California Prison Inmates.* Santa Monica, California: Rand.

President's Commission on Law Enforcement and Administration of Justice. 1967. *The Challenge of Crime in a Free Society.* Washington D.C.: Government Printing Office.

Press, S. J. 1971. *Some Effects of an Increase in Police Manpower in the 20th Precinct of New York City.* New York: Rand.

Quinney, R. 1970. *The Social Reality of Crime.* Boston: Little, Brown.

Rau, R. M. 1975. 'Westinghouse consortium - crime prevention through environmental design'. *Proceedings of Policy Development Seminar on Architecture, Design and Criminal Justice.* Law Enforcement Assistance Administration. U.S. Department of Justice. Washington D.C.: Government Printing Office.

Reppetto, T. A. 1974. *Residential Crime*. Cambridge, Mass.: Ballinger.

Reppetto, T. A. 1976. 'Crime prevention and the displacement phenomenon'. *Crime and Delinquency*, April, 166–177.

Research Bureau Limited. 1977. *Car Theft Campaign Evaluation, 1976–1977*. Prepared for Central Office of Information. Job No. 94066–11352.

Research Bureau Limited. 1979. *Evaluation of an Anti-Vandalism Advertising Campaign*. Prepared for Central Office of Information. Job No. 11500.

Rettig, S. 1966. 'Group discussion and predicted ethical risk-taking'. *Journal of Personality and Social Psychology*, **3**, 629–633.

Riccio, L. J. 1974. 'Direct deterrence - an analysis of the effectiveness of police patrol and other crime prevention technologies'. *Journal of Criminal Justice*, **2**, 207–217.

Riley, D. & Mayhew, P. (In press) *Crime Prevention Publicity: an Assessment*. Home Office Research Study No. 63. London: H.M.S.O.

Ross, L. 1977. 'The intuitive psychologist and his shortcomings: distortions in the attribution process'. In: Berkowitz, L. (Ed.), *Advances in Experimental Social Psychology (Vol. 10)*. New York: Academic Press.

Rouse, W. V. & Rubenstein, H. 1978. *Crime in Public Housing: a Review of Major Issues and Selected Crime Prevention Strategies (Vol. 1)*. American Institutes for Research. Report for the Department of Housing and Urban Development. Washington D.C.: Government Printing Office.

Rutter, M. 1979. *Changing Youth in a Changing Society*. London: Nuffield Provincial Hospitals Trust.

Schneider, A. L. 1976. 'Victimisation surveys and criminal justice system evaluation'. In: Skogan, W. G. (Ed.), *Sample Surveys of the Victims of Crime*. Cambridge Mass.: Ballinger.

Scottish Council on Crime. 1975. *Crime and the Prevention of Crime*. Scottish Home and Health Department. Edinburgh: H.M.S.O.

Smith, C. S., Farrant, M. R. & Merchant, H. J. 1972. *The Wincroft Youth Project*. London: Tavistock Publications.

Sturman, A. 1978. 'Measuring vandalism in a city suburb'. In: Clarke, R. V. G. (Ed.), *Tackling Vandalism*. Home Office Research Study No. 47. London: H.M.S.O.

Sunderland Crime Prevention Panel. 1975. *Campaign to Reduce Thefts and Taking of Motor Vehicles without the Owners' Consent*. Northumbria Police.

Suttles, G. D. 1968. *The Social Order of the Slum: Ethnicity and Territory in the Inner City*. Chicago, Illinois: University of Chicago Press.

Taylor, I., Walton, P. & Young, J. 1973. *The New Criminology*. London: Routledge and Kegan Paul.

Tennent, T. G. 1971. 'School non-attendance and delinquency'. *Educational Research*, **13**, 185–190.

Tien, J. M., O'Donnell, U. F., Barnett, A. & Mirchandani, P. B. 1979. *Street Lighting Projects*. National Evaluation Program Phase 1 Report. National Institute of Law Enforcement and Criminal Justice, Law Enforcement Assistance Administration, U.S. Department of Justice. Washington D.C.: Government Printing Office.

Times Educational Supplement. 1974. 'DES seek the facts on truants'. 18 January.

Tizard, J. 1976. 'Psychology and social policy'. *Bulletin of the British Psychological Society*, **29**, 225–233.

Trasler, G. B. 1979. 'Delinquency, recidivism, and desistance'. *British Journal of Criminology*, **19**, 314–322.

Turner, B. (Ed.). 1974. *Truancy*. London: Ward Lock.

Tyerman, M. J. 1968. *Truancy*. London: University of London Press.

Wade, A. L. 1967. 'Social process in the act of juvenile vandalism'. In: Clinard, M. B., and Quinney, R. (Eds.), *Criminal Behaviour Systems*. New York: Holt, Rhinehart and Winston.

Walker, N. D. 1979. 'The efficacy and morality of deterrents'. *Criminal Law Review*, March, 129–144.

Wallach, M. A., Kogan, N. & Bem, D. J. 1965. 'Group decision-making under risk of adversive consequences'. *Journal of Personality and Social Psychology*, **1**, 453–460.

Waller, I. & Okihiro, N. 1978. *Burglary: The Victim and the Public*. Toronto: University of Toronto Press.

Wallis, C. P. & Maliphant, R. 1967. 'Delinquent areas in the county of London'. *British Journal of Criminology*, **7**, 250–284.

Walsh, D. P. 1978. *Shoplifting: Controlling a Major Crime*. London: MacMillan.

White, T. W., Regan, K. J., Waller, J. D. & Wholey, J. S. 1975. *Police Burglary Preventive Programs (Prescriptive Package)*. National Institute of Law Enforcement and Criminal Justice, Law Enforcement Assistance Administration, U.S. Department of Justice. Washington D.C.: Government Printing Office.

Wilkins, L. T. 1964. *Social Deviance*. London: Tavistock.

Wilkinson, P. 1977. *Terrorism and the Liberal State*. London: MacMillan.

Williams, P. 1974. 'Collecting the figures'. In: Turner, B. (Ed.), *Truancy*. London: Ward Lock.

Wilson, J. Q. 1975. *Thinking about Crime*. New York: Basic Books.

Winchester, S. W. C. 1978. 'Two suggestions for developing the geographical study of crime'. *Area,* **10,** 116–119.

Yin, R. K., Vogel, M. E., Chaiken, J. M. & Both, D. R. 1977. *Citizen Patrol Projects*. National Evaluation Program Phase 1 Summary Report. National Institute of Law Enforcement and Criminal Justice, Law Enforcement Assistance Administration, U.S. Department of Justice. Washington D.C.: Government Printing Office.

Young, P.A. 1974. 'An experiment in observation'. *Police Research Bulletin,* No. 23, 56–59.

Zaharchuk, T. & Lynch, J. 1977. *Operation Identification: a Police Prescriptive Package*. Ottawa: Ministry of Solicitor General.

Zimbardo, P. G. 1973. 'A field experiment in auto-shaping'. In: Ward, C. (Ed.), *Vandalism*. London: Architectural Press.

Subject Index

In this index, H.O. and H.O.R.U. refer respectively to the Home Office and to the Home Office Research Unit. Closed circuit television is also abbreviated to C.C.T.V.

Alcohol
  breathalyser systems in cars, 7
  sale at football matches, 10
Anti-climb paint, 156
Architectural design
  and crime prevention, 8 *see also* Defensible
  space
Autocrime *see also* Car thieves
  anti-theft devices, 11, 19n (1), 114, 117,
  122, 123
  car radios, theft of, 6, 106, 108
  commercial vehicles 22, 24n, 27
  defined, 19n (2), 99n
  demand for cars, 23, 25
  and displacement, 11, 20, 22–3, 27–8, 29,
  104, 107, 110
  duplicate keys, 108, 110, 125
  electronic security devices, 6, 110n
  future levels, vii, 22–3, 25, 27, 110
  in German Federal Republic *see under*
  Steering column locks
  ignition keys, 13–14, 21, 23, 30
  and insurance, 19, 27, 29, 108, 125
  legislation (on car security), 13–14, 30,
  110
  lorry-loads, thefts of, 17
  methods of, 23, 108, 110, 125
  in Metropolitan Police District, v, 19, 22,
  24 (Fig. 2:1), 27, 108
  motorcycles *see under* Theft
  number of vehicles on the road, 20, 23,
  25
  in Plymouth, 102, 105
  and the police, 19, 22, 29, 113
  prevention of, 6, 9, 30, 108–10 *see also*
  Steering column locks
  publicity campaigns *see* Autocrime
  publicity
  risk of *see* Victimisation
  and road safety, 19, 29
  security carelessness, v, 15, 20, 21, 22, 30,
  99, 105, 106, 107, 109, 121
  statistics, 19n (2) (3), 20–1, 105n (2), 115n
  (2)
  steering column locks *see* Steering column
  locks

  thefts from vehicles, 21n, 23n (2), 30, 106,
  107, 114
  thefts of vehicles, 20–1, 22, 23n (2), 105n
  (2), 115n (1)
  unauthorised taking, 20–1, 21n, 22, 23n (2),
  105n (2), 115n (1)
Autocrime publicity *see also* Plymouth
autocrime publicity campaign, 1977; H.O.
autocrime publicity campaign, 1979
  evaluations of, 99–101, 113
  H.O. publicity 99, 102, 113
  H.O. 1976 campaign, 99, 100, 107, 113
  police campaigns, 99–100, 102
  public complacency, 107
  'talking car', 103
Avon and Somerset Constabulary, 86
  role in H.O.R.U. study of truancy patrols,
  vii, 87

Bank robbery, 11
Breathalyser systems in cars, 7
British Transport Police (London Transport
Division)
  patrols by, 78
  records kept on crime, 75–6, 77n (3)
Burglar alarms, 11, 13
Burglary
  and insurance, 14
  Operation Identification, 7
  risk of, 15
  'sting' operations, 7
Buses, crime on
  flat-fare collection, 6
  vandalism *see* Bus vandalism
Bus vandalism
  and accidental damage, 32, 34
  cost of, 38
  H.O.R.U. study, v, 9, 31–8
  location of damage on different types of
  bus, 33–6
  prevention of, 37–8
  records on, 32
  seat choice, 36–7, 38
  staircase position, effects of, 35–6, 38
  supervision by crew, effects of, v, 9, 31,
  33–6, 38

Bus vandalism (cont.)
supervision by passengers, effects of, 35
Bystander intervention *see* 'Natural'
surveillance

Car security campaigns *see* Autocrime
publicity
Car radios, theft of, 6, 106, 108
Car theft *see* Autocrime
Car thieves
age, 19
opportunist/'joyriders', 22, 23, 25, 27–8,
30, 108
professionals, 22, 23, 25, 27, 108
'Career' criminals, 5, 11 *see also* Car thieves
(professionals)
Caretakers
on housing estates, 9, 46, 57, 60
in schools, 9, 16
Central Office of Information
car security publicity, 113, 124
vandalism publicity, 128, 135
Cheque books, theft of, 7
City of Manchester *see* Manchester City
Children's play
research on, 60
Closed circuit television (C.C.T.V.)
on buses, 38
effectiveness of, 75, 82
on London Underground, viii, 9, 11, 75,
79–83
on Metro system, Washington, D.C., 87
objections to, 6, 13
in shops, 75, 82
Commercial vehicles, theft of, 22, 24n, 27
Community policing, 139
Community surveillance, 8
supervision of children, 60
Computer crime, 12
Constabularies of police *see* Police forces
Containment, 2
Cost-effectiveness
bus vandalism prevention, 37–8
C.C.T.V. on the London Underground,
82
Plymouth autocrime publicity campaign,
1977, 103, 107n
situational crime prevention, 13, 16, 17
steering column locks, 28–9
Crash helmets *see* Theft (motorcycles)
Credit cards, theft of, 7
Crime *see also* Autocrime; Crime on the
London Underground; Theft; Vandalism;
Victimisation
bank robbery, 11
burglary *see* Burglary
bus vandalism *see* Bus vandalism
computer crime, 12
'causes' of, 5, 17, 69
drunken driving, 7, 11

extent of, 11, 17
football hooliganism, 9–10
hijacking, 6, 17
income tax evasion, 11
'joyriding' *see* Car thieves
'mugging', 75, 76, 77
parking offences, 12
shoplifting *see* Shoplifting
subway crime, 79, 82 *see also* Crime on the
London Underground
Crime on the London Underground
alarms, 80, 82
assaults on staff, 83
C.C.T.V., viii, 9, 11, 75, 79–83
H.O.R.U study, viii, 9, 75–83
'mugging', 75, 76, 77
reliability of records, 76, 79
risk of theft and robbery, 76–7
special policing, 75, 78–9, 82
Crime Policy Planning Unit (H. O.), viii, 141
see also Manchester School Vandalism
Project
Crime prevention *see also* Publicity;
Situational crime prevention
and criminal justice system, 2–3, 16, 17
definition, 1
displacement effects *see* Displacement
and the Home Office, 16, 141
legislative prevention 139, 142
and local authorities, 16, 150
'physical' prevention, 1
'social' prevention, 1, 3, 13, 139, 142, 150,
152, 160
Crime Prevention Centre, Stafford, 142, 153
Crime Prevention Officers, 1, 14, 99, 101,
107n (1), 139 *see also under* Manchester
School Vandalism Project
Crime prevention publicity *see* Publicity
*Crime Prevention Through Environmental
Design*, 2, 58
'Crime specific' studies, 2
Criminal damage *see under* Criminal
Statistics
Criminal justice system
crime preventive potential of, 2–3, 16, 17,
139
Criminal statistics
autocrime, 19n (2) (3), 20–1, 105n (2), 115n
(2), 118 (Fig. 9:1)
criminal damage, 47, 129, 133, 134
(Fig. 10:2), 157
Criminology
controlled experiments, 101
correctional bias, 3
dispositional bias, 3, 5, 10, 17
ecological research, 2
neglect of situational factors in, v, 1, 3,
17

Damage on buses *see* Bus vandalism

174

Author Index

Publications

Titles already published for the Home Office

Postage extra

Studies in the Causes of Delinquency and the Treatment of Offenders

1. Prediction methods in relation to borstal training. Hermann Mannheim and Leslie T. Wilkins. 1955. vi + 276 pp. (11 340051 9) £3.

2. † Time spent awaiting trial. Evelyn Gibson. 1960. 46pp. (34-368-2) 27p.

3. † Delingquent generations. Leslie T. Wilkins. 1960. 20pp. (11 340053 5) 16p.

4. † Murder. Evelyn Gibson and S. Klein. 1961. 44pp. (11 340054 3) 30p.

5. Persistent criminals. A study of all offenders liable to preventive detention in 1956. W. H. Hammond and Edna Chayen. 1963. x + 238pp. (34-368-5) £1.25.

6. † Some statistical and other numerical techniques for classifying individuals. P. McNaughton-Smith. 1965. 34pp. (34-368-6) 17½p.

7. Probation research: a preliminary report. Part I. General outline of research. Part II. Study of Middlesex probation area (SOMPA). Steven Folkard, Kate Lyon, Margaret M. Carver, Erica O'Leary. 1966. vi + 58pp. (11 340374 7) 42p.

8. † Probation research: national study of probation. Trends and regional comparisons in probation (England and Wales). Hugh Barr and Erica O'Leary. 1966. viii + 52pp. (34-368-8) 25p.

9. † Probation research. A survey of group work in the probation service. Hugh Barr. 1966. viii + 96pp. (34-368-9) 40p.

10. † Types of delinquency and home background. A validation study of Hewitt and Jenkins' hypothesis. Elizabeth Field. 1967. vi + 22pp. (34-368-10) 14p.

11. † Studies of female offenders. No. 1 - Girls of 16–20 years sentenced to borstal or detention centre training in 1963. No. 2 - Women offenders in the Metropolitan Police District in March and April 1957. No. 3 - A description of women in prison on January 1, 1965. Nancy Goodman and Jean Price. 1967. vi + 78pp. (34-368-11) 30p.

12. † The use of the Jesness Inventory on a sample of British probationers. Martin Davies. 1967. iv + 20pp. (34-368-12) 11p.

13. † The Jesness Inventory: application to approved school boys. Joy Mott. 1969. iv + 28pp. (11 340063 2) 17½p.

Home Office Research Studies

1. † Workloads in children's departments. Eleanor Grey. 1969. vi + 75pp. (11 340101 9) 37½p.

2. † Probationers in their social environment. A study of male probationers aged 17–20, together with an analysis of those reconvicted within twelve months. Martin Davies. 1969. vii + 204pp. (11 340102 7) 87½p.

3. † Murder 1957 to 1968. A Home Office Statistical Division report on murder in England and Wales. Evelyn Gibson and S. Klein (with annex by the Scottish Home and Health Department on murder in Scotland) 1969. vi + 94pp.

4. Firearms in crime. A Home Office Statistical Division report on indictable offences involving

† Out of print. Photostat copies can be requested from Her Majesty's Stationery Office upon request.

183

firearms in England and Wales. A.D. Weatherhead and B.M. Robinson. 1970. viii + 37pp. (11 340104 3) 30p.

5. † Financial penalties and probation. Martin Davies. 1970. vii + 38pp. (11 340105 1) 30p.

6. Hostels for probationers. Study of the aims, working and variations in the effectiveness of male probation hostels with special reference to the influence of the environment on delinquency. Ian Sinclair. 1971. iv + 199pp. (11 340106 X) £1.15.

7. Prediction methods in criminology including a prediction study of a young men on probation. Frances H. Simon 1971. xi + 233pp. (11 340107 8) £1.25.

8. † Study of the juvenile liaison scheme in West Ham 1961–1965. Marilyn Taylor. 1971. vi + 45pp. (11 340108 6) 35p.

9. † Explorations in after-care. I - After-care units in London Liverpool and Manchester. Martin Silberman (Royal London Prisoners' Aid Society), Brenda Chapman. II - After-care hostals receiving a Home Office grant. Ian Sinclair and David Snow (HORU). III - St Martin of Tours House. Aryeh Leissner (National Bureau for Co-operation in Child Care). 1971. xi + 168pp. (113401094) 85p.

10 A survey of adoption in Great Britain. Eleanor Grey in collaboration with R.M. Blunden. 1971. ix + 168pp. (11 340110 8) 95p.

11. † Thirteen-year-old approved school boys in 1962. Elizabeth Field, W.H. Hammoned and J. Tizard. 1971. ix + 45pp. (11 340111 6) 35p.

12. Absconding from approved schools. R.V.G.Clarke and D.N.Martin. 1971. vi + 145pp. (11 340112 4) 85p.

13. An experiment in personality assessment of young men remanded in custody. H. Sylvia Antony. 1972. viii + 79pp. (11 340113) $52\frac{1}{2}$p.

14. Girl offenders aged 17–20 years. I - Statistics relating to girl offenders aged 17–20 years from 1960 to 1970. II - Re-offending by girls released from borstal or detention centre training. III - The problems of girls released from borstal training during their period on after-care. Jean Davies and Nancy Goodman. 1972. v + 77pp. (11 340114 0) $52\frac{1}{2}$p.

15. † The controlled trial in institutional research - paradigm or pitfall for penal evaluators? R.V.G.Clarke and D.B.Cornish. 1971. v + 33pp (11 340115 9) 29p.

16. A survey of fine enforcement. Paul Softley. 1973. v + 65pp. (11 340116 7) 47p.

17. † An index of social environment designed for use in social work research. Martin Davies. 1973. v + 61pp. (11 340117 5) 47p.

18. † Social enquiry reports and the probation service. Martin Davies and Andrea Knopf. 1973. v + 47pp. (11 340118 3) 50p.

19. † Depression, psychopathic personality and attempted suicide in a borstal sample. H. Sylvia Anthony. 1973. viii + 44pp (0 11 340119 1) $36\frac{1}{2}$p.

20. The use of bail and custody by London magistrates' courts before and after the Criminal Justice Act 1967. Frances Simon and Mollie Weatheritt. 1974. vi + 78pp. (0 11 340120 5) 57p.

21. Social work in the environment. A study of one aspect of probation practice. Martin Davies, with Margaret Rayfield, Alaster Calder and Tony Fowles. 1974. x + 164pp. (0 11 340121 3) £1.10.

22. Social work in prisons. An experiment in the use of extended contact with offenders. Margaret Shaw. 1974. viii + 156pp. (0 11 340122 1) £1.45.

23. Delinquency amongst opiate users. Joy Mott and Marilyn Taylor. 1974. vi + 54pp. (0 11 340663 0) 41p

24. IMPACT. Intensive matched probation and after-care treatment. Vol.I. The design of the probation experiment and an interim evaluation. M.S.Folkard, A.J.Fowles, B.C.McWilliams, W.McWilliams, D.D.Smith, D.E.Smith and G.R.Walmsley. 1974. vi + 54pp. (0 11 340664 9) £1.25.

25. The approved school experience. An account of boys' experience of training under differing regimes of approved schools, with an attempt to evaluate the effectiveness of that training. Anne B.Dunlop. 1974. viii + 124pp. (0 11 340665 7) £1.22

† Out of print. Photostat copies can be purchased from Her Majesty's Stationery Office upon request.

26. Absconding from open prisons. Charlotte Banks, Patricia Mayhew and R.J.Sapsford. 1975. viii + 92pp. (0 11 340666 5) 95p.

27. Driving while disqualified. Sue Kriefman. 1975. vi + 138pp. (0 11 340667 3) £1.22.

28. Some male offenders' problems. I - Homeless offenders in Liverpool. W McWilliams. II - Case-work with short-term prisoners. Julie Holborn. 1975. x + 150pp. (0 11 340668 1) £2.50.

29. Community service orders. K.Pease, P.Durkin, I.Earnshaw, D.Payne, J.Thorpe. 1975. viii + 80pp. (0 11 340669 X) 75p.

30. Field Wing Bail Hostel: the first nine months. Frances Simon and Sheena Wilson. 1975. viii + 56pp. (0 11 340670 3) 85p.

31. Homicide in England and Wales 1967–1971. Evelyn Gibson. 1975. iv + 60pp. (0 11 340753 X) 90p.

32. Residential treatment and its effects on delinquency. D.B.Cornish and R.V.G.Clarke. 1975. vi + 74pp. (0 11 340672 X) £1.00.

33. Further studies of female offenders. Part A: Borstal girls eight years after release. Nancy Goodman, Elizabeth Maloney and Jean Davies. Part B: The sentencing of women at the London Higher Courts. Nancy Goodman, Paul Durkin and Janet Halton. Part C: Girls appearing before a juvenile court. Jean Davies. 1976. vi + 114pp. (0 11 340673 8) £1.55.

34. Crime as opportunity. P.Mayhew, R.V.G.Clarke, A.Sturman and J.M.Hough. 1976. vii + 36pp. (0 11 340674 6) 70p.

35. The effectiveness of sentencing: a review of the literature. S.R.Brody. 1976. v + 89pp. (0 11 340675 4) £1.15.

36. IMPACT. Intensive matched probation and after-care treatment. Vol. II - The results of the experiment. M.S.Folkard, D.E.Smith, and D.D.Smith. 1976. xi + 40pp. (0 11 340676 2) 80p.

37. Police cautioning in England and Wales. J.A.Ditchfield. 1976. iv + 31pp. (0 11 340677 0) 65p.

38. Parole in England and Wales. C.P.Nuttall, with E.E.Barnard, A.J.Fowles, A.Frost, W.H.Hammond, P.Mayhew, K.Pease, R.Tarling and M.J.Weatheritt. 1977. vi + 90pp. (0 11 340678 9) £1.75.

39. Community service assessed in 1976. K.Pease, S.Billingham and I.Earnshaw. 1977. vi + 29pp. (0 11 340679 7) 75p.

40. Screen violence and film censorship. Stephen Brody. 1977. vi + 179pp. (0 11 340680 0) £2.75.

41. Absconding from borstals. Gloria K.Laycock. 1977. v + 82pp. (0 11 340681 9) £1.50.

42. Gambling - a review of the literature and its implications for policy and research. D.B.Cornish. 1978. xii + 284pp. (0 11 340682 7) £4.25.

43. Compensation orders in magistrates' courts. Paul Softley. 1978. vi + 42pp. (0 11 340683 5). 90p.

44. Research in criminal justice. John Croft. 1978. vi + 18pp. (0 11 340684 3) 50p.

45. Prison welfare: an account of an experiment at Liverpool. A.J.Fowles. 1978. v + 32pp. (0 11 340685 1) 75p.

46. Fines in magistrates' courts. Paul Softley. 1978. v + 42pp. (0 11 340686 X) £1.00.

47. Tackling vandalism. R.V.G.Clarke (editor), F.J.Gladstone, A.Sturman, Sheena Wilson (contributors). 1978. vi + 91pp. (0 11 340687 8) £2.00.

48. Social inquiry reports: a survey. Jennifer Thorpe. 1979. vi + 55pp. (0 11 340688 6) £1.50.

49. Crime in public view. P. Mayhew, R. V. G. Clarke, J. N. Burrows, J. M. Hough and S. W. C. Winchester. 1979. v + 36pp. (0 11 340689 4) £1.00.

50. Crime and the community. John Croft. 1979. v + 16pp. (0 11 340690 8) 65p.

51. Life-sentence prisoners. David Smith (editor), Christopher Brown, Joan Worth, Roger Sapsford, Charlotte Banks (contributors). 1979. v + 52pp. (0 11 340691 6) £1.25.

52. Hostels for offenders. Jane E. Andrews with an appendix by Bill Sheppard. 1979. v + 30pp. (0 21 340692 4) £1.50.

53. Previous convictions, sentence and reconviction: a statistical study of a sample of 5,000 offenders convicted in January 1971. G. J. O. Phillpotts and L. B. Lancucki. 1979. v + 55pp. (0 11 340693 2) £2.25.

54. Sexual offences, consent and sentencing. Roy Walmsley and Karen White. 1979. vi + 77pp. (0 11 340694 0) £2.75.

55. Crime prevention and the police. John Burrows, Paul Ekblom and Kevin Heal. 1979. v + 37pp. (0 11 340695 9) £1.75.

56. Sentencing practice in magistrates' courts. Roger Tarling with the assistance of Mollie Weatheritt. 1979. vii + 54pp. (0 11 340696 7) £2.25.

57. Crime and comparative research. John Croft. 1979. iv + 16pp. (0 11 340697 5) £1.00.

58. Race, crime and arrests. Philip Stevens and Carole F. Willis. 1979. v + 69pp. (0 11 340698 3) £2.75.

59. Research and criminal policy. John Croft. 1980. iv + 14pp. (0 11 340699 1) £1.75.

60. Junior attendance centres. Anne B. Dunlop. 1980. v + 47pp. (0 11 340700 9) £2.75.

61. Police interrogation: an observational study in four police stations. Paul Softley with the assistance of David Brown, Bod Forde, George Mair and David Moxon. 1980.

62. Co-ordinating crime prevention efforts. F.J. Gladstone. 1980.

63. Crime prevention publicity: an assessment. D. Riley and P. Mayhew. 1980.

64. Taking offenders out of circulation. Stephen Brody and Roger Tarling. 1980.

HMSO

The above publications can be purchased from the Government Bookshops at the addresses listed on the reverse of title page (post orders to PO Box 569, London SE1 9NH) or through booksellers.

The following Home Office research publications are available on request from the Home Office Research Unit, Information Section, 50 Queen Anne's Gate, London, SW1H 9AT.

Research Unit Papers

1. Uniformed police work and management technology. J. M. Hough. 1980.

2. Supplementary information on sexual offences and sentencing. Roy Walmsley and Karen White, 1980.

Research Bulletin

The Research Bulletin is published twice a year and consists mainly of short articles relating to projects which are part of the Home Office Research Unit's research programme.

Printed in England for Her Majesty's Stationery Office at the Alden Press, Oxford Dd 696854 K 2011/80